Event Sponsorship

The Wiley Event Management Series

SERIES EDITOR: DR. JOE GOLDBLATT, CSEP

Event Sponsorship

Bruce E. Skinner, CFE
Vladimir Rukavina, CFE

JOHN WILEY & SONS, INC.

Library of Congress Cataloging-in-Publication Data:

Skinner, Bruce E.
    Event sponsorship / Bruce E. Skinner, Vladimir Rukavina.
      p. cm.— (The Wiley event management series)
Published simultaneously in Canada.
      ISBN 0-471-12601-2 (cloth : alk.paper)
  1. Corporate sponsorship. 2.   Special events.   I. Rukavina, Vladimir.
    II. Title. III. Series.
      HD59.35 .S55 2003
      659.2′85—dc21   2002010348

Printed in the United States of America.

20 19 18 17

Contents

Foreword

The renowned writer Fyodor Dostoevski was once asked to give his opinion about the value of ideas. Dostoevski promptly answered, "Neither man nor nation can exist without a sublime idea." This excellent and comprehensive resource for international event organizers and their sponsors is the perfect example of hundreds of sublime ideas that cross every international border to advance the art and science of event sponsorship.

Bruce E. Skinner, CFE, of the United States and Vladimir Rukavina, CFE, of Europe worked together to conduct the groundbreaking research that unites the entire industry of event sponsorship for the first time in this pioneering new book. They have literally removed the walls that previously separated countries and event destinations and produced the first ever comprehensive guide for event organizers and their sponsors worldwide.

Whether you are a novice event organizer or "an old pro," you will greatly benefit from this book. Skinner is one of the most respected and experienced consultants in the field of event management and event sponsorship in the world. He has studied events on many continents and consulted with both large and small event organizations in countries throughout the world. His advice and counsel are highly valued, and now you can benefit from his consultation in this book.

The field of event sponsorship has dramatically expanded during the past 25 years. As traditional advertising has diminished in popularity, marketers are constantly seeking new marketing channels to promote their products and services. Skinner and Rukavina have provided a step-by-step, easy-to-use model for shifting marketing efforts to a more effective and efficient response mechanism: international event sponsorship. As global brands have emerged, so has the need for local promotion of those brands. That is, in fact, the genius within these pages. You will learn how to assess the need for sponsorship for your event, utilize the proven tools that have worked for thousands of successful events, and then apply your global perspective to achieve localized results that will amaze and impress your sponsors.

Another important aspect of this book is that it is designed for both event organizers and their sponsors. Whether you are vice president of marketing, a chief executive officer, or a local brand manager, this book will provide you with the tools, templates, and techniques to make a productive sponsorship purchase decision. Furthermore, by learning why and how events ensure effective marketing outcomes, you will be able to provide even greater value for your organization as you continually seek new ways to increase name recognition, lengthen brand recall, and produce better and faster buying decisions.

Dostoevski also wrote, "The second half of a man's life is made up of nothing but the habits he has acquired during the first half." Through this most excellent book you will learn the important, effective, and valuable habits that will enrich you and your organizations in the future. As we enter a new century, in which lifelong learning is no longer optional but now mandatory for continuous growth and advancement, this book will provide you with the essential information and inspiration needed to become a global leader in the field of event sponsorship. The entire event industry owes an enormous debt of gratitude to Bruce Skinner, CFE, and Vladimir Rukavina, CFE, for their careful and comprehensive collaboration. They are living examples of how an event world with the artificial borders removed can create a bigger and better marketplace for all. From the Pacific Northwestern United States to Maribor, Slovenia, and beyond, this book has encircled the world with new opportunities for creative, imaginative, and financially successful events through sponsorship. The next time you see the words "sponsored by," you may silently thank Skinner and Rukavina for enlarging and improving this field through their exceptionally well-researched and well-written book. May the habits you form as a result of the many chapters in this book make the next stage of your event or marketing career even more successful than those already accomplished. And may you contribute to the continued globalization of event sponsorship through the lessons you will learn and use as a direct result of this valuable new book.

Dr. Joe Goldblatt, CSEP
Series Editor, The Wiley Event Management Series
Dean, Alan Shawn Feinstein Graduate School,
Johnson & Wales University

Preface

One of the most vivid memories of my professional career is my visit to Valley National Bank, then the largest financial institution in the Southwestern United States, in September 1984.

This wasn't my first visit to the bank for event funding. Each time, I had veered to the left after getting off the elevator on the 10th floor of the Valley National Bank Building in downtown Phoenix, where the corporate contributions department was located. I had gone hat in hand to ask for donations to our nonprofit event, and as a big community contributor, the Bank had always come through.

But this time a new phenomenon was sweeping the country—corporate event sponsorship—and instead of turning left, I turned right, into the marketing department.

And my life, and the lives of many other event professionals, changed. Now I wasn't "begging" for money, I was forming a partnership with the Bank. Although one of the reasons that the Bank would continue to give the Fiesta Bowl money was to support a great community activity, its criteria for giving changed dramatically.

It now wanted return on investment, just as it did when it spent money on any other marketing venture, such as advertising, special promotions, and the like. The return for us, however, was that the donations that became event marketing dollars were now much larger.

Nothing has made a greater impact on the festival/special events industry than corporate sponsorship. It has fueled incredible growth for numerous events and provided start-up monies for many new ones. Many of those who have not grasped its principles—sometimes by choice—have watched their events slip as event attendees have developed a desire to go to events that are climbing to the next level, made possible by sponsorship dollars.

Corporate America has provided those dollars, increasing its sponsorship participation from $171 million in 1982, according to the International Events Group (IEG) in Chicago, to $5.9 billion in 2001.

The basic structure of the community event has changed. Events, especially new ones, are better because they are able to invest dollars in new and exciting programming. Festivals are no longer assigned to companies' personnel who deal with contributions; they are now administered by corporate marketing departments, where greater revenues are distributed. And event staffs have become much larger and more professional—gone are the days when festival jobs were glorified clerical positions.

What follows are the nuts and bolts of developing sponsorship as seen through the eyes of some of the world's top event professionals (see Figure 1).

Chapter 1 deals with the definition of sponsorship and the most important requirement in selling sponsorship—you must have a good event to start with.

In Chapter 2 you learn why sponsors sponsor what they do and how to develop a sponsorship marketing plan. Chapter 3 shows how to research your sponsors by seeing sponsorship through their eyes, and in Chapter 4, you discover how to create an effective proposal.

Chapter 5 shows you how to expand the value of your sponsorship, Chapter 6 demonstrates how important the image of your event is, and Chapter 7 explores the reasons that you need to be creative.

After you have done your homework by reading the first seven chapters, Chapter 8 tells you how to close the deal. Chapter 9 explores the legal issues surrounding the sponsorship industry, and in Chapter 10 you learn the importance of having qualified event managers on your professional staff.

In Chapter 11 you will discover how to retain your sponsors year after year, and Chapter 12 shows you how to place value on your sponsorships. Vladimir Rukavina offers a European view on sponsorship in Chapter 13, and Chapter 14 demonstrates the power of networking with other event professionals.

Finally, Chapter 15 delves into the future and the predicted trends for the sponsorship industry.

A number of appendixes are included at the end of this book, listing resources for event managers—books, periodicals, organizations, directories, Web sites, and video productions. There are also samples of various documents.

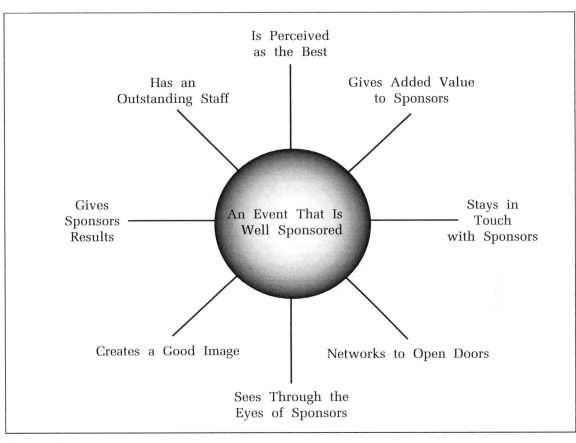

Figure 1
For the Ultimate in Event Sponsorship

How to Use This Book

Each chapter has a standard format that can help you discover this exciting industry:

- At the beginning, there is a list of what you will learn in the pages that follow.
- In the middle, figures, models, and success stories emphasize the underlying principles.
- At the conclusion, "The Keys . . ." summarize.

- "Sponsorship Activities" lists additional ways in which you can learn.
- "Sponsorship Tool Kit" lists more reading and discovery opportunities.

Bruce E. Skinner, CFE
Former President, International Festivals and Events Association
current President, Bruce Skinner and Associates
and
Vladimir Rukavina, CFE
General Manager, Narodni Dom Cultural Center, Maribor, Slovenia
President/CEO, International Festival of Lent

Acknowledgments

I have been very fortunate in my professional career: first, to serve as assistant executive director and then, for ten years, as executive director of one of America's top college football bowl games, Arizona's Fiesta Bowl.

It was here that I learned about sponsorship. In 1985 we were fortunate enough to become not only one of the country's top bowl games, but also one of the leaders in the sponsorship arena when we signed a deal with Sunkist to be the first title sponsor of a bowl game.

After serving 17 years at the Bowl, I went on to serve as president/CEO of the International Festivals and Events Association (IFEA), a trade association that grew from 400 to 3000 members during the ten years I was there. It was at the IFEA that I learned sponsorship from hundreds of events, large and small. Because of my position, I probably hold the distinction of having attended more, and more varied, events than anyone else. It is this background that I have used to develop knowledge about event sponsorship.

However, even with all my contacts, I couldn't have written this book myself. First, I am indebted to the following people who worked on the form of this manuscript—Jim Austin, President and Chief Operating Officer of the Houston International Festival; George Hill from ABC Sports; Heather Bloyer, the current editor of *Festivals,* the official publication of the IFEA; Sue McCabe, another IFEA staffer, and Teresa MacDonald, my longtime assistant.

I am also indebted to my family, Kathy, Alison, and Emily, who allowed me the time to complete this manuscript, which, I hope, will allow some people to go to the next level in their quest to sell sponsorship.

Finally, I want to thank the following people for their assistance throughout my career:

Janet Ahreneberg, Ericsson
K Alferio, Capital One, Richmond, Virginia
Jo Ann Andera, Texas Folklife Festival, San Antonio
Sylvia Allen, Allen Consulting, Holmdel, New Jersey
Jim Austin, Houston International Festival
Kathi Austin, Houston International Festival
Dennis Bash, U.S. Bank, Portland
Jill Bell, Acordia of Louisville
Mike Berry, Kentucky Derby Festival, Louisville
Elizabeth "Bo" Black, Summerfest, Milwaukee
Doug Blouin, The Fiesta Bowl, Tempe, Arizona
Heather Bloyer, International Festivals and Events Association, Port Angeles, Washington
Dennis Boese, The Miller Brewing Company, Milwaukee
Nancy Bove, Burlington Parks and Recreation, Vermont
Mike Brennan, Bellingham Ski to Sea Festival
Mary Bridges, Bridges Marketing & PR, Brookfield, Wisconsin
Jim and Barb Bunger
Gaylene Carpenter, University of Oregon
Nancy Chapman, Milestone Products, Monrovia, California
Bill Charney, Bill Charney & Associates, Denver
Thor Christensen, *Dallas Morning News*
Karen Churchard, Fiesta Bowl, Tempe, Arizona
Cindy Ciura, Cierra Creative Marketing Services
Dick Clark, Portland Rose Festival
Ray Cole, Sunkist
Bill Collins, Chesapeake Bay Region Festivals and Events Association
William Cone, Knight Ridder Newspapers, Miami
Melanie Conty, *Shopping Centers Today*
John Cordova, Coca-Cola Company, Atlanta
Ken and Fossie Coulter, Mammoth Lakes Jazz Jubilee, California
Pat Craig-Corda, Gator Bowl, Jacksonville, Florida

Dianna Craven, SunFest of West Palm Beach, Florida
Carolyn Crayton, The Macon Cherry Blossom Festival, Georgia
Mo Dana, Pioneer Hi-Bred International
Ida D'Errico, Three Rivers Regatta
Jean David, Cirque du Soleil, Montreal
Charlotte DeWitt, International Events Limited, Stockholm
Mitch Dorger, Pasadena Tournament of Roses
Jay Downie, Downie Productions
Bruce Erley, Creative Strategies Group, Denver
Tim Estes, Fiesta Parade Floats
Derrick Fox, Sylvania Alamo Bowl, San Antonio
Howard Freeman, New Jersey Festival of Ballooning
Wayne Friedman, *Advertising Age*
Michele Gauthier, Canadian Tulip Festival, Ottawa
Tom and Julie George, Tempe, Arizona
Dr. Joe Goldblatt, Johnson and Wales University, Providence, Rhode Island
Richard Goldstein, Unilever
Tony Greener, Guinness
Skye Griffith, Skyline Talent & Events, Denver
Jack Guthrie, Guthrie/Mayes Public Relations, Louisville
Ned Harden, Circleville, Ohio
Kirk Hendrix, Kirk Hendrix & Associates
Julie Hester
Dave Hilfman, Continental Airlines
Brian Hill, Centenial Olympic Park
George Hill, George Hill & Associates, Port Angeles, Washington
Hans Horsting, Communis Opino, Rotterdam, the Netherlands
Dave Howell, Bank of America, San Francisco
Janet Hyrne, Aloha Festivals, Honolulu
Dan Ison, Philip Morris U.S.A., Louisville
Robert Jackson, *Special Events: Inside and Out*
David Jacobson, The Exordium Group
Paul Jamieson, SunFest of West Palm Beach
Dale Johnson, K & K Insurance, Fort Wayne, Indiana
Swede Johnson, Coors
John Junker, Fiesta Bowl, Tempe, Arizona
Blaine and Barry Kern, Kern Studios, New Orleans
Tom Kern, The National Cherry Festival
Beth Knox, Boise River Festival

Elizabeth Kraft-Meek, Indy Festivals, Indianapolis
Eleanor Krusell, Florida Festivals and Events Association
Valerie Lagauskas, Synergistic Concepts, Philadelphia
Norm Langill, One Reel
Pierre-Paul Leduc, Festivals et Evenements Quebec
John Lloyd, The Great Circus Parade, Milwaukee
Bill Lofthouse, Phoenix Decorating, Pasadena, California
Steve Long, Pepsi Cola, Denver
Rhonda Lopresti, Olympia Memorial Hospital
Kerry Luginbill, America West Airlines, Tempe, Arizona
Virginia Mampre, Media International, Houston
Dan Mangeot
Mickey Markoff, MDM Group, Fort Lauderdale, Florida
John Marks, San Francisco Convention and Visitors Bureau
Eric Martin, Bands of America, Schaumburg, Illinois
Christine Matthews-Sheen, Edinburgh International Festival,
    Scotland
Rochelle McHugh, Olympic Memorial Hospital Foundation
Annette Meisl, La Gala—Internationale Kulturprojekte, Cologne,
    Germany
Janice C. Meyer, Canton, Ohio
Phil Motta, The Motta Company, Phoenix
Jeroen Mourik, Evenementen en Festivals, Utrecht, the Nether-
    lands
Scott Nagel, Washington Festivals and Events Association
Robin Nelson, Utah Arts Festival
Dick Nicholls, Gilroy Garlic Festival
Dick Nunis, Walt Disney World
Chuck O'Connor, The National Cherry Festival, Traverse City,
    Michigan
Ron Okum, Pasadena Tournament of Roses
Steve Oliver, Hurricane Ridge Public Development Authority
Al Parisi, Fremont Fair, Seattle
Eileen Pawlak, *The Arizona Republic,* Phoenix
Carolyn Pendergast, the Arizona Biltmore Hotel, Phoenix
Penny Perrey, IEG, Chicago
Eric Poms, Federal Express Orange Bowl
N. W. "Red" Pope, Red Pope and Company, Scottsdale, Arizona
Jon Proctor, Delta Airlines
Mindy Rabinowitz, Southwest Airlines

Michael Rea, Haas & Wilkerson Insurance, Shawnee Mission, Kansas

Mary Hutchings Reed, IEG Legal Guide to Cause Marketing

John Reid, Holiday Bowl, San Diego

Steve Remington, Eugene Celebration, Oregon

Sandra Risk,Wildflower! Festival in Richardson, Texas

Carol Romine, Bank of America Coconut Grove Arts Festival, Florida

Ira Rosen, Entertainment on Location, Matawan, New Jersey

Nathalie Sauvanet, CEREC

Eric Schechter, Great American Merchandise and Events, Scottsdale, Arizona

Karen Scherberger, Norfolk Festevents, Virginia

Steven Wood Schmader, International Festivals and Events Association

Ruth Schnabel, California Festivals and Events Association

Mark Schonberg, Macy's Parade

Jurgen E. Schrempp, DaimerChrysler

Willard Scott, NBC *Today Show*

Lynn Settje, Greeley Independence Stampede, Colorado

Trevor Sheahan, Brisbane, Australia

Bridget Sherrill, Kentucky Derby Festival, Louisville

Dr. Annie Sidro, Carnavals Sans Frontieres, Nice, France

Larry Sinclair, Churchill Downs, Louisville

David Skinner

Ed and Doris Skinner

Hanne Sondegaard, Wonderful Copenhagen, Denmark

Alexis Sorensen, International Festivals and Events Association, Boise

Laura Stitt, Colorado Lottery, Denver

Rafael Stone, Foster, Pepper & Shefelman PLLC, Seattle

Terese St. Onge, National Capital Commission, Ottawa

Bruce Storey, Storey Event Consulting, Denver

Gail Logan Strange, Brown and Williamson Tobacco Company, Louisville

Carl Stressman, Wrangler Jeans, Greensboro, North Carolina

David Sullivan, First Night International, Boston

Jim Tarman, Pennsylvania State University

Margaret Y.B. Teo, Singapore Tourism Board

Rand Thomas, Thomas Building Company, Sequim, Washington

Chic Thompson, *If It Ain't Broke, Break It*
Wright Tilley, RCS Productions, Atlanta
Rick Tittermary, Frito-Lay, Cincinnati
Peter Tolini, Gateway Computers, Hampton, Virginia
Mark Tucker, Greeley Independence Stampede, Colorado
Sue Twyford, The Twyford Group, North Palm Beach, Florida
Lesa Ukman, IEG, Chicago
Pete Van de Putte, Dixie Flag, San Antonio, Texas
Dr. Paul Van Gessel, Netherlands Board of Tourism
Belinda Venuti, Seneca Lake Whale Watch, Geneva, New York
Bruce Wicks, University of Illinois
Dan Wilder, Wilder Toyota
Barry Wilkins, Mt. Barker, Australia
Beth Wojick, Seattle SEAFAIR
Bill Youngberg, *Newsweek*
George, Marcie, and Danabeth Zambelli, Zambelli Internationale
    Fireworks, New Castle, Pennsylvania
Peter Zapf, Siemens Mobile Devices

—*Bruce Skinner*

The History
of Sponsorship

1 B.C.–1600—The Era of Patronage

Sponsorship in this era was not sponsorship in its modern-day sense, as individuals, not companies, sponsored artists. However, they did expect a "return on investment," such as support from their subjects.

In the Roman period, patronage of the arts was in the hands of the rulers and army commanders. Later, the central role was played by the church, statesmen, and aristocratic patrons.

Shakespeare created his Royal Theatre Group. The Roman popes and other church dignitaries were clients or supporters of artists such as Michelangelo and Leonardo da Vinci. The Medici family in Florence and the Sforci family in Milan are among the most famous families of the time who encouraged the arts through their patronage.

1631—The Advent of Advertising

Once again, sponsorship during this period was not sponsorship as we know it—only the benefit of exposure was offered through advertising. However, it was a necessary step in the development of modern-day sponsorship, and, as everyone knows, it still thrives today in the media world.

Important first steps: In 1631, a French newspaper ran a classified ad; in 1704, a Boston newspaper printed a display advertisement.

1910–1970—The Early Pioneers

The Eveready Hour was the first sponsored radio program in 1924. Motor sports, golf, and tennis were the forerunners of modern-day sponsorship. Cigarette, alcohol and automobile companies became the first to sponsor events. Firestone and Bosch have been sponsors of the Indianapolis 500 since 1911. The Goodyear Tire and Rubber Company developed the Goodyear blimp and started using it extensively in 1959 because of the vision of the company's vice president of public relations, Bob Lane. In 1956, The Kentucky Derby Festival was the first festival to have a title sponsor for one of its events: the Philip Morris Festival of Stars.

1970–1984—The Era of Development

Although many event managers refused to accept corporate sponsorship (they were afraid of their events being tainted), motor sports, golf, and tennis and their sponsors continued to build on their relationships. However, most sponsorship in this era was provided because sponsors could get free exposure on television or were afforded hospitality opportunities, or because the CEO wanted to play golf with Arnold Palmer. Sponsorship was never activated or leveraged (see Chapter 5).

1983—THE SPONSORSHIP EXPLOSION

Faced with a situation of very few government funding sources, Peter Ueberroth sold more than $400 million worth of sponsorship for the Los Angeles Olympic Games. That led to an explosion of sponsorship marketing. Companies found that they could increase sales through sponsorship, and many event managers forgot the notion that their events could be tainted. They increased their sponsorship levels dramatically, and approximately 40,000 events were created in the next ten years because of sponsorship funding.

People like Ben Barkin of the Schlitz Brewing Company teamed up with festival organizers like George Wein of the Newport Jazz Festival, paving the way for sponsorship of free festivals. Jerry

1B.C.– 1600	1631	1924– 1970	1970– 1984	1984	1990	2000
The Era of Patronage	The Advent of Advertising	The Early Pioneers	The Era of Development	The Sponsorship Explosion	The Era of Added Value	The Technological Era

Figure 2
Skinner-Rukavina Sponsorship Historical Time Line

Welsh of American Express introduced new ways of marketing through events and more or less invented cause marketing. He got his company involved in the Statue of Liberty restoration, the first national cause marketing initiative. Event managers, too, contributed to the sponsorship explosion. CEOs Jack Guthrie and Dan Mangeot of the Kentucky Derby Festival led the way to increased participation by sponsors at festivals around the world.

In May 1983, Lesa Ukman of the International Events Group (IEG) published the first sponsorship newsletter (see Chapter 14), and sponsors and event managers begin to learn about sponsorship and all of its forms from an industry publication.

1990s—The Era of Added Value

When the explosion hit in 1984, most sponsors were still happy if they received only signage and hospitality opportunities. In the 1990s sponsors became more sophisticated. Things like business-to-business (B2B) opportunities, measured results and sales, activation and providing incentives became increasingly important. Hospitality and mentions in connection with an event were still vital, but more value was desired.

2000–Present—The Technological Era

Just as technology has affected all other areas of society, it has had a great impact on events. Website sponsorship partners are starting to become commonplace. On July 17, 2001, Microsoft Network U.K. and Elton John made history (see Chapter 15). The former sponsored Sir Elton's July 17 concert from the ancient Great Amphitheatre in Ephesus, Turkey, and the latter sponsored a cybercast of the concert on pay-per-view for broadband users only. (See Figure 2.)

CHAPTER 1

Outstanding Events Sell Sponsorships

If you do things well, do them better. Be daring, be first, be different, be just.

ANITA RODDICK, FOUNDER, BODY SHOP INTERNATIONAL

IN THIS CHAPTER YOU WILL LEARN:

- The definition of commercial sponsorship
- The most important thing you must do to be a successful event sponsorship manager
- Why you need to update your event
- Attributes of outstanding events
- What you need to do to stage a great sponsored event

Over the past 25 years there have been many definitions of *sponsorship.*

The International Events Group (IEG) located in Chicago and the industry's leading company among those that track and analyze sponsorship, defines it as "cash and/or an in-kind fee paid to a property (typically in sports, arts, entertainment or causes) in return for access to the exploitable commercial potential associated with that property."

The Exordium Group, an industry strategy company headquartered in Cupertino, California, describes it as "a mutually beneficial relationship most often between a corporation and event or rights holder, for the purpose of enhancing a product or corporate brand."

Another way to look at sponsorship is that it is like any other form of marketing—*it is an activity that puts buyers and sellers together, with both receiving certain benefits.* In other words, if you have the right people coming to your event as far as your sponsors are concerned (their potential customers), you are probably going to have happy sponsors.

However, even though creating that match is very important, it is still not the most important thing an event manager needs to do if he or she is going to sell sponsorship.

Most everything written or said about successful sponsorship stresses that event managers must work on creating the best packages, writing the best proposals, creating added value, and learning the proper selling techniques. It is also important to establish a good relationship with your sponsors and research them very well.

But the most important thing to remember before you even attempt to sell sponsorship is that you must create an event that is better than the rest. You have to be very good at what you do in your community, no matter what its size.

This does not mean that you have to be the biggest, but it does mean that you have to be the best in a particular niche, or that you present something extremely creative, unique, or entertaining.

"Developing our brand is very important to us right now," said Capital One's "K" Alferio. "When people use their Visa or MasterCard, they readily recognize those brands. But they might not know that Capital One is the bank behind them. We want everyone to see Capital One, Capital One, Capital One."

"In this era of bank mergers, brand awareness and enhancement are critical," says Dennis Bash of U.S. Bank. "U.S. Bank was an almost completely unknown brand when the company entered the state of Washington market. We became an official sponsor of Seattle's Goodwill Games in 1990 and used that sponsorship to establish our brand using Games themed advertising, merchandising, and hospitality."

Bash, vice president and western region manager of corporate sponsorship for U.S. Bank in Portland, looks to creative, professional event staff to bring new ideas to the table. "In many markets our brand is well established so branding is a secondary or tertiary concern. But we do need to achieve ROI [return on investment] on our sponsorships, and we do that in part by selling product. It's a huge help to us when an event's staff comes to us with ideas on how we can sell product. That speaks volumes of their commitment to us as a sponsor."

U.S. Bank also seeks to build unique experiences through sponsorships. "We're in the third year of a deal with the hottest team in baseball," said Bash in July 2001. "We've created an affinity checking program around that sponsorship and have increased our sale of checking products tremendously due to tying our brand with the Seattle Mariners."

The bank also looks for nontraditional hospitality opportunities in which the only way people can have certain experiences is through their relationship with the bank.

"We did a batting practice event with the Triple A baseball team in Sacramento, the River Cats," said Bash. "We gave customers the opportunity to take batting practice, take infield/outfield, receive a special jersey, and have lunch at the ballpark. We never fail to get business when we do this type of event."

U.S. Bank also sponsors "Blues by the Bay" in Eureka, California. It invites musicians to come and join its customers at a lunch. "To blues fans, having a chance to talk with a name musician is just as important as a sports fan talking to a sports star, those experiences creating lasting memories for our customers," said Bash.

Tradition and Change

Many events are very tired—they present the same program year after year, and fail to add interesting and new elements to their programs.

"Change for the sake of change is not good," state Steven Wood Schmader and Robert Jackson in *Special Events: Inside and Out*. "But change to keep an event fresh and growing is essential.

"Before hitting the streets to begin selling an event to potential sponsors, the first thing you must do is take a long, hard look at the event itself . . . like your child, you can love your event, but still recognize its faults. . . .

"Don't ask Mack Truck to sponsor the Royal Canadian Ballet," say these authors. "It just doesn't fit. A good fit, on the other hand, is Pepto Bismol and the World Championship Chili Cook-off."

The Best of the Best

The following are examples of events that have risen to the top, as either large or niche events.

EVENTS IN LARGE MARKETS

Roses and Hydros

Two events located in the Pacific Northwest are extremely successful at selling sponsorship. One was founded in 1907 and the other in 1948, and both have, at times, bucked change.

The Portland Rose Festival has always been one of the best events in the country. Its parade, featuring numerous floral displays, is one of the top five in the United States according to *USA Today*. It has had two other parades for years—the Starlight, which is the second largest illuminated parade in the Northwest, and the Junior Rose Festival Parade, which is the oldest and largest children's parade in the country.

On the waterfront of the Willamette River, a carnival midway has drawn substantial numbers of people, including U.S. Navy, Coast Guard, and Royal Canadian Navy personnel from the many large ships that dock near the midway site. It also has featured a rose show that began in 1891.

With that lineup, it would have been very easy for the Portland Rose Festival to rest on its laurels and retain the status quo. But its event managers have not stopped there. While keeping the events described earlier, they have made improvements and added others. There is now a CART automobile race and a huge air show, as well as a large festival.

Because the Rose Festival has changed and remained the top festival in the state of Oregon, its lineup of sponsors is extremely impressive—this is an event that everyone wants to be a part of (see Figure 1-1). *In 2001 the Festival sold $4.1 million in cash sponsorship and another $2 million in in-kind trade!*

Seattle SEAFAIR is another old-time Northwest event that could have rested on its laurels. But it too has not. For years SEAFAIR has featured one of the best night parades in the United States and the largest unlimited hydroplane race in the country.

Over time, it has made changes and added to its mix of events. It has changed its controversial queen coronation to a scholarship pageant for women. It has added a preparade torchlight run, which is held on the parade route before hundreds of thousands of parade viewers.

Like the Rose Festival, SEAFAIR is very successful at selling sponsorship. Its sponsored events include:

- Southwest Airlines Torchlight Parade
- General Motors Cup
- SEAFAIR Milk Carton Derby presented by Navy Recruiting
- Benaroya Research Institute Triathlon
- Talgo Criterium
- UPS Torchlight Run

It is easy to say that SEAFAIR and the Rose Festival are successful at selling sponsorship because they are in large markets. But there are many other large markets that do not have festivals equal in quality to these events, and there are many events in

---

- Fred Meyer Opening Weekend Celebration featuring the STARsmATM Fireworks Spectacular
- Pepsi Waterfront Village
- KeyBank Starlight Run
- Portland General Electric/SOLV Starlight Parade presented by Southwest Airlines
- George Morlan Plumbing/1190 KEX Festival of Bands
- Southwest Airlines Grand Floral Parade
- Portland Arts Festival presented by Verizon Wireless
- G.I. Joe's 200
- Rose Festival Air Show presented by Intel

Figure 1-1
2002 Portland Rose Festival Sponsored Events

Seattle and Portland that sell few sponsorships because they do not measure up.

International Celebration

Started in 1947, Scotland's Edinburgh International Festival is recognized as one of the most important celebrations of the arts in the world.

The Festival brings to Edinburgh some of the best in international theater, music, dance, and opera and presents the arts of Scotland to the world. It is held for three weeks in August each year and comprises more than 180 performances, including 78 different productions and concerts featuring arts from around the world.

This celebration is so big that a recent survey shows that it generates almost $200 million for the economy of Edinburgh and sustains more than 4000 jobs in Scotland. It has also led to the creation of several other great festivals that are held at the same time

SUCCESS STORY

THE SALZBURG MUSIC FESTIVAL

The Salzburg Festival in Austria is universally regarded as the world's best-known musical and theatrical event. It runs for five weeks each year, starting in late July.

After World War I, several German-speaking cultural figures, including Richard Strauss and Max Reinhardt, developed the idea of an annual summer cultural festival to be held in Salzburg. It debuted on August 22, 1920, and from the beginning the main focus of the festival has been on Mozart, who was born in Salzburg.

The Festival first achieved its great brilliance in the 1930s, when Arturo Toscanini and Bruno Walter were its leading conductors. Vienna State Opera productions of works by Mozart, Beethoven, Wagner, and Verdi directed by these maestros were especially distinguished. When the Nazis took over Austria in 1938, the Festival declined

in significance, as many musicians could not (Walter) or would not (Toscanini) participate. Nevertheless, the Festival continued through 1943.

It was revived as an international event in the summer of 1945, immediately following the Allied victory in Europe, and has been held every summer since then. Close to a quarter of a million people attend the event annually.

Because of its brilliance, sponsors flock to the event in order to be tied with such a magnificent event. Nestlé says it is involved to "establish consumers' trust." Audi sponsors many music festivals, but especially Salzburg. This company says that "cultural involvement expresses the corporate culture of Audi." The company portrays itself as being creative by sponsoring projects that seek to treat new themes and expand dramatic creativity.

in Edinburgh: the infamous Edinburgh Fringe Festival, the Military Tattoo, a jazz festival, a film festival, and a book festival.

No destination in the world has so many good events going on at the same time except for the Olympic Games. For this reason, the Festival is an opportunity that sponsors cannot afford to miss. In fact, 28 percent of the Festival's budget is sponsorship revenue.

EVENTS IN SMALLER MARKETS

There are many smaller market festivals that have become extremely good events and are very successful at selling sponsorship.

National Cherry Festival

Perhaps the best example of a good event in a small market is the National Cherry Festival in Traverse City, Michigan. Located in the northern part of the state, the city has only 15,800 people, but there are few events that have as high-quality programming as the Cherry Festival.

It was founded in 1926, and more than 500,000 people visit the Festival over an eight-day period. It features 150 events and creates $30 million in economic impact for the area. It has a diverse lineup of events that are extremely well run.

Event managers include activities for kids, such as cherry pie eating contests and turtle races, and a large number of events for special populations and seniors. There are events designed to expand the public's awareness of the cherry industry and its products: a Taste of Cherries event, the Cherry Farm Market, the Grand Cherry Buffet, and the Cherry Connection.

The Cherry Festival annually brings in top-name entertainment that few markets the size of Traverse City ever see. Bonnie Raitt, the Beach Boys, Christina Aguilera, Bad Company, Tim McGraw, Faith Hill, and many others have played on Festival stages.

However, probably the most impressive thing its managers do is sell sponsorship. They are able to do this because the Cherry Festival is one of the top events in the country, despite the size of its market.

The festival's official sponsors include CenturyTel, Pontiac-GMC, Northwest Airlines, and Pepsi.

There are more than 70 event sponsors, such as Blue Cross/Blue Shield, Touchstone Energy, Domino's Pizza, Country Fresh Ice Cream, Nabisco, Home Depot, Kentucky Fried Chicken, MetLife, Miller Lite, Budweiser, and Sara Lee Bakery.

All told, each year the Cherry Festival brings in more than $850,000 in sponsorship.

The Sequim Irrigation Festival

Consider an even smaller market in the state of Washington. Sequim has a population of only 4000 people, but for its annual festival, the Sequim Irrigation Festival, event managers sold $185,000 in cash sponsorship for their 100th anniversary event in 1996.

They were able to do so because they took their event to a higher level. They staged the largest fireworks show in the region's history. They brought in the Shirelles and Fabian—big names for a city the size of Sequim. The parade featured Macy-style inflatables.

Many sponsors who for years "donated" to the festival at the $250 level became sponsors at the $5000 level. In Chapter 7 of this book you will read more on how they were able to do that.

The International Festival of Lent in Maribor, Slovenia, is located in a mid-sized European market and is only 10 years old, but it already is one of the best events in the world—and the best at selling sponsorship. *Photo courtesy of Rich Riski.*

EVENTS IN MIDSIZED MARKETS

The International Festival of Lent

Midsized markets produce good events too. Not only is the International Festival of Lent the largest open-air multicultural event in Slovenia, it is also the biggest in Eastern Europe.

SUCCESS STORY

THE ANATOMY OF THE BOISE RIVER FESTIVAL

As with the other events cited in this chapter, there is something special about the Boise River Festival. It was started in 1990 by a visionary board of directors consisting of the movers and shakers of Boise.

Before creating the Festival, they knew they first had to have a top-notch staff. They immediately started a nationwide search, which led them to hire Steven Wood Schmader away from Up With People. Schmader led the festival as president and CEO for more than ten years. The International Festivals and Events Association board, however, thought so much of him that they lured him away to become their president and CEO in 2001. Following Schmader, the board selected Beth Knox, who had a tremendous amount of event experience working for SEAFAIR and One Reel in Seattle.

A visionary board and quality staff meant that in the Festival's very first year it became the signature event of Boise. They produced an event that was not only the best in the state of Idaho, but also became one of the best in the country. When they started parades for the event, they did not choose just any float builder. They picked Tim Estes of Fiesta Floats in California—one of the top float builders for the Pasadena Tournament of Roses Parade and one of the best in the world. The Festival's fireworks show was produced by one of the industry's top producers, Zambelli Internationale of New Castle, Pennsylvania. It has presented top-notch entertainment each year, including Patty Loveless, Big Bad Voodoo Daddy, and John Tesh, which was the lineup for 2001. It has also had great entertainment for children. In fact, the event calls itself "America's Finest Family Festival."

The American Bus Association has named the Boise River Festival as one of the top 100 events in North America, and members of the International Festivals and Events Association (IFEA) picked it as one of the top 10 summer festivals in the country. *Travel & Events U.S.A.* chose it as one of the top 40 events in the United States, and *Special Events: Inside and Out* named it as the top regional event in the country.

What does all this have to do with sponsorship? Boise River Festival event managers have created an event that sponsors want to be part of. In fact, 54 percent of their budget is revenue from sponsorship—$884,000 from 371 corporate partners.

The Festival was not started until 1993, but it features annually approximately 300 performances and 450 different events (classical music; opera; theater; folk and jazz music; jam sessions; rock, pop, and country music; street theater; carnival performances; exhibitions; dance performances; folklore dances; fashion shows; children's workshops; sporting events; and fireworks).

It is held on 18 different stages, with the main venue being the floating stage on the River Drava. Performers such as Ray Charles, Jose Feliciano, James Brown, B. B. King, Paquito D'Rivera, the United Nations Orchestra, and others have all played at the festival.

Despite being in a market of only 140,000 people, the event has a budget of $1.3 million, with *80 percent of revenues coming from sponsorship!*

The Macon Cherry Blossom Festival

Macon, Georgia, stages its International Cherry Blossom Festival each March, when the city is ablaze in pink. It is successful because it has something no other city has—millions of cherry blossoms.

The Festival is a tribute to William A. Fickling Sr. He, and his family after he passed away, have donated 271,500 cherry trees to the residents of Macon since 1973. In 1982, Carolyn Crayton founded the festival to honor Fickling for his gift and served as the event's executive director until November 2001.

What has evolved is a special event, which featured Jimmy Carter *and* James Brown as grand marshals of its parade one year. There is an abundance of pink at the festival—pink pancakes, ice cream, dental floss, and many other pink items. The whole community gets into the act; the city even has a pink garbage truck and pink buses. Yellow Cab paints its cabs pink, and mailboxes, porches, and automobiles have pink decorations.

"Florists tell us that they are as busy during the Festival as they are during Christmas and Easter," says Crayton.

And what does all the pink mean? *It helps the Festival to sell $355,000 worth of sponsorship each year.*

Sporting Events

Sporting events that are able to rise above the rest are also the most successful at selling sponsorship.

FIESTA BOWL

Before it became the first bowl game to sign a title sponsor, the Fiesta Bowl was a fledgling but growing event that had a vision to be the best. Beginning as a pre-New Year's game, it was one of the lower-ranked bowls in the first ten years of its existence. In 1982 the day of the game was moved to New Year's Day, then the magic date for college bowl games, and the Bowl immediately began recruiting better teams.

Once it was scheduled for New Year's, it fared well against other televised bowl competition. Because of its success and the promise of future success (it landed national championship games in 1987 and 1989), it was able to sell its title sponsorship to Sunkist Growers of Arizona and California.

In addition to the game, the Bowl has 34 events, sponsored by the likes of Ernst & Young, Insight.com, Nordstrom, Honeywell, Blue Cross/Blue Shield, and the current game title sponsor, Tostitos.

NATIONAL FINALS RODEO

When Las Vegas leaders decided to recruit a rodeo to come to town, they went after the best. What followed was a competition that attracts 115 contestants who compete for $4.6 million in prize money, the largest purse for a U.S. event. Every one of the ten events is a sellout (175,000 tickets sold).

Staged alongside the rodeo are the Bucking Horse and Bull Sale, the World's Champion Banquet, and the Spikes and Spurs Golf Tournament. Because the event is a good one, many sponsors—Dodge, Copenhagen, Jack Daniels, Justin Boots, and Wrangler—have stepped up to the plate.

The Arts

Good arts events, like the Houston International Festival, Seattle's Bumbershoot, and the Washington Mutual Coconut Grove Arts Festival in Florida, attract sponsors too.

HOUSTON INTERNATIONAL FESTIVAL

The $7.4 million Houston International Festival sells $1 million in sponsorship. Approximately 550,000 attend the event, which features nine Festival stages highlighting regional, national, and international performers, including Celtic, country, blues, rock, Tejano, zydeco, and other diverse musical forms.

The Festival also stages the highly successful Art Car Parade, featuring wildly decorated automobiles.

What makes the event unique is that it features a different country every year as its central theme. In 2001, the Festival showcased Ireland, thus including many Irish performing groups as well as a visit by the president of Ireland. For sponsors who do business in Ireland, this was an opportunity to interact with a head of state—a tremendous benefit to them and to the Festival itself.

BUMBERSHOOT

One of the many events produced by One Reel of Seattle, Washington, Bumbershoot has been called the "Mother of All Festivals" by *Rolling Stone* magazine. The entertainment at this performing arts event is diverse—the Black Crowes, Loretta Lynn, David Lee Roth, Taj Mahal, and the Lily Cai Chinese Dance Company have all performed on the event's stages.

Bumbershoot calls itself the "granddaddy of all parties," and each year the Labor Day event features the wacky, the wonderful, the artful, and the outrageous and sells $600,000 in sponsorship.

WASHINGTON MUTUAL COCONUT GROVE ARTS FESTIVAL

This event's title, the Washington Mutual Coconut Grove Arts Festival, already tells you that it is successful at selling sponsorship. It is also successful as a visual arts festival, held Presidents' Day weekend in the community of Coconut Grove, located next to Miami.

The Festival began in 1963 as a small clothesline art show featuring a few dozen artists and several thousand browsers. Today it attracts more than 750,000 visitors and generates approximately $20 million for the local economy. It is consistently ranked as one of the top art shows in the United States by leading publications. The festival features artists adept at working in watercolor, clay, fiber, digital art, glass, sculpture, painting, photography, wood, jewelry, metalwork, mixed media, printmaking, and drawing.

"Washington Mutual's [a new company in Florida when it first became a sponsor, and therefore very interested in strengthening its brand] commitment to the Coconut Grove Arts Festival is the company's largest ever financial commitment in support of a community event in Florida," said Gwynn Virostek, the company's senior vice president group manager for Florida.

MUSIC FESTIVALS

Two of the nation's top music festivals also do well in the sponsorship arena.

SunFest

SunFest of West Palm Beach, Florida, was created in 1982 to extend the Palm Beach County tourism season to the beginning of May. It draws 300,000 people annually and is one of the best-produced festivals in the country. Members of the International Festivals Association selected it as the best event in the state of Florida in 2000.

What separates SunFest from most festivals, besides its exceptional staff and volunteer organization, is its music. Whereas most festivals are content to have one or perhaps two name acts, Sun-Fest had George Clinton, Chuck Berry, Melissa Etheridge, the Black Crowes, Tower of Power, and several other performers during the four-day event in 2001 alone.

Summerfest

Summerfest is the ultimate music festival—in fact, it was dubbed "the biggest music festival" in the world by the *Guinness Book of World Records* in 1999.

This festival evolved from an idea inspired by networking. After visiting Oktoberfest in Munich, Germany, in 1968, the late former mayor Henry W. Maier dreamed about bringing a festival to reenergize the downtown area of Milwaukee.

What followed was an incredible event that has featured almost every major group. In the year 2001 alone, the festival featured Prince, Paul Simon with Brian Wilson, BoDeans and Joan Osborne, Poison, Destiny's Child, Tom Petty and the Heartbreakers, Jackson Browne, Tim McGraw, and Bon Jovi.

In 1990, Summerfest had Huey Lewis, the Temptations, and Michael Bolton, *all playing at the same time on different stages.* And, of course, along with this array of stars comes an incredible level of sponsorship—approximately $5.6 million.

"We always look for the predominant event in a market," says Dennis Boese, corporate manager of fair and festival marketing for the Miller Brewing Company. "If the event is featured in the six

The spires of Churchill Downs have inspired two outstanding events that conclude with the Kentucky Derby horse race each year on the first Saturday in May. The first is the Derby itself, while the second is the Kentucky Derby Festival, a series of events that lead up to the U.S.'s most famous horse race. The Derby Festival was one of the forerunners in the selling of sponsorship in the festival world. *Photo courtesy of Churchill Downs Incorporated.*

o'clock news, and in the hearts and minds of everyone all day long, that's where we want to be. That's why we're involved in events like Summerfest and the Kentucky Derby Festival."

THE KENTUCKY DERBY FESTIVAL

The Kentucky Derby Festival organization is entirely separate from the Kentucky Derby horse race, which is run by Churchill Downs. In fact, the Festival is so good, it would still exist if the Derby ceased to operate.

The Festival has many very large events (most festivals are lucky to have one): the Great Steamboat Race, the Pegasus Parade, and the largest annual U.S. fireworks show, Thunder over Louisville.

Sponsorship Selling

The Indy 500 Festival is similar to the Kentucky Derby in that it surrounds another celebrated event—in this case, the Indianapolis 500 automobile race. Like the Derby, it would continue even if there were no car race. This festival, too, has many large events. The Derby and Indy 500 festivals are both adept at selling sponsorship; in fact, the Derby Festival set the standard for sponsorship selling in the early 1980s under the leadership of the late CEO Dan Mangeot and is continuing this trend with current CEO Mike Berry.

All the events that are chronicled in this chapter—and many others that are too numerous to mention in this book—have one thing in common: They are so good that sponsors feel that they have to be a part of them. *So set a goal to make your event the very best!*

Yet it must be said that sponsorship is not for everyone. Mardi Gras in New Orleans does not have corporate sponsorship in the traditional sense. The event has more than 50 parades, all run by Krewes—clubs supported by individual members' dues. It is the dues that provide the funds to build Mardi Gras floats and to purchase beads.

Although membership in these clubs offers great opportunities for business networking (see Chapter 5 on benefits), it does not constitute sponsorship (see definitions at the beginning of this chapter).

Individuals who are members of Krewes receive benefits, but the sponsorship goals of their companies, besides the business-to-business opportunities, do not come into play. Brands are not strengthened, there is no sponsor visibility, and there is no return "for access to the exploitable commercial potential associated with [the] property."

There are also the cases of Stanford University and the University of California. The former cut back on sponsorship sold by its athletic department, and the latter also questioned its athletic department's sale of corporate sponsorship, concerned that it would lead to "excessive corporate entanglement."

Volker Kirchberg, in *Arts and Business,* writes that many German companies seek to maintain a low profile in arts sponsorship. "They do not ask for big plaques at restored buildings or an ostentatious display at a performing arts event (e.g., naming the event after the sponsor or displaying the name of the sponsor on stage)," says Kirchberg.

Choosing to Go Noncommercial

There have also been instances in which successful events elected to go noncommercial after selling sponsorship for many years, and the decision backfired on them.

In October 2001, CNN reported that the use of Adolf Hitler's image to advertise the Adelaide Arts Festival, Australia's most prestigious arts festival, triggered a $500,000 snub from Telstra, the country's largest telecommunications company.

A black-and-white television commercial showed the German World War II dictator behind a camera, apparently taking a photograph, then with his head superimposed on the body of the painter Pablo Picasso, and again sitting in a film director's chair.

A voice said, "In 1908, Adolf Hitler was turned down by Vienna's Academy of Fine Arts. If only his artistic side had been embraced and nurtured, who knows what he might have put his energies into? The arts do make a difference, as you are about to find out."

Telstra pulled its sponsorship of more than $500,000 when organizers hesitated to cancel the Hitler advertisements immediately. Even after the commercials were canned, the telco company still elected not to be involved with the event.

"Telstra is not prepared to be associated in any way with an organization using this person's name or image to obtain publicity for itself," a spokesman said.

Telstra had been a festival naming-rights sponsor for many years, until festival organizers decided that year on a deliberately anticommercial approach. "It appears they have succeeded beyond expectations," CNN reported.

The festival, regarded as Australia's finest, had already been cut by almost half following a decline in international tourism since the September 11 terrorist attack, and the demise of the country's second carrier, Ansett Airlines.

Despite the rare cases cited here, sponsorship is now sold by almost every significant event, as well as by several other entities. Needless to say, sponsorship is here to stay.

Now that you have determined that you are going to have an outstanding event, you are ready to move on to the nitty-gritty of sponsorship sales. That is what the remaining 14 chapters of this book are about.

The Keys to Creating a Strong Event

To create a sponsor-wowing event, make sure you:

- Present the dominant event in your community, or at least the best in your category (arts festival, music event, etc.).
- Appear on the six o'clock news often.
- Position the event in the hearts and minds of a good portion of your community.
- Do something that others cannot—present something special about your community (like the Gilroy Garlic Festival—90 percent of the garlic in the United States is processed in Gilroy).
- Develop an event that is held in high regard, and that has value.
- Change your event (keep the good things you do, but make them better and add to your program).
- Always strive to take your event to the next level each year.

- Act visionary.
- Research and adopt ideas from other events, and adapt them to your own situation.
- Make your event something that sponsors cannot stay away from.

Sponsorship Activities

1. Read Dr. Joe Goldblatt's book, *Special Events: Twenty-first Century Global Event Management,* especially Chapter 2, "The Five Critical Stages for All Successful Events."
2. Visit the following Web sites to learn more about the top events mentioned in this chapter.
   Portland Rose Festival—*www.rosefestival.org*
   SEAFAIR—*www.seafair.com*
   Salzburg Music Festival—*www.salzburgfestival.com*
   Edinburg International Festival—*www.eif.co.uk*
   National Cherry Festival—*www.cherryfestival.org*
   Sequim Irrigation Festival—*www.irrigationfestival.com*
   International Festival Lent—*www.lent.slovenia.net*
   Macon International Cherry Blossom Festival—*www.cherry-blossom.com*
   Fiesta Bowl—*www.tostitosfiestabowl.org*
   National Finals Rodeo—*www.lasvegasevents.com*
   Houston International Festival—*www.hif.org*
   Bumbershoot—*www.onereel.com*
   Washington Mutual Coconut Grove Festival—*www.coconut-groveartsfest.com*
   SunFest—*www.sunfest.org*
   Summerfest—*www.summerfest.com*
   Kentucky Derby Festival—*www.kdf.org*
   Churchill Downs—*www.kentuckyderby.com*
   Mardi Gras—*www.kernstudios.com*
   Boise River Festival—*www.boiseriverfestival.org*
3. Read Steven Wood Schmader and Robert Jackson's book, *Special Events: Inside and Out,* especially Chapter 4, "A Matter of Quality."
4. For a European perspective, read Rosanne Martorella's book, *Arts and Business: An International Perspective on Sponsorship.*
5. Using the events in this chapter, make a list of the common characteristics of successful events.

Sponsorship Tool Kit

Goldblatt, Dr. Joe, CSEP. (2002). *Special Events: Twenty-first Century Global Event Management.* New York: John Wiley & Sons, Inc.

Grey, Anne-Marie, and Kim Skildum-Reid. (1999). *The Sponsorship Seeker's Toolkit.* New York: McGraw-Hill.

Hoyle, Leonard H. (2002). *Event Marketing: How to Successfully Promote Events, Festivals, Conventions and Expositions.* New York: John Wiley & Sons, Inc.

Martorella, Rosanne. (1996). *Arts and Business: An International Perspective on Sponsorship.* Westport, CT: Prager Publishers.

Schmader, Steven Wood, and Robert Jackson. (1997). *Special Events: Inside and Out.* Champaign, IL: Sagamore Publishing.

CHAPTER 2

The Sponsorship Marketing Plan

Plans are nothing, planning is everything

DWIGHT D. EISENHOWER, 34TH PRESIDENT OF THE UNITED STATES

IN THIS CHAPTER YOU WILL LEARN:

- Why sponsors sponsor certain events
- What types of sponsorship events sell
- How to create a sponsorship menu
- What types of companies to target for sponsorship sales
- How your event can fit a sponsor's needs

In 1981, Jovan and the Rolling Stones joined together in an historic plunge into the world of sponsorship. Three years before the sponsorship explosion that began with the 1984 Los Angeles Olympics, the men's fragrance company and the legendary group combined for the first sponsored rock tour and, more important, forecast what was to come in the world of music sponsorship.

This sponsorship was modest by today's standards. Jovan paid only a paltry $100,000 in exchange for the "presenting sponsorship" of the 1981 North American Tour of the Rolling Stones. The company received two meager on-site benefits: mention on the event ticket and *one* sign in each stadium where the Stones performed.

Jovan sponsored the tour in order to heighten its visibility and strengthen its brand. In the early years of sponsorship, that was all that corporate America wanted—it treated sponsorship much like it treated advertising in the newspaper. Signage, television and other media coverage, and other mentions were used to create impressions.

Reasons for Sponsoring Events

Heightening visibility is still a strong motive for companies to sponsor events, but sponsorship has come a long way in the last 20 years. There are many more reasons that sponsors sponsor what they do in the twenty-first century, and we must first understand these before we develop a marketing plan: *Event managers must look at sponsorship through the eyes of the sponsor.*

According to the International Events Group (IEG) of Chicago, there are ten reasons that companies sponsor events (see Figure 2-1).

- Heighten visibility
- Shape consumer attitudes
- Narrowcasting
- Provide incentives for retailers, dealers, and distributors
- Entertain clients
- Recruit/retain employees
- Create merchandising opportunities
- Showcase product attributes
- Differentiate their product from competitors
- Drive sales

Source: Courtesy IEG.

Figure 2-1
IEG's Ten Reasons That Companies Sponsor Events

HEIGHTENING VISIBILITY

Visibility is often the first reason that companies sponsor events. Larger events enjoy the wide exposure that is provided, particularly by television, but also by print media, and the traditional sponsor benefits of signage, brochure mentions, and so forth.

"Outside of traditional television advertising spots, Sylvania received other benefits, ranging from the 10- and 15-second spot promotions ESPN ran during the month of December to promote the bowl game, to identify it on the field, along with score graphics and verbal references on team jersey patches," said Alamo Bowl executive director Derrick Fox.

Visibility was a major reason that the Colorado Lottery decided to sponsor the Capital Hill People's Fair located in Denver. Bruce Erley of Creative Strategies Group, a leading sponsorship sales company in Denver, created the Powerball Dance Hall at the Fair. The 40- by 80-foot tent included a swing stage, wooden dance floor, and various contests and promotions to appeal to the lottery's core customer.

SUCCESS STORY

HEIGHTENING VISIBILITY FOR SYLVANIA

Improving visibility was a leading reason that Sylvania chose to sponsor the Alamo Bowl in San Antonio. As title sponsor, Sylvania gained tremendous brand name awareness by the consumer. Led by the Bowl's ESPN television coverage, the company received $3.8 million in exposure (of which more than $3.6 million was provided by television).

Furthermore, Sylvania received recognition for providing funding for higher education and exposed its name/brand before a very targeted audience—school alumni and students (future employees, especially from schools that have engineering students).

Sponsorship Summary—Sylvania Alamo Bowl

Television Exposure	$3,643,548
Radio Exposure	60,215
Print Exposure	56,700
Website Exposure	18,150
Game Exposure	51,000
Hospitality/Event Benefits	63,507
Total Sponsorship Value:	$3,893,120

Visibility is often the first reason that companies sponsor events. Sponsors of larger events enjoy the wide exposure that is provided, particularly by television, but also by print media, and the traditional sponsor benefits of signage, brochure mentions, and the like.

As a result, lottery sales went up, and the branding heightened the visibility of the lottery's upcoming participation with the national Powerball lottery.

Carlsberg Brewing uses events to strengthen its global position. The company's global marketing activities have increased significantly in order to strengthen the consumer's close relationship with the brand worldwide. The brand achieved overall growth in 2000, experiencing a particularly strong sales development in the United States, Sweden, Portugal, several markets in Asia, and the duty-free trade.

Although traditional advertising forms the backbone of its brand communication strategy in most key markets, Carlsberg has pursued an active strategy toward developing direct contact and communication with consumers.

In keeping with a strategy for association with prestige sports, Carlsberg has made great efforts to expand its involvement in golf in Asia by developing sponsorship programs for the Maylasian Open, Singapore Masters, and Hong Kong Open.

Carlsberg continues to participate actively in the international world of soccer, generating great brand visibility and at the same time appealing to the hearts of the supporters of probably the most popular sport in the world.

The company was the main sponsor of the European Football Championships in 2000. This was the biggest event in the company's history—48 markets implemented the activity locally.

SHAPING CONSUMER ATTITUDES

It is in shaping consumer attitudes that sponsorship can create or change a brand image. Sponsors such as Coca-Cola and Pepsi do not need any more visibility, but they do like to tie in with particular lifestyles.

Conoco Oil sponsored Denver's Cherry Creek Arts Festival's environmental program, which included the industry's best recycling program created by then executive director Bill Charney. This sponsorship followed the Exxon Valdez oil spill in Alaska. By being proactive, Conoco gained a large amount of publicity and an environmentally friendly image.

AT&T became the presenting sponsor of the same festival. "They said that the festival was the perfect venue to help dispel a 'long distance' or far off perception about the long-distance phone company in the Denver area," said Charney.

NARROWCASTING

Sponsorship gives companies an opportunity to reach a niche market. Sylvania was certainly able to do that in the "Success Story" chronicled in this chapter.

Carolyn Pendergast, formerly with the University of California's athletic department, also achieved this objective by allowing her sponsors to gain positioning among students at arguably the top public institution in America. Companies like Cisco Systems highly valued the opportunity to participate in the university's career night for its 900 student-athletes. As sponsors, they were the exclusive corporate representatives who were allowed to attend the event. They set up recruiting booths, provided keynote speakers, and had one-on-one meetings with the student-athletes.

Ericsson, a manufacturer of mobile phones, sponsored the MTV Network's Europe Music Awards because it wanted to target a youth audience. Broadcast from the Festhalle in Frankfurt, Germany, the awards had a European distribution to more than 100 million homes and reached an estimated two-thirds of the world's population. The show featured a star-studded lineup that included Destiny's Child, Dido, and Janet Jackson.

As part of its sponsorship, Ericsson launched a limited edition of its A2618 mobile phone that enabled consumers to vote for their favorite stars via these mobile phones. Ericsson's "Make Yourself Heard" theme was used to increase brand awareness and brand perception among 16- to 25-year-old consumers. The event was also an opportunity to promote the usage of the mobile Internet and highlight its advantages for a modern, young consumer.

"MTV is the only music property available on a global basis, and together with other music-related marketing activities, MTV helps us to communicate our comprehensive youth-oriented product portfolio," said Jan Ahreneberg, vice president of marketing and communication at Ericsson's consumer division.

INCENTING RETAILERS, DEALERS, AND DISTRIBUTORS

Within the walls of retail stores, products are constantly fighting for shelf space. Some companies use sponsorship to ensure good shelf presence, which guarantees the ever-so-important eye contact with their products as customers wheel their carts down the aisles of stores.

The Beach Music Festival on Jekyll Island, Georgia, distributes thousands of tickets through Friendly convenience store locations. Coca-Cola works with the stores and the event to supply banners in front of all locations and point-of-purchase displays, and it offers a discount on its products.

Incentives for employees are tied to talent/entertainment by allowing the top five store managers and employees who sell the most tickets a chance to meet the entertainers and have their pictures taken.

These efforts create a win-win situation for everyone. The event receives more publicity and higher ticket sales, Coca-Cola gains valuable point-of-purchase locations, and the convenience store chain ties in with a popular event and provides perks for employees.

CLIENT ENTERTAINMENT

The opportunity to host clients at an event, especially those for which it is almost impossible to get tickets, sometimes pays for the entire sponsorship.

Lloyds Private Banking of London, a division of Lloyds Bank, was established to meet the financial needs of wealthy individuals. It provides a highly personal and discreet service to more than 26,000 clients.

The Lloyds Private Banking Playwright of the Year Award was launched in February 1994 as an entirely new initiative to support the arts. Lloyds Bank has long been at the forefront of arts sponsorship, but this award marked the first time a subsidiary company had created a significant and innovative scheme for an area of the arts that had been poorly served by commercial sponsorship.

The specific objectives were to provide support and encouragement to British and Irish writing talent and to help widen interest in regional as well as London theaters. The sponsor also had clear commercial objectives in mind. At the core of the company's marketing strategy was to demonstrate an unwavering commitment to excellence.

More important, establishment of the award created business-to-business development opportunities with key clients through corporate hospitality events. More than 20 of these events proved a great success in further strengthening relationships with clients as well as supporting regional theaters. The annual award ceremony has also provided a further opportunity to successfully host important clients.

When Sunkist Growers became the first bowl game title sponsor in 1985 for the Fiesta Bowl, this was a key ingredient in its sponsorship plan. The organization flew top supermarket executives to Phoenix from around the country—people who made the decisions about how much Sunkist produce their stores would purchase.

Guests received complimentary rooms at the five-star Arizona Biltmore Resort Hotel, free rounds of golf, exclusive opportunities to meet coaches and players, and 50-yard-line tickets to the game, a prime commodity when the Bowl hosted the national championship game in 1987 (Penn State vs. Miami) and 1989 (Notre Dame vs. West Virginia). There was a further advantage for Sunkist when the guests happened to be alumni of one of these schools. For its part, the Fiesta Bowl hired an employee for three months whose only job was to work with Sunkist to make sure that guests had the best possible time.

RECRUITING/RETAINING EMPLOYEES

During times of low unemployment, companies are required to go to greater lengths to recruit and keep employees, and they often use the sponsorship arena to help them.

When Intel wanted to promote its story and recruit new employees in a tight labor market, it sponsored the Portland Rose Festival's Air Show, which helped it grow to be Oregon's largest employer.

RCS Productions in Atlanta produced an event, the Memorial Musicfest, at Stone Mountain Park in Georgia. The financial backer of the event, Z-93 radio, sold the presenting sponsorship to one of its clients/advertisers, Cracker Barrel. Cracker Barrel utilized the sponsorship opportunity to recruit new employees by having a job fair on-site during the event. Besides banner rights, sampling, radio ads, and client and VIP hospitality, the company had a captive audience of more than 50,000 people who had the option to go to its tent.

The University of California athletic department and the Sylvania Alamo Bowl also used the recruitment incentive to their advantage in the examples mentioned earlier.

SUCCESS STORY

BARCLAYS SPONSORSHIP WINS EMPLOYEE SUPPORT

Barclays has been a long-term supporter of the arts, recognizing their value at a national and local level. In 1995 the company reviewed its sponsorship program to bring it more in line with its business objectives.

The key objectives were developed around positioning Barclays as a leading, enabling, and innovative organization, responsive to a recognized regional need. The arts provided a platform to reach existing employees.

Barclays Stage Partners, a specially created title sponsorship, was developed in collaboration with the Arts Council of England. Its purpose was to enable top-quality theater productions to tour the United Kingdom, and through this scheme Barclays has become the largest sponsor of regional theater in the country. As a result, a total of 39 plays have been produced, touring at 130 venues and reaching an audience of more than 1 million people.

And because the productions occur in all sizes of communities where Barclays has employees, the sponsorship has won widespread support and endorsement from that group.

MERCHANDISING OPPORTUNITIES

Sponsors can use events as merchandising opportunities—they provide something an event has to offer in exchange for purchases of their products.

In Florida, Pat Craig Corda of Events by Craig utilized something that is not rare in most of the country—but was unique in this location—an outdoor ice skating rink. She used it for a ten-day event that had a different sponsor each night, many of whom gave a $1.00-off skating coupon when their products were purchased.

From 1988 to 1992, Maxwell House Coffee was the title sponsor of the Portland Rose Festival Air Show. It increased its market share from 10 to 35 percent during the 90 days around the Show by distributing a commemorative Air Show poster with each purchase of a three-pound can of coffee.

SHOWCASING PRODUCT ATTRIBUTES

One of the truly tremendous things about sponsorship is that companies can actually see their products in action at a festival or event, which they cannot do with other forms of media. Event managers who showcase product attributes are doing a great service for sponsors, as they actually show their products to potential customers during an event. Wireless cell phone companies benefit from being in-kind sponsors by donating telephones to event producers, which are then seen in action by attendees.

Pontiac showcases its vehicles by lending them to the National Cherry Festival in Michigan. It supplies courtesy cars for Festival board members, VIPs, and guests to drive during the event, placing a logo on each for all to see.

The Cowboy Poetry and Music Festival receives a rent-free venue from the Melody Ranch Motion Picture Studio in Santa Clarita, California. The movie studio, which was used for filming Westerns such as *High Noon* and *Wyatt Earp,* is now the Festival's official sponsor, in exchange for a $20,000 in-kind sponsorship. With an attendance of 15,000, the Festival enables the studio to showcase its facility.

SunFest of West Palm Beach, Florida, works this angle well, providing booths for sponsors to promote one-on-one interaction. Each sponsor offers an activity, such as a rock climbing wall, a virtual baseball game, golf, and body painting (in good taste).

DIFFERENTIATING PRODUCTS FROM COMPETITORS'

Differentiating products from those of competitors is another area in which sponsorship scores high, inasmuch as an event usually ensures category exclusivity, which enables financial institutions and other service industries to stand out from their competitors.

Visa became the presenting sponsor of Baltimore's First Union Harbor Music Festival for $25,000. Not only did Visa's deal include on-site advertising and inclusion in print and media spots, it also encouraged use of the charge card.

Concertgoers who make Visa charges for lawn seats at any of seven designated shows in July and August receive two tickets for the price of one. The shows run the gamut from rap to Christian music because of Visa's desire to encourage use of its card across several demographic groups.

DRIVING SALES

An increasing number of companies are using sponsorship to drive sales.

As mentioned earlier, Pontiac is a major sponsor of the National Cherry Festival in Traverse City, Michigan. The 80 courtesy

During its coupon promotion with the Macon Cherry Blossom Festival, fast food sponsor Chick-fil-A saw a 13 percent increase in local sales. *Photo courtesy of Mary Huff.*

vehicles that the event receives for use during the event are sold as part of a major sales promotion after the event is over.

The Kentucky Derby Festival has a pin program that is unmatched. Each year it sells more than 500,000 pins at $2.00 each. In each pin envelope is a coupon worth more than $2.00, so the buyer knows that the pin will pay for itself. Sponsors who put coupons in the envelope have seen a significant increase in sales.

Another festival that benefits from a pin program is the Macon Cherry Blossom Festival. During its coupon promotion with the festival, fast-food sponsor Chick-fil-A saw a 13 percent increase in local sales.

The Marketing Plan

Once you understand what motivates sponsors, you can develop an effective marketing plan (see Figure 2-2). Before you begin the process, you have to create a list of sponsorships you would like to sell, paying particular attention to the items that would interest a sponsor (see Figure 2-3). There may be something that you need to have underwritten, but that would be of no interest to a sponsor because it has no value to that sponsor. There may also be items that do not need underwriting that a sponsor *may* be interested in sponsoring.

You should never sell something based on how much it costs you; you should sell it based on its value.

Keeping this maxim in mind, write down every possible thing that might be sponsored, including title sponsorship of your event (if appropriate), areas, stages, services, and so forth. Break down the event into as many areas as you can, because each entity can have a sponsor. If you have more than one stage, each can have a sponsor. For example, the Fiesta Bowl not only has Tostitos as a title sponsor, but hundreds of other sponsors. Floats are sponsored for the parade, and the Bowl has 34 other events, each with a sponsor(s). You can also have official beverages and other products.

Once you determine what you have to sell, it is time to determine to whom you want to sell these items—or for whom you can create the right fit.

---

1. Break down your event and determine what you have to sell.
2. Start by selling sponsorship to media.
3. Determine the categories of companies you want to approach (beverage, communications, financial institutions, etc.).
4. Make a list of companies that are already sponsoring in your market.
5. Find out what companies are doing in similar-sized markets.
6. Look at your accounts payable.
7. Look out for new categories when mergers occur.

Figure 2-2
Skinner's Elements of a Sponsorship Marketing Plan

Title Sponsor	$75,000
Presenting Sponsor	35,000
Stage Sponsorship (5)	10,000
Official Product	5,000
Fireworks	6,000
Title—International Food Fair	6,000
Information Center	4,000
Arts/Crafts Fair	5,000

Figure 2-3
Sample Sponsorship Menu

MEDIA SPONSORSHIP

First and foremost, sponsorship starts with the various media, because they can help you sell other sponsorships. Media are so important that many festivals that have multiple events attempt to get an official radio station for each. Although cash is king, event managers are most interested in the in-kind services a station can provide.

Radio stations can produce and broadcast advertising messages regarding your event, thus serving as a great promotional vehicle. When making a deal with a radio station, be sure that the spots are placed during times when most people are listening to the radio, preferably during morning and afternoon drive times. Radio stations are likely to be most cooperative if you contact them with sufficient information on an event, which will require little work on their part.

In addition, it is important for an event manager to make sure that a sponsoring station is permitted to mention the names of other sponsors in its spots. This can help to sell other sponsorships.

Good sponsors also augment their tie-in with an event by purchasing time and space from radio, television, and print media and, increasingly, on the Web. If a sponsor chooses to purchase radio time to promote its sponsorship, everyone wins. The radio station gets a good promotion and additional advertising revenue, the sponsor gets additional promotion via the event's radio spots, and the event receives much needed publicity.

Many events, like the North Olympic Peninsula Festival of Trees in Port Angeles, Washington, get their local newspaper to become a media sponsor by getting them to do a supplement that is inserted into the paper. *Photo courtesy of Rich Riski.*

SPONSORSHIP CATEGORIES

There are many categories of sponsorship that can be sold (see Figure 2-4 for types of sponsors). All types of beverage companies sponsor events—makers of soft drinks, beer, wine, water, juices, and so on. An event can really help a new product. There are two restaurants in Carefree, Arizona, just north of Phoenix, called the Horny Toad and the Satisfied Frog, that experienced nearly instantaneous success in event sponsorship. They introduced a microbrew—Frog Light—at an event in Phoenix.

The product became a success overnight, as people not only saw the product but actually tasted it. Because of the cost of traditional media, it was out of the question for Frog Light to attempt to compete with Budweiser's and Miller's substantial advertising budgets, but by sponsoring an event, it achieved its objectives.

Restaurants can be good sponsors, providing better and more diverse fare than the typical carnival-type food. Many events, especially tasting festivals, include restaurants. Not only do they provide food, they provide great food because they are already

1. Title Sponsor—Sponsor is part of the name of the event (Tostitos Fiesta Bowl).
2. Presenting Sponsor—Mentioned after the name of the event (The Rose Bowl, presented by AT&T). Not as valuable for the sponsor as title sponsorship, as most times the media in writing about the event will drop the name of the sponsor.
3. In-kind Sponsor—Cash is not provided, but service is. This is often as good as cash, as you are saving money on things you would have purchased anyway (airline tickets, food, beverage, etc.).
4. Official Sponsor—A product that is an event's exclusive sponsor.
5. Media Sponsor—Print, radio, television, Web site sponsors.
6. Co-sponsor—Company that is part of an event with other sponsors.

Figure 2-4
Types of Sponsors

accustomed to providing it for regular customers. In addition, many restaurant sponsors do not care how they do financially at an event, but provide even more and better food because their major objective is to generate traffic for their establishments months after the event is over.

Financial institutions and insurance companies also make great sponsors. They all provide basically the same products, so becoming involved in events where their competitors are not present is important. When Bank of America first entered the Phoenix market, it became the title sponsor of the local duck race. Not only did it provide cash up front, but it also adopted a $5.00 duck for each person who opened a checking account, which amounted to $70,000 in additional sales.

Retail outlets, airlines, communication companies—*just about every company that needs exposure*—can make good sponsors.

TARGETING COMPANIES

Focus on the large advertisers in your market, particularly those that sponsor other events. It is not necessary to sell them on the value of event marketing, just the value of the event.

Also focus on companies that sponsor similar events in other markets. This is where organizations such as the International Festivals and Events Association (IFEA), the International Events Group (IEG), and the International Special Events Society (ISES) can be useful, because you can network with other event organizers, particularly at their conferences and conventions, to identify likely sponsors.

Las Vegas Events hosted World Cup 2000, the world's top equestrian show jumping championship. President and CEO Kirk Hendrix saw that Budweiser was the largest sponsor of this type of event in the United States and approached the company with the title sponsorship of the event, to which it agreed.

Its sponsorship took Budweiser to another level, because the World Cup is the Super Bowl of the sport. All Grand Prix events the company had sponsored prior to the World Cup became the road to the World Cup.

The Cherry Creek Arts Festival's Bill Charney attended the Coconut Grove Arts Festival in Miami and saw that Häagen-Dazs was a major sponsor. He got a testimonial from the product's distributor in Florida and used it to sell the sponsorship to his Denver event.

"I also read trade journals," Charney said, "and not only went after companies that were listed, but also their competitors." He made them aware of what other companies in the category were doing, and it became the "added value" to what sponsors found in the relationship.

Many corporate contacts are not entrepreneurial and event managers may take the easy way out by making traditional media buys instead of putting together a difficult sponsorship package. Charney developed equity in his relationships by making sponsors more aware of what was happening in their own industries in regard to sponsorship and thus made them look smart.

Events like the National Cherry Festival focus on their accounts payable departments to seek additional in-kind sponsorship. "Every fall I look at the past year's payables to determine likely barter leads," said the Festival's Chuck O'Connor.

These events also focus on new categories, which are created when industries such as telecommunications, banking, and energy are deregulated. It was not long ago that the Cherry Festival had no energy-related sponsors, but now that customers have a choice in their purchase of energy, it has three such sponsors.

SPONSORS CAN BRING OTHER SPONSORS

Retail stores can bring in other sponsors in the form of products that are on their shelves. We will go into this in more detail in Chapter 8, "The Keys to Successful Sales." Retail stores have a tremendous amount of leverage in regard to the products in their stores and can help you increase your sponsorship levels by helping you sell to those vendors who are fighting for all-important shelf space.

You can also use entertainers to sell sponsorship. By working with an artist and touring sponsor early, an event can turn an entertainer's existing endorsement into a new participating sponsor.

Three Keys to Developing a Good Sponsorship Marketing Plan

To develop a good sponsorship marketing plan:

1. Learn which of the ten reasons for sponsoring an event motivates a potential company, and then develop your sales pitch around those reasons.
2. Determine the right fit for a sponsor in your event. Make sure your demographic matches the company's demographic.
3. Determine which companies are already sponsors in your community, both locally and nationally; then you do not have to sell them on sponsorship in general, but just on sponsoring your event.

Sponsorship Activities
1. Read Chapter 3, "Winning Markets: Market-Oriented Strategic Planning," in Philip Kotler's book, *Marketing Management: The Millenium Edition.*
2. Visit *www.event-solutions.com* and read steps 1 and 3 in the "10 Steps to Sponsorship Success."
3. Read *The Ultimate Guide to Sport Event Management and Marketing,* by Stedman Graham, Dr. Joe Goldblatt, and Lisa Delpy, Ph.D.
4. Read Chapter 6, "How to Start Evaluating Your Property," in Sylvia Allen and C. Scott Amann's book, *How to Be Successful at Sponsorship Sales.*

5. Create a hypothetical event and develop a list of the types of sponsorship you could sell for the event.

Sponsorship Tool Kit

Allen, Sylvia, and C. Scott Amann. (1998). *How to Be Successful at Sponsorship Sales.* Holmdel, NJ.

Beckwith, Harry. (1997). *Selling the Invisible: A Field Guide to Modern Marketing.* New York: Warner Books.

Graham, Stedman, Dr. Joe Goldblatt, and Lisa Delpy, Ph.D. (1994). *The Ultimate Guide to Sport Event Management and Marketing.* Burr Ridge, IL: McGraw Hill.

Kotler, Philip. (2000). *Marketing Management: The Millenium Edition.* Upper Saddle River, NJ: Prentice-Hall.

Schmader, Steven Wood, and Robert Jackson. (1997). *Special Events: Inside and Out.* Champaign, IL: Sagamore Publishing.

Sleight, Steve. (1989). *Sponsorship: What It Is and How to Use It.* New York: McGraw-Hill.

Web Sites

www.event-solutions.com

CHAPTER 3

Research: The Sponsor's Perspective

Last year our customers bought over one million quarter-inch drill bits and none of them wanted to buy the product. They all wanted quarter-inch holes.

ANONYMOUS

IN THIS CHAPTER YOU WILL LEARN:

- How to research your sponsor's needs
- How to discover how your sponsor's mind operates
- Why ongoing sponsorship research is important
- What is important and valuable to sponsors

In a city of 18,000 people like Port Angeles, Washington, it is very difficult to sell sponsorship at even modest financial levels to local sponsors, because most are small businesses with relatively miniscule marketing budgets. So when the Olympic Memorial Hospital Foundation wanted to get the sponsorship of a car to offer as first prize for its duck race fund-raiser, it found it had to do considerable research on a potential sponsor.

A duck race is a glorified way to do a raffle. People are asked to adopt (pay for) a rubber duck, which is numbered and dropped into a body of water that flows, if all goes well. The first ducks across the finish line win prizes (for which the fund-raiser tries to get sponsors) for their owners, including the typical first-place automobile.

The Foundation approached Wilder Toyota to donate the car, because the owner was on the board of the hospital foundation, the major recipient of funds for the event. The owner definitely wanted to do something for the race because of his interest in the community—a typical trait of a local sponsor—but did not want to donate a car, a heavy expenditure in such a small market.

Therefore, the Foundation knew that it had to do the research and help the owner to do business in order to get the coveted top prize. In their first meeting, dealership owner Dan Wilder told Foundation leaders that he tried to do two things to sell cars:

- Get people into the dealership—"It's very difficult to sell a car over the phone," Wilder said (people buy from people).
- Even more important, get people to test-drive a vehicle—If they do, he continued, "I've just greatly increased my chances to sell."

To assist him in achieving his goals, the Foundation helped Wilder establish a side event in conjunction with the duck race, in which people came by the dealership and guessed how many ducks were in the back of a Toyota pickup. That brought more business traffic to the dealership, and he adopted a duck for each person who test-drove a vehicle.

Once Wilder saw how the sponsorship could pay for itself, he gladly donated the vehicle.

Creating a Win-Win

Wilder had to advertise the contest, which became a win-win for everyone. He placed ads with two local media sponsors, the *Peninsula Daily News* and Radio KONP, which gave them additional revenue. The Foundation received more publicity for the race, and

Many events are able to get more sponsors by researching a company's needs. Duck races, like this one found in Singapore, can drive traffic into an automobile dealership, which leads to increased automobile sales. *Photo courtesy of Great American Merchandise and Events.*

Wilder got more traffic into his store. And the best news of all? Wilder had his best month in history. Now, without fail, he approaches Foundation organizers each year and asks, "We will get to be the car sponsor next year, won't we?"

That is sponsorship at the ultimate grassroots level, and even though sponsorship on a national level is more complex, the same principles still apply—you have to help a sponsor do business.

ANOTHER WIN-WIN AT A HIGHER LEVEL

In 1985, the Fiesta Bowl became the first college football bowl game to sell a title sponsorship—to Sunkist Growers of California and Arizona. At first glance, you may not think that Sunkist would make a good sponsor for a football game—it is mainly men who watch football, and mainly women who buy oranges. However, when Fiesta Bowl event managers further explored Sunkist's marketing goals and objectives, they found that the event did provide a good fit.

At first glance, Sunkist Growers of California and Arizona wasn't the ideal match to become the first title sponsor of a college football bowl game in 1985. However, Fiesta Bowl organizers found out their hot buttons and made the sponsorship work. *Photo courtesy of Jeff Stanton.*

Sunkist had a relatively small advertising budget, so making an ad buy on television was out of the question, as that would create very little impact. What interested it most were the following:

- Sunkist marketing executives wanted to be where no one else was, separated from the clutter of television advertisers. Obviously, being the first sponsor of a college football bowl game would accomplish that.
- They wanted to be with an event where they could entertain their major customers, the Safeways, Albertsons, and Krogers of the world.
- The Bowl included a televised parade, which had a large female viewing audience, to whom they wanted to appeal.

And so Sunkist did become the sponsor of the Fiesta Bowl, and the Sunkist Fiesta Bowl featured a national championship game twice in a three-year period, including the 1987 game between Penn State and Miami, which still is the most-watched college football game of all time.

Sunkist and Wilder Toyota? We're talking about a $3,000,000 sponsorship versus a $12,000 one, but you use the same principle with both: You have to look at sponsorship through the eyes of sponsors and accomplish their marketing objectives.

The Most Overlooked Step in the Sponsorship Process

Many event managers make the fatal error of not researching their potential sponsors, stumbling into corporate offices with little knowledge of the companies' marketing and other objectives.

One event that avoids this mistake is the Houston International Festival, one of the most important performing arts festivals in the country. Jim Austin, and many other marketers like him, go to one of the best sponsorship research tools of all time—the Internet.

"We attempt to understand the company's industry and environment," said Austin. "If Shell Oil, for example, is having trouble with the Nigerian government over payments for pipeline services, that knowledge endears us to the top brass at the company.

"It says, 'I care about your business and the issues that you face day-to-day.' It definitely reinforces that we are not a bunch of carnies who are looking for a big American corporation to pay our bills."

CORPORATE SPONSORSHIP PHILOSOPHY

Many sponsors have developed a corporate sponsorship philosophy. For example, if an event manager were to research Germany's DaimlerChrysler, he or she would discover that the company's approach to sponsorship includes three components:

- Corporate sponsorship focuses on community-related issues and chooses subjects suited to the company as a whole.
- Brand sponsorship is target-group oriented and focuses on marketing particular brands as well as defining brand image.
- Community relations programs are carried out at key DaimlerChrysler locations.

DaimlerChrysler currently works with the Berlin Philharmoniker, among others, to achieve its objectives. The company initiated the European Concerts in 1991 and has sponsored the concert as performed by the Philharmoniker every year of its ten-year history.

Traditionally, these concerts take place on May 1, the founding date of the orchestra in 1882, in a different European cultural metropolis each year. After Petersburg, Versailles, Stockholm, and Cracow, Berlin was chosen for the 2000 event. The concert is broadcast on television worldwide, and approximately 400 million people around the world watch it.

The first European Concert was held in Prague's Smetna Hall, and the company, then Daimler-Benz AG, and the Philharmoniker laid the foundations for an invaluable shared tradition. Since that time, this series of concerts, which transcends all language and cultural barriers, has been dedicated to European integration.

"Over the past ten years, the vision of European unity has become reality, not only in economic terms, but also culturally," said Jurgen E. Schrempp, chairman of the board of management of DaimerChrysler. "The cultural exchange between nations has played a crucial role in helping the member states of the European Union grow closer together."

Seeing Them Face-to-Face

The next step in the sponsorship process is the best way to research sponsors—meeting with them in person.

The Portland Rose Festival staff used that strategy to sell a significant sponsorship to General Motors. Before they pitched their event, they found out that GM's latest strategy was to generate leads for dealers to call on after the event. The staffers asked the company about its success stories and then tailored key traffic locations at Festival events for them to collect leads by distributing Festival-provided premium items. They landed a six-figure sponsorship that also allowed them to further market the festival through the giveaways.

Bill Charney also used the strategy at the Cherry Creek Arts Festival in Denver. Many sponsors were surprised that he did not have a proposal in hand when he came for the first meeting with them. It was important to him to develop the relationship and to determine the proper fit before even suggesting a deal.

Sometimes Charney gained the feeling that the prospect was not going to be a good fit, but he still achieved his goal of building positive relationships and developing a larger population of marketing personnel who had respect for the Festival sales team.

Ongoing Research

It is crucial to remember that research, like other phases of the sponsorship selling process, never ends.

The first title sponsor of the Alamo Bowl in San Antonio was Builders Square. Derrick Fox learned the company's hot buttons and then sold the sponsorship. But even after the sponsor said yes, Fox spent a considerable amount of time with the company learning its business.

In the process, he discovered that the Builders Square budget was very limited and that it was necessary to generate dollars in order to offset its sponsorship fee and, at the same time, generate additional dollars for the Bowl.

The Bowl entered into an agreement with Builders Square, accepting a reduced rights fee on the front end of the agreement, with the understanding that the parties would develop a mutually beneficial vendor program. At the height of the program, Builders Square secured support from 103 of its vendors, which raised $164,000 to offset part of its title sponsorship fee, and generated an additional $435,000 in sponsorship support for the Bowl.

The vendor program really helped the Bowl when the company began its downward spiral toward bankruptcy. During the last year of the sponsorship, the Bowl and Builders Square ended up with just six vendors to support the sponsorship. However, one of them was Sylvania, which became the next title sponsor, a position it still holds today.

GETTING INTO THE SPONSOR'S MIND

During the research process, it is important to get to know your sponsors so you know how they think. Often you can sell sponsorship in the strangest ways.

The Michigan Thanksgiving Day Parade knew that Chrysler was concerned about its image in Detroit when it moved its corporate headquarters to a northern suburb, angering many people in the city. The Parade sold the auto manufacturer the presenting sponsorship of the event, which became a good public relations tool for Chrysler, allowing it to show its investment and interest in the city and its people.

Doug Blouin of the Fiesta Bowl believes that there is always one person in an organization who can "carry the ball" for an event organizer. "It is crucial," he says, "to determine who that is and to build a solid rapport with him or her."

Because the Bowl works with the Big 12 and other conferences, Blouin always tries to find out the alma mater of a potential sponsor.

One of the Bowl's sponsors is a major telecommunications company that has a major executive who attended one of the Big 12 Conference's universities. The Bowl's relationship with the Big 12 provided a tremendous opportunity to establish a relationship with him on a more personal level.

HOT BUTTONS

Learning a sponsor's personal interests can be a big help too. As an event manager, you need to discover the interests of the marketing executives you are meeting, which can be any of a number of things—children, education, health and human services, sports, culture and the arts, quality of life, and so on. You should also

SUCCESS STORY

INFORMATIONAL INTERVIEWS

Bruce Erley of Creative Strategies Group in Denver explains "informational interviews." He arranges meetings with potential sponsors—not to pitch a specific sponsorship (he has not started the actual sales process yet)—but to learn from them about their marketing and communications objectives, past event marketing activities, annual sponsorship budget, communications objectives, and so forth. He then returns to his office and formulates a sponsorship of an event that best suits the needs of the potential sponsor.

"Our whole approach to sales is relationship building," said Erley. "We spend time with the sponsor contact and get to know his or her style of operating, interests, activities, and hot buttons."

learn about their hobbies, recreational interests, family, locale, and the like. It is no accident that golf enjoys a high level of sponsorship participation, due in large part to corporate America's desire to play golf with Tiger Woods and other professional golfers in pro-am events, for example.

By thinking outside the box, managers of festivals and other events can sell sponsorship appealing to personal interests too.

The Wildflower! Arts & Music Festival in Richardson, Texas, used to have a difficult time selling sponsorship to Nortel Networks. The answer to their proposals continually came back as "no" until Festival organizers met with Nortel and really listened to what would interest its VIPs and employees.

Out of that meeting came the Corporate Battle of the Bands. A major executive of the company was a professional horn player, and all of a sudden, Nortel Networks became a festival sponsor. After Nortel, Ericsson followed.

Wailing "Louie Louie" and crooning "Ba-Ba-BarbrAnn," corporate executives can now relive the garage band days of their youth at the festival while backing the event as a sponsor and promoting their company in the process. They get their five minutes of fame, as families and co-workers crowd in to cheer on "their" band.

Festival director Sandra Risk went further and increased visibility for these sponsors. She broke down the Festival into ten different zones, each named after a different sponsor. Each area has its own entrance—for example, "The Nortel Networks Gate"— which helps visitors to identify the location where they parked. The area surrounding each entrance carries the theme of the same company, and all those entering have a hand stamped with the company's logo.

A zone sponsor is also treated similarly to a title sponsor or a stage sponsor. The company name appears several times in publicity materials and the festival program, extending the sponsor's visibility throughout the event.

Events that feature children have strong sponsor potential. Family is very important to sponsors because, in many instances, both parents in a family are employed and are interested in doing top-quality things for children. Heather Bloyer, writing in *Festivals,* the official magazine of the International Festivals and Events Association (IFEA), gave an example of this approach concerning the Bank of America Coconut Grove Arts Festival in Florida. In order to beautify Festival grounds and to develop additional sponsorship revenues, the Festival uses an often wasted resource—its trash cans.

Each year the Festival and some of its sponsors hold a youth art competition called the "Dare to Design Art Program." Hundreds of kids from dozens of Miami-area schools submit original creations related to Coconut Grove, the arts, the Festival, and their awareness of the environment.

Selected entries adorn the event's trash receptacles, which are made from empty Coca-Cola syrup cans because of their smooth exterior and portability. Winners receive $100 savings bonds, $200 donations to their schools' arts programs, and a year's supply of Coke products for themselves and their schools.

Businesses jumped at the chance to sponsor the program when it began in 1999. Not only does it provide artsy trash cans that blend better with the arts festival environment, it also gives Festival sponsors a much desired, although hesitant, market, said president and CEO Carol Romine.

"The sponsors also love it because it gives them a presence in the school," Romine said. "These days getting into the school system is delicate for corporate sponsors. Parents don't want logos and advertising all over everything."

Festival sponsors get to send representatives to explain the program to schoolchildren, judge entries, and present the awards, which they donate. Because the sponsors work together, they have also formed friendships, which lead to additional accounts.

Bloyer writes in *Festivals* about another example of the growing number of children's events, made possible by a sponsor's interests, KidSpree in Aurora, Colorado. Event managers went a step further here and found a new way to convince business leaders of their festival's marketing charms.

By staging a special adults-only preview of their kid-oriented festival, they secured their first presenting sponsor, among others. They also raised scholarship funds and liberated a few inner-city children to boot.

Planners held the preview, called PreSpree, the night before KidSpree. They invited business and community leaders to leave their business suits behind and scamper through special adult-sized versions of children's activities.

In return for each $10 scholarship donation, participants received a commemorative pin and admittance to the event, where they scaled a climbing wall, boxed with padded gloves in a bouncy air castle, navigated through a 2500-square-foot maze, and created the silliest hats imaginable, among other activities.

The city enlisted the help of other community organizations, including the co-host, the Aurora Chamber of Commerce, to produce the new event. To get the word out to the adult business community, coordinators visited service club meetings. The Chamber also publicized the festival in its monthly newsletter and sent postcard invitations to all business leader members. Both organizations distributed a series of press releases and e-mail to local media and city employees to encourage attendance.

"The preview helped planners target businesses that would normally not have seen KidSpree's marketing benefits," said Laura Stitt, former city special events coordinator. After the event, the Aurora Credit Union Alliance agreed to become Kid Spree's first presenting sponsor and Adolfson Peterson became PreSpree's first sponsor.

USING DEMOGRAPHICS

While researching your sponsors, make sure you also research your own event. If your audience demographic matches up—*that is, if you have the right fit*—with those of your potential sponsor's customers, you almost always have an interested company. Often, the only thing that remains to be settled is the price.

"Don't ask Mack Truck to sponsor the Royal Canadian Ballet," write Steve Schmader and Bob Jackson in *Special Events: Inside and Out.* "It just doesn't fit. A good fit, on the other hand, is Pepto Bismol and the World Championship Chili Cook-off."

In *Shopping Centers Today,* Melanie Conty writes about how malls are getting into the sponsorship arena and how one of them is using research as a valuable tool.

Cindy Ciura, SCMD, and president of Cierra Creative Marketing Services in Bloomfield, Michigan, first researched a sponsorship program with GM MasterCard at malls in Palm Beach, Florida and Troy, Michigan.

"Once I knew that the GM Card really wanted the markets that my shopping centers were in, it made things a lot easier," she said.

"Once they saw the malls' traffic counts and demographics were exactly what they sought, GM officials were happy to pay half a million dollars to be there."

ASSOCIATIONS, CONVENTIONS, AND TRADE SHOWS

No matter what type of event or venue you are attempting to sell a sponsorship for, research is very important. Many associations that stage conventions and trade shows have begun to sell sponsorship, particularly to their vendor members.

Once again, you have to look at the needs of vendors. Here are some strategies used by the International Festivals and Events Association:

- Keep in mind that sponsorship sales depend on building a trusting relationship with vendor members. People buy from people.
- Listen to vendor member needs, and tailor sponsorships to suit their individualized marketing strategies.
- Ask yourself these important questions: What types of organizations are you trying to reach? What would you like to communicate to them?
- Look for ways to create win-win situations for both your organization and the potential sponsor.
- Package benefits. Make sure you give potential sponsors the ones they really need.

SUCCESS STORY

IFEA AND THE PARADE COMPANY

The Parade Company in Detroit rents and sells floats, inflatables, and costumes to parades. The company's goal was to actually show these inflatables and costumes to parade decision makers. Therefore, the sponsorship proposal from the International Festivals and Events Association not only contained valuable advertising opportunities, but also the unique opportunity to stage a parade at the association's annual convention.

The parade led delegates down a half-mile route to a social/dinner function. Each delegate became part of the spectacle, and many felt it was a special honor to have the streets closed and a police escort. As a result, The Parade Company significantly increased its business, as many parade event managers who attended the convention started to lease products from the company.

1. Research the company well—Companies are responding less and less to random appeals. They are looking for partners in major projects to work with over a long period of time. Fund seekers should not approach major companies without doing initial market research.
2. Locate a number of tools to use—Companies' Web sites include anything from a paragraph to several pages on their sponsorship policy. Also read company publications, directories, and documents published by national associations promoting business sponsorship of members of CEREC.
3. Find the point of contact at the company—It may be someone who is in charge of your geographic area, or someone who is interested in your issues (e.g., education, environment, etc.).
4. Know what different people in a company are interested in when they are sponsoring your event—for example: sponsorship officer (direct or indirect returns), foundation director, marketing manager (increasing brand awareness), development manager (increasing market shares), or corporate affairs manager (social investment).
5. Be careful about timing—Sponsorship has to be budgeted for in advance.

Figure 3-1
Five Key Issues for European Fund Solicitors

EUROPEAN RECOMMENDATIONS

The European Committee for Business, Arts and Culture (CEREC), headquartered in Barcelona provides support and advice to arts organizations in Europe in developing relationships (predominantly sponsorships) with businesses. This network of associations, agencies, and businesses exists to promote partnerships between the private sector and the arts to their mutual benefit across Europe. At the 2nd European Sponsorship Congress staged in London in March 2000, CEREC cited five recommendations that apply to event managers worldwide in researching sponsors (see Figure 3-1).

We discuss demographics further in the next chapter, "The Effective Sponsorship Proposal," but your own research can be used to help you sell a sponsorship and also to price it for what it is worth.

Six Keys to Researching Your Sponsors

There are a number of ways to research sponsors:

1. Read about your sponsors in annual reports and other documents, and be sure to use the best research tool of all—the Web.
2. Always try to meet your sponsors in person and to see their sponsorships through their eyes.
3. To further research your potential sponsors, set up "informational interviews."
4. Learn the interests of your sponsor—family, sports, education, hobbies, and so on—get into the sponsor's mind.
5. Never stop researching the businesses of your sponsors.
6. Match the demographics of your event with those of your potential sponsor.

Sponsorship Activities

1. Read Part III, "Know Thy Sponsor," in Sylvia Allen and C. Scott Amann's book, *How to Be Successful at Sponsorship Sales.*
2. Look at the Web site of CEREC, the European Committee for Business, Arts and Culture, *www.aedme.org,* and read its tips for researching sponsors.
3. List the reasons that it is important to research your sponsors.
4. For your hypothetical event, explain how you would research potential sponsors.

Sponsorship Tool Kit

Allen, Sylvia, and C. Scott Amann. (1998). *How to Be Successful at Sponsorship Sales,* Holmdel, NJ.

CEREC, the European Committee for Business, Arts and Culture, *www.aedme.org*

CHAPTER 4

The Effective Sponsorship Proposal

Don't sell the steak, sell the sizzle!

ELMER WHEELER, AMERICAN *advertiser*

IN THIS CHAPTER YOU WILL LEARN:

- How to customize a sponsorship proposal for a business category and a business within the category
- How to present added value and benefits that will get a sponsorship proposal noticed
- How to present demographic information about your event to help you match the demographic of your sponsor—called "creating the right fit"
- How to help sponsors differentiate themselves from their competitors—known in the marketing world as "separating from the clutter"

The best proposals are those that utilize all of the techniques mentioned in the first seven chapters of this book. If you are successful in researching and in developing added value and, most important, if you have *looked at sponsorship through the sponsor's eyes,* your proposal will be almost like a letter of agreement.

You have already agreed on almost every point in your last face-to-face meeting. Not only has the company agreed to be your sponsor, but details of the agreement have already been negotiated and only final tweaking needs to be done.

Unfortunately, once again, many properties skip all of the aforementioned procedures and mail off tens and even hundreds of proposals that pay little, if any, attention to the wants and needs of the sponsors. These presentations cover only what the event needs, and not what the sponsor desires. The proposals are generic—no matter whom the event manager is sending them to, they read exactly the same.

Proposals like these most often end up in the potential sponsor's trash can. Even if an event gets lucky once in a while, it will only receive a small amount of cash. Figure 4.1 is an example of one of those presentations, which, unfortunately, is what all too many sponsorship proposals look like. The event is a festival of trees, one of many similar events that are held across the country between Thanksgiving and Christmas.

A typical tree festival displays Christmas trees that are sponsored by companies and then designed by interior decorators or artists. They are typically auctioned off at a black-tie gala event at high prices, which are thus among the most successful fundraising events in the country. However, many tree festivals are staged by hospital foundations and other philanthropic organizations. These organizations are good at raising money through contributions, but many do not understand the sponsorship game.

Obviously, in this example the president made no attempt to find out about the telecommunications company's business. That is why his presentation violated many of the principles of creating a good proposal. This presentation:

- Was not customized to the sponsor's business category.
- Was not customized to the individual sponsor within the business category—what are its target markets as compared with its competition?

September 5, 2002

Telecommunications Company

Anywhere U.S.A.

Dear Sue:

I am writing you hoping that your company will once again be a sponsor for the 2003 Festival of Trees.

Since its inception in 1991, the Festival of Trees has grown to be the most successful event in the state. More than 5000 people now attend it over a three-day period, and it raises vital monies for equipment at the hospital.

Because the Hospital District encompasses two cities, this event is an excellent vehicle for you to cover both communities. Next year's event will be held November 21–23.

If you choose to be a seven-foot tree sponsor for $550.00 (our cost), you will receive:

1. A seven-foot, fully decorated tree, which can be designed by you or by a designer that we will find
2. Two special guest admissions to the Festival Gala held Friday, November 21
3. Ten Festival admission tickets for public days (November 22–23)
4. Recognition in the special festival program and at the event itself
5. Mention in the official publication of the hospital, which is distributed to every home in two counties
6. An eight-page advertisement in the local newspaper.

Thank you for your consideration. I will call you in the near future to discuss this further.

In the meantime, if you have any questions, please don't hesitate to give me a call.

Sincerely,

Foundation President

Figure 4-1
Proposal for a Communications Company by a Festival of Trees Organization

- Did not mention any items that would give added value, and did not consider the company's marketing goals.
- Did not price the sponsorship correctly. Just because a tree cost the Foundation $550 does not mean that the sponsorship is worth that amount—its value may be higher or lower, depending on the sponsor.
- Did not contain any demographic information on the event or whether that audience will fit the customers of the sponsor.
- Did not provide for product category exclusivity—the sponsor's competition might be in the same room.

There are, however, numerous examples of good proposals, such as that in Figure 4-2, developed by Bruce Erley of Creative Strategies Group in Denver.

In contrast to the presentation for the festival of trees, this proposal was developed after several meetings with the sponsor. It is a great example of what you can achieve by listening and addressing the needs of the sponsor. This proposal:

- Places Coors at a special level, separating the brewer from its competition. This is especially important at a beer festival that features many different beers. The proposal raises Coors above other beer sponsors by giving the company "recognition as industry leader and benefactor."
- Presents demographic information on the event and indicates how the audience fits one of the target markets of Coors.
- Includes the opportunity to build brand promotions within the festival.
- Suggests that Coors become the sponsor of the Educational Pavilion (which it did), which describes the process of making beer. This also places Coors as an industry leader.
- Gives Coors substantial media and Internet exposure.
- Allows Coors to show a video that Creative Strategies learned it wanted shown during an earlier meeting.
- Provides the sponsor with hospitality benefits that will be of interest to its key customers, clients, and employees.
- Concludes by looking at the needs of the sponsor: "an excellent investment in the achievement of Coors Brewing Company's key marketing and communication objectives."

Another top-notch proposal comes from the National Cherry Festival in Traverse City, Michigan, which, once again, addresses the needs of the sponsor, as shown in Figure 4-3.

(text continues on page 64)

An Ensemble of Rights and Benefits

The Great American Beer Festival (GABF) has designed our sponsorship program to provide you with the greatest possible exposure and opportunity to reach and impact your key target groups. Among the marketing and communications rights and benefits Coors Brewing Company will receive as an Official Sponsor are:

- **Top Level Industry Sponsorship of the Great American Beer Festival**
  - Sponsor name receives presenting recognition with nation's leading beer tasting event (e.g., "Coors Brewing Company . . . Official Sponsor of the Great American Beer Festival").
  - Guaranteed dominant presence to a highly desirable Male 21–34 audience of 22,000 people attending three sold-out public tastings between August 16 and 18, 2003, at the Colorado Convention Center in Denver, Colorado.
  - Recognition as industry leader and benefactor.
  - Multiyear agreement with first right of refusal allows for strategic implementation of sponsorship benefits and the opportunity to build brand promotions with GABF.
- **Proprietary Naming Opportunity for Exclusive GABF Program or Venue**
  - Sponsor receives first right for proprietary naming rights for specific events or venues within the festival (e.g., "Coors Brewing Company Educational Pavilion"). Key naming opportunities for Official Sponsors include:
    - Education Pavilion
    - Exhibition Area
    - Volunteer Program
    - Brewer's Hospitality Area
    - Brewer's Gathering
    - Judges' Reception
- **Guaranteed Media Coverage**
  - Primary logo recognition in Denver ADI paid and promotional advertising, valued at $135,000+, by media partners: ($204,000 in 2002)
    - *Denver Rocky Mountain News* (renewal pending)
    - The Hawk Radio (renewal pending)

Figure 4-2
The Great American Beer Festival and Coors

- Official Sponsor status in all press kits and general news releases
- **Internet Exposure**
  - Logo recognition on GABF's homepage on gabf.org
  - Hot link from GABF Festival Homepage to sponsor's Web site
- **Extensive On-Site Dominance**
  - Dominant name position on exterior of the Colorado Convention Center marquee banner, seen by 8500 downtown drivers daily
  - Dominant logo position on sponsor marquee banner inside Hall A of the Colorado Convention Center
  - Rotating logo recognition and acknowledgment on Video Wall
  - Opportunity to give video presentation on Video Wall *(maximum running time: 10 minutes)*
  - Dominant on-site signage through prime placement of four aisle or wall logo banners throughout Exhibition Hall
  - Logo recognition on industry sponsor marquee banner inside Brewers Hospitality Area and at Awards Ceremony attended by 2000 brewing industry executives from across the nation
- **Full Promotional Rights**
  - Top-level, Official Sponsor trademark recognition in all GABF collateral promotional materials including:
    - 5000 GABF Promotional Posters distributed throughout Colorado prior to the event
    - 5000 Promotional Kiosk Cards distributed locally and mailed nationally
    - 1500 Volunteer T-shirts
    - Full-page, four-color ad in premium location in 10,000 Programs (can do front/back inside cover)
  - Opportunity to participate in GABF Special Offers
    - Right to create and promote GABF sweepstakes and contests
  - Opportunity to create cross-promotions with other GABF corporate sponsors and media partners
- **Customer Relations and Staff Benefits**
  - Hospitality Benefits for distribution to key customers, clients, and employees, including:
    - 100 GABF Public Session Tickets
    - 20 Invitations to Awards Ceremony

Figure 4-2
(Continued)

- 10 Invitations to Judges' Reception
- 10 Tickets to private Brewers' Gathering

An Excellent Marketing Value

Your sponsorship of the Great American Beer Festival is an excellent investment in the achievement of Coors Brewing Company's key marketing and communications objectives.

Source: Courtesy of Bruce Erley, Creative Strategies Group.

Figure 4-2
(Continued)

Pontiac-GMC
2002 National Cherry Festival Sponsorship Proposal

Acclaimed by Travel Michigan as Michigan's number one event, and as one of the nation's top festival events by *USA Today* and *Private Clubs* and *Coast to Coast* magazines, the National Cherry Festival is attended annually by more than 500,000 people. Scheduled for July 5 through 12, 2002, the 75th National Cherry Festival will offer nearly 150 events and activities, including chances to win brand new *Pontiac-GMC* vehicles. Guests will enjoy family and children's events, free *GMC* Truck Air Shows, sporting events, band competitions, three colorful parades, fishing contests for the kids, an arts and crafts fair, and a high-profile music concert series, all in Traverse City, Michigan. In addition, there are various forms of free, live entertainment and activities all week long at multiple Festival venues, including the Festival Open Space Park, located on the beautiful shores of Lake Michigan.

The following benefits will be coordinated for *Pontiac-GMC:*

I. National Cherry Festival to provide advertising and promotion to *Pontiac-GMC:*
   A. *Pontiac-GMC* will be granted automotive exclusivity and recognized as the "Official Automotive Sponsor of the National Cherry Festival."

Figure 4-3
The National Cherry Festival and Pontiac-GMC

B. All public identification and recognition of *Pontiac-GMC* during the NATIONAL CHERRY FESTIVAL will be made as follows: "*Pontiac-GMC,* Official Vehicles of the NATIONAL CHERRY FESTIVAL . . ."

C. *PONTIAC-GMC* name/logo will be denoted in official NATIONAL CHERRY FESTIVAL PROGRAM, produced by *Traverse City Record Eagle* newspaper, as Official Sponsor (45,000 subscribers plus handout overrun).

D. *PONTIAC-GMC* name/logo attachment to NATIONAL CHERRY FESTIVAL advance postcard (50,000).

E. *PONTIAC-GMC* name/logo will be attached to *Michigan Lodging Directory* advertisement (inside back cover), circulation of one million (1,000,000).

F. *PONTIAC-GMC* sponsorship affiliation will be included in annual media and press relations program.

G. One (1) full-page, four-color *PONTIAC-GMC* ad in the NATIONAL CHERRY FESTIVAL'S *Official Pocket Guide* (50,000).

H. *PONTIAC-GMC* name/logo attachment, as Official Sponsor, to a minimum of two (2) painted Lamar Advertising outdoor billboards on prime highway arteries for months of May, June, and July—daily effective circulation of 27,000 to 2.4 million impressions.

I. Minimum of one thousand (1000) *PONTIAC-GMC* exclusive: 30-second television commercials on Charter Communications Cable Network.

J. Two :30-second spots each in the NATIONAL CHERRY FESTIVAL Heritage Parade, Junior Royale Parade, and Cherry Royale Parade live television broadcasts on Northern Michigan ABC affiliates.

K. Live and taped radio and television media interviews with *Pontiac-GMC* corporate representatives, and NATIONAL CHERRY FESTIVAL spokespersons on behalf of *PONTIAC-GMC,* throughout the eight-day event.

L. Web site/on-line: Year-round *PONTIAC-GMC* links to NATIONAL CHERRY FESTIVAL Internet homepage (www.cherryfestival.org), and related interactive Internet activities. *The Festival's interactive site received more than four million hits in an 11-month measured period*

Figure 4-3
(Continued)

from October 18, 2000, to September 7, 2001, including over 1,000,000 hits during the eight-day event in 2001, which featured live audio and video streaming, an on-line "Safari & Win!" contest featuring Pontiac-GMC contest clues, and our new Cherry Festival on-line store.

   M. *PONTIAC-GMC* will have the right to use the new NATIONAL CHERRY FESTIVAL logos (with prior written approval).

II. *PONTIAC* Title Sponsorship of the NATIONAL CHERRY FESTIVAL Commemorative Pin Program:

   A. NATIONAL CHERRY FESTIVAL and area civic group volunteers will conduct a six-week "Go for the Gold" *Pontiac* Commemorative Pin sales campaign.

   B. Exclusive automotive logo rights on 65,000 2002 Commemorative Pins and packaging.

   C. A comprehensive media plan will emphasize the giveaway and *PONTIAC-GMC* as the official automotive sponsor of the NATIONAL CHERRY FESTIVAL:

      1. Includes a minimum of two thousand (2000) :30-second cable television spots featuring the grand prize vehicle

      2. Inclusion in all television, radio, and print news stories relating to the *Pontiac* giveaway event

   D. Expanded *Pontiac* giveaway exposure through a trailered display, with the Grand Prize vehicle moving from various NATIONAL CHERRY FESTIVAL venues and pre-event sites with *Pontiac* Commemorative Pin sales representatives.

   E. *Pontiac-GMC* corporate representative to award the grand prize vehicle in the Commemorative Pin giveaway show on Saturday evening, July 13, in front of a live NATIONAL CHERRY FESTIVAL audience. Winner of the grand prize *Pontiac* and presenters to be interviewed for television broadcast on 11:00 P.M. local news.

   F. The Festival and *Pontiac* will donate fifty percent (50%) of the proceeds from the sale of *Pontiac* Commemorative Pin sales to the Kiwanis Club of Traverse City for the Boys and Girls Club.

   G. NATIONAL CHERRY FESTIVAL designated Event Director to coordinate Pontiac Commemorative Pin sales: Jim Bard.

Figure 4-3
(Continued)

III. *GMC* title sponsorship of the NATIONAL CHERRY FESTIVAL Air Shows:
  A. Both Saturday and Sunday, July 6 and 7, Air Show will be referred to as the *"GMC Truck Festival Air Show"* in all promotion.
  B. *GMC* logoed banner/signage at the Air Show center point and VIP area adjacent to Clinch Park Marina on West Grandview Parkway in Traverse City, Michigan, for two (2) days—Saturday, July 6, and Sunday, July 7.
  C. Exclusive *GMC* vehicle display at the Air Show center point for two (2) days—Saturday, July 6 and Sunday, July 7.
  D. A minimum of twenty-five (25) VIP viewing area tickets.
  E. Live interviews with *GMC* representatives from show center on Sunny 102 WLDR Radio (100,000 watts), radio co-sponsor.
  F. *GMC* name/logo attachment to Air Show editorial in the Official NATIONAL CHERRY FESTIVAL program.
  G. *GMC* name/logo attachment to Air Show media campaign including:
    1. One (1) ¾-page, two-color ad in TC *Record Eagle* newspaper
    2. Broadcast promotional schedule leading up to event
    3. *GMC* attachment as Air Show title sponsor in April NATIONAL CHERRY FESTIVAL Press Conference
    4. *PONTIAC-GMC* name/logo attached to related press releases
  H. *PONTIAC-GMC* name/logo on VIP area Air Show passes (2000).
  I. NATIONAL CHERRY FESTIVAL designated Air Show Event Director: Steve Plamondon.
IV. On-site exposure to *PONTIAC-GMC*
  A. A tented display area, minimum of twenty-five feet by fifty feet (25' × 50'), will be provided for a *PONTIAC-GMC* vehicle display in the Open Space Park for eight (8) days.
  B. Space for the *Pontiac Aztek* (or other) trailered display in the Open Space Park will be provided for all eight days.
  C. Space for three (3) *Pontiac* and three (3) *GMC* Official Vehicle banners. (These and additional banners will be moved

Figure 4-3
(Continued)

to various venues and perimeter fencing throughout the week, reflecting crowd traffic and guest opportunities.)

  D. Inclusion of *PONTIAC-GMC* specialty unit in the Cherry Royale Parade (fee waived). (The trailered Pontiac give-away car may be entered in all three Festival parades.)

V. Additional provisions to *PONTIAC-GMC*

  A. Use of related mailing lists and databases. *NATIONAL CHERRY FESTIVAL will provide PONTIAC-GMC with the Pontiac "Go for the Gold" Pin Program database/mailing list.*

VI. Tickets and Hospitality to *PONTIAC-GMC:*

  A. Hosting and hospitality packages for eight (8) representatives at the following VIP events: *GMC* Air Show, Sponsor Fireworks VIP Reception, Cherry Royale Parade VIP viewing area

  B. One (1) foursome in the Sponsor golf tournament (Pontiac vehicle display as hole-in-one prize)

VII. NATIONAL CHERRY FESTIVAL will return all *PONTIAC-GMC* courtesy vehicles by July 15, 2002, to Bill Marsh Motors, located at 1621 South Garfield, Traverse City, MI 49686. NATIONAL CHERRY FESTIVAL will provide *PONTIAC-GMC* with two (2) proof of performance ROI summary binders.

Pontiac—GMC Sponsorship Investment:

I. The Agreement will commence as of the signing of the agreement by both parties and end on December 31, 2002.

II. *PONTIAC-GMC* to pay a sponsorship fee of _____ to NATIONAL CHERRY FESTIVAL.

  Payment as follows:

  A. _____ within thirty (30) days after invoice upon execution of the contract.

  _____ within thirty (30) days after invoice upon receipt of proof of performance packages.

III. Loan TBD 2003 model year, factory equipped PONTIAC-GMC vehicles for use as courtesy vehicles by the NATIONAL CHERRY FESTIVAL. The NATIONAL CHERRY FESTIVAL will

Figure 4-3
(Continued)

> pick up vehicles at time and location determined by PON-TIAC-GMC. Models and option content to be determined and mutually agreed upon by both parties.
>
> IV. Loan a minimum of four (4) 2002 model year, factory equipped PONTIAC-GMC vehicles for limited static display purposes only. Specific models and option content to be determined by PONTIAC-GMC.
>
> V. Deliver one (1) 2002-model year *Pontiac* to raffle prizewinner.
>
> VI. Provide a minimum of three (3) *"Pontiac-Official Vehicle"* and three (3) *"GMC-Official Vehicle"* banners.
>
> VII. NATIONAL CHERRY FESTIVAL to use descriptive copy and artwork for appropriate advertising and publicity items to maximize *PONTIAC-GMC* exposure.
>
> *Source:* Courtesy of the National Cherry Festival.

Figure 4-3
(Continued)

Most people will tell you that proposals should be short. This one is not, because, again, it looks more like a letter of agreement. Its creation followed several meetings between the Festival's marketing director, Chuck O'Connor, and the sponsor. It includes all of the benefits that the sponsor, in this case Pontiac-GMC, wanted to receive.

This is an effective proposal because it addresses the needs of an automobile sponsor *and* the needs of Pontiac-GMC dealers in Michigan. Key parts of the proposal include:

- Section I.A.—Pontiac-GMC is granted automotive exclusivity at the festival, which enables the company to separate itself from other automobiles and dealers.
- Section I.L.—Web site/on-line links featuring a contest that activates the sponsorship with Pontiac-GMC contest clues.
- Section II.D. and E.—The opportunity to showcase product, which is extremely important to automobile sponsors. This is a good example of customizing a proposal according to the business category.
- Section III.A. and C.—Title sponsorship is granted, which

greatly heightens visibility, and, once again, the product is showcased.

- Section IV. B., C., D.—More showcasing.
- Section VII.—Features the most important benefit for any automobile sponsor—a promotion to drive traffic into the dealership. The courtesy cars were part of a special sales promotion once they were returned. Another great example of customizing!

Of course, both the Coors and Pontiac-GMC proposals were made after face-to-face meetings, and although we highly recommend such an approach over "cold calling," you will not get in the door every time. In fact, more than once you will be faced with a sponsor telling you, "Send us a proposal, and then we will see whether we need to set up a meeting."

In that case, a proposal must be concise, relatively short, and hard-hitting. You are counting on a potential sponsor being hit quickly between the eyes with one of your points that fits with his or her marketing goals and objectives (see Figure 4-4 for the European Committee for Business, Arts and Culture's tips for developing a good sponsor proposal).

Figure 4-5 is a good example of a generic proposal from the International Festival of Lent in Maribor, Slovenia. It was developed before it was tailored to a sponsor's needs and desires, but represents a good place to start.

- Be careful about timing—sponsors budget months in advance.
- Be businesslike in your approach.
- Write in clear and short sentences—send ten pages of material at the most.
- Be prepared to negotiate.
- Don't just ask for cash—include possible in-kind support too.

Figure 4-4
European Committee for Business, Arts and Culture's (CEREC)
Tips for Developing a Good Sponsor Proposal

Dear Sir,

The International Festival of Lent is the largest summer open-air event in Slovenia. It is organized by the public institution Cultural Centre Narodni Dom Maribor, established by the City of Maribor.

In seventeen days more than 400 different cultural performances take place every year. More than 400,000 visitors from Slovenia and abroad enjoy opera, ballet, classical music, jazz, theater, dance performances, folklore dances, jam sessions, rock and country music, carnival performances, exhibitions, musicals, fashion shows, children's workshops, street theater and fireworks.

Many esteemed musicians and artists have performed at the Festival. They include Ray Charles, B. B. King, Lester Bowie, Stephane Grappelli, Jimmy Witherspoon, Howard Johnson, Maynard Ferguson, Jose Feliciano, and Paquito D'Rivera, as well as the great street theater group Plasticiens Volants and many others.

The International Festival of Lent will take place in Maribor, in the old part of the city called Lent, which is located by the banks of the Drava River. The main stage is a large floating stage on the river, supported by many other activities in the Lent area.

The main parts of the Festival of Lent are the jazz music festival JazzLent, the Children's Festival, the Street Theatre Festival, and the international C.I.O.F.F. folklore festival FolkArt, in which groups from all over the world take part.

This year's Festival will be perpetuated with names like Simple Minds, David Sanchez, Tania Maria, the Blues Brothers, Paquito D'Rivera, Vocal Samplings, Dr. John, the Kiev Ballet, and folklore groups from Portugal, Italy, Armenia, the United States, Poland, Brazil, Ukraine, and the Russian republic of Kalmykia. There will also be outstanding street theater group performances, including the fantastic French group Cie Eclat Immediat et Durable.

It is our belief that our festival offers many unique business opportunities for sponsors, and that you will have numerous possibilities to position yourself with our audience.

The following is our sponsorship price list:

MAIN GENERAL SPONSOR	(already closed deal)
GENERAL SPONSOR	50.000 DEM
SPONSORS OF INDIVIDUAL EVENTS	20.000 DEM
COSPONSORS	10.000 DEM

Figure 4-5
Sample Proposal Letter from the International Festival of Lent

GENERAL SPONSORS AT THE FESTIVAL OF LENT or sponsors of a single program block or stage (JAZZLENT, FOLKART, PROGRAMME FOR CHILDREN, SPORT LENT, STREET THEATRE FESTIVAL, THE OLD VINE STAGE, LENT STAGE) will receive:

- Formal signing of the contract at a press conference
- Announcement of the sponsor at every program presentation of the Festival in the daily newspaper *Večer*, on Radio Maribor, Radio City, and on national television
- Logo on the background wall in the press center and in the VIP pavilion.
- Logo on festival posters
- Three panels on the main stage on the Drava river for all 16 days of the Festival (on the sponsor's day, the panel is moved to the central location of the main stage)
- Publication of the logo several times a day on two big screens during the festival
- Recognition when events are announced
- Logo on two jumbo panels located at the Festival
- Recognition in the daily newspaper *Večer*, on Radio Maribor, Radio City
- Publication of the logo in the Festival of Lent program
- Publication of a sponsor's coupon with logo in the Festival of Lent booklet
- Publication of the logo on the Festival of Lent 2003 homepage, *http://lent.slovenija.net/,* with a link to the sponsor's homepage
- Possible catering of approximately 100 business partners in the VIP lounge, with reservation of VIP seats to watch the performance
- Ride on VIP raft for guests of the sponsor (up to 50)
- 20 VIP passes for every day use
- Possible setup of a commercial hot air balloon at the event
- Press conference in the press center on the day of the performance
- 100 festival booklets
- 50 "Sponsor of Festival of Lent" badges for the sponsor's employees
- Possible selling or distribution of products of the sponsor during the Festival
- Distribution of the sponsor's commercial material
- Publication of the sponsor's logo on the Festival of Lent postcards

Figure 4-5
(Continued)

> - Possible recognition of sponsor on official T-shirt or hat at cost
> - One-time complimentary use of the Narodni dom Cultural Center venue
> - Other benefits also to be considered
>
> For any other information please contact us at ++386 62 229-4001 or by fax, ++386 62 225-376, or by E-mail: *nd@nd-mb.si.*
>
> Please visit our Web site http://lent.slovenija.net.
>
> Best regards,
>
> CULTURAL CENTER
> NARODNI DOM MARIBOR
> Director
> Vladimir Rukavina

Figure 4-5
(Continued)

Five Keys to Developing a Good Proposal

A proposal must:

1. Be filled with added value and benefits, meeting the company's marketing goals.
2. Contain pertinent demographic information about your event that matches the potential sponsor's target audience.
3. Be highly customized for the business category and for the sponsor within the category—if it is not, it is in the wastebasket.
4. Provide for the opportunity to be exclusive, thus separating the sponsor from its competitors.
5. Provide plenty of exposure, not just signage and brochure mentions, but substantial media exposure.

As stated earlier, the proposal itself should be short. However, feel free to include any background material on your event, preferably in a notebook that is well tabbed. In addition, you need to include several high-quality photos of your event.

The Portland Rose Festival was creative in developing its proposal for Verizon Wireless. Not only did they prepare a well-documented and graphically pleasing document, they accompanied it with a cookie decorated like a cellular phone. *Photo courtesy of Portland Rose Festival Association.*

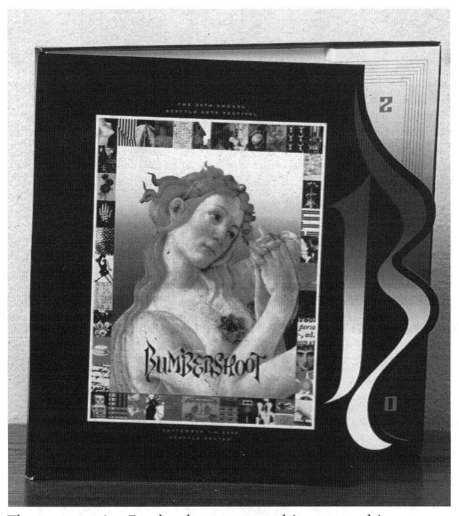

The ever-creative Bumbershoot presented its proposal in a package that resembled a record album. *Photo courtesy of One Reel Productions.*

"The point is not to make them arty," said Bruce Storey, former CEO of the Cherry Creek Arts Festival in Denver, in the *IFEA's Official Guide to Sponsorship.* "Rather, show brand names adjacent to crowds representative of the demographics your prospect needs. Spend the money this year to employ a good professional photographer so that you will have the correct tools for next year's proposals."

Sponsorship Activities

1. Read Chapter 3, "Creating an Effective Proposal," in the International Festivals and Events Association book, *IFEA's Official Guide to Sponsorship.*
2. Read the section "Pricing: Determining What a Sponsorship Is Worth" in *IEG's Complete Guide to Sponsorship.*
3. List the main components of an effective proposal.
4. Create a proposal to a potential sponsor for your fictitious event.

Sponsorship Tool Kit

IFEA's Official Guide to Sponsorship. (1992). Boise, ID: The International Festivals and Events Association.

Ukman, Lesa. (2001). *IEG's Complete Guide to Sponsorship,* Chicago, IL: IEG.

CHAPTER 5

Benefits: The Formula for Sponsorship Success and Growth

There will always, one can assume, be a need for some selling, but the aim of marketing is to make selling superfluous. The aim of marketing is to know and understand the customer so well the product or service hits him and sells itself.

PETER DRUCKER, AMERICAN BUSINESS PHILOSOPHER AND AUTHOR

IN THIS CHAPTER YOU WILL LEARN:

- How to add value to your event sponsorship packages
- How to use sponsorship exclusivity to your advantage
- How to use the demographics of your event to improve your properties
- How to provide business-to-business (B2B) opportunities
- How to activate your sponsorships
- How to provide the best in sponsorship hospitality

Even when corporate America was deeply involved with sponsoring events following the 1984 Los Angeles Olympics, it still found it difficult to get out of the "contributions" mode.

For decades, companies supported events, "donating" money to them each year (at much lower levels than they do now). In return, they received merely a listing in the event's program, which would appear in 10-point type along with hundreds of other contributors. The only extra benefit those early contributors might have expected is a few tickets to an event, and if they were big sponsors, to be listed in 12-point type.

So when contributors started becoming sponsors in droves in the mid-1980s, most were very happy with the now minimal additional benefits they received. Instead of the 10- or 12-point type listings, all of a sudden they were getting huge signs at the events they sponsored, with their names and logos on posters, brochures, and tickets.

The Growth of Added Value

When sponsors started to gain more experience in event marketing, things started to change. More sophisticated sponsors and properties got together and took a smarter approach—creating added value to agreements.

When Sunkist and the Fiesta Bowl became partners in 1985, the signatories included new, value-added benefits in their agreement, which would later become commonplace in the world of sponsorship (although the number of benefits the citrus grower received does not come close to those provided today).

First, they took signage to a new level. The Bowl placed street pole banners in three strategic locations—on the Bowl's parade route on Central Avenue in Phoenix, around the stadium where the game was played in Tempe, and perhaps most important, at Sky Harbor International Airport. That first impression at the airport struck Sunkist executive Ray Cole. "When I arrived in Phoenix, I thought we owned the town. I was blown away," Cole remembers.

And so were the 600 guests Sunkist flew into town—many of them buyers of large quantities of citrus products.

Hospitality, as it is for many events today, was a key part of the Sunkist sponsorship's strategic plan: Marketing executives wanted to provide a memorable experience for the select group of invited guests. The Bowl and Sunkist worked very closely to achieve this geniality.

For its part, Sunkist paid the bills, treating each guest at the then five-star Arizona Biltmore Resort Hotel to a room, golf, tennis, and other amenities.

The Bowl hired an employee for three months whose only job was to take care of Sunkist. In addition, it invited guests to already established and exclusive events and to others it created—all top-notch and original. The goal of each event was to develop a one-of-a-kind affair. All of the guests were accustomed to attending many social functions both in and out of their own communities, so *creativity* was the word of the day.

The Bowl was already famous for providing hospitality for the official parties of the competing teams, so it simply included top executives in these established events. When the official parties of the competing teams flew to the Grand Canyon on donated corporate planes, top Sunkist officials and guests were included too.

The Bowl's media party—huge at any major sporting event—was held in a hotel ballroom. A feeling of being in a football stadium was created, complete with typical game-day food concessions.

Immediately following the game, guests attended a party in the Arizona Biltmore Grand Ballroom, which also had a game-day atmosphere. A football "stadium" was constructed, complete with bleachers, Astroturf, and yard markers. But instead of watching a live game, guests viewed the Orange Bowl on a giant television screen.

The topper was an event sponsored by Golden State Foods, the largest distributor of McDonald's restaurant products in the world. Dress was black tie only, entertainment was provided by the Phoenix Symphony Orchestra, and Willard Scott of the NBC *Today Show* was the guest speaker. He had been the first Ronald McDonald, and event managers showed footage of him in his "Ronald" attire.

Yet as good as these preparations were, they were not what made the event special. The location, the Golden States Foods warehouse, was a distinguishing factor, but the icing on the cake was the meal served:

> *Big Mac under Glass, with French Fries and*
> *Chicken McNuggets!*

The Bowl also helped Sunkist with its business-to-business opportunities. Until 1985, the parade had a policy that only two politicians—Arizona's governor and Phoenix's mayor—could appear in the parade. Otherwise, every politician in the state would have to be included, taking advantage of the parade's large attendance along the route and its national television coverage.

However, it was of great interest to Sunkist that politicians who were important to it on the state and federal level be included, so the Bowl found ways to achieve that. It also created opportunities for Sunkist to meet with these elected officials one-on-one.

CREATING REAL VALUE

Before creating added value, it is important to consider what sponsors do *not* want to hear. You have to take time to listen to sponsors before you can develop top-shelf benefits (see Figure 5-1).

- Look beyond the traditional sponsorship benefits of signage, brochure mentions, etc. Go to the next step and create added value.
- Provide the best in hospitality. Let your sponsors receive and visit places that no one else can (VIP hospitality tents, private parties, etc.).
- Create business-to-business opportunities—get your sponsors together with other business leaders or government officials through your event, which will provide additional business opportunities for them.
- Exclusivity provides for excellent value. Sponsors like to be where their competitors aren't!
- Make your demographics fit your sponsors', which allows them to target their customers.
- Activate sponsorship—give your sponsors the opportunity to do promotions and other things at your event.
- Help your sponsors. They often do not have the expertise or knowledge about how to maximize sponsorship at your event— you know your event better than anyone else.

Figure 5-1
Skinner's Secrets for Creating a Benefits Package

Sylvia Allen and C. Scott Amann, in *How to Be Successful at Sponsorship Sales,* cite actual examples from recent sponsorship packages received by potential sponsors:

- *Your logo on all banners.* "OK, now what?" say Allen and Amman. "What is the exposure, what is the competition, where are the banners being placed, etc.?"
- *Your logo on all promotional material.* "What material? Who does it go to? What is the value to me as the sponsor?"
- *Right to place banner at your booth.* "I hope so! They are paying for the space!"

Business-to-Business Opportunities

Today, creating business-to-business opportunities is extremely important. This is something event organizers can do that other traditional forms of media may not.

The National Cherry Festival struck a deal with a company, providing a 46-foot sailing catamaran with sponsor logos on the mainsail to take corporate decision makers on a day cruise. For many business leaders this would be worth the price of the sponsorship in itself—an opportunity to visit with other executives with whom they would like to do business.

CEREC, the European Committee for Business, Arts and Culture, located in Barcelona, Spain, gives helpful tips to event managers, urging them to create business-to-business opportunities for sponsors.

The CEREC publication *The Business of Heritage* cited, "One of the main audiences for the business world is the private sector. Show business that you can deliver public sector contacts. Make sure that businesses know that the public sector (local or regional or national European ones) supports your project."

While Bill Charney was at the Cherry Creek Arts Festival, he made developing such opportunities a priority. "We got serious in this area," Charney said. "I think this is one of the most underperforming aspects of most festival sponsorship programs."

Charney asked a graphic design firm to provide logo/trademark supplies to all other sponsors, which gave the designers business leads for the future. Camera supply stores joined forces with photo labs. Catering companies sponsored VIP areas, and taxi companies shuttled VIPs.

The Portland Rose Festival started a relationship with a local top classic rock station to sell booth space in a large exhibit tent as part of a radio package for its customers. It brings the Festival another $40,000, but most important, it provides another sales inventory piece with which the radio station can distinguish itself in a tight market.

The Michigan Thanksgiving Day Parade has a pre-event, a 10K run called the Turkey Trot. Two vendors of Arbor Drugs were looking to get better shelf placement in drugstore chains in Detroit between Thanksgiving and Christmas. A three-way deal gave Arbor title sponsorship of the event, and Kimberly-Clark (Huggies) and Duracell (batteries) paid the sponsorship fee.

Because of its title sponsorship, Arbor increased its in-store traffic, Huggies sold more diapers, and Duracell more batteries, and the parade organization received sponsorship dollars.

The Houston International Festival features a different country each year for its ten-day event. Organizers put together extremely valuable one-on-one time between leaders from these countries and the Festival's sponsors, especially those who might be doing business overseas.

Also in Houston, a manufacturer of a chocolate syrup wanted to do business with an ice cream manufacturer. The chocolate company decided to place an advertising buy in an event sponsored by the ice cream company. Not only did the former get exposure from the ad buy, it was also invited to a party hosted by the ice cream company for event participants and sponsors. At that venue the chocolate company executives were able to meet with the company targeted for its business, the ice cream company.

Many event managers also hold sponsorship workshops, which can achieve many goals. For these workshops, they typically get all of their sponsors together and stage educational sessions on event sponsorship. Sponsors talk to each other and exchange ideas on how they can do a better job of being sponsors at the festival, which leads to discussions on how they can do better business with each other after the festival is over.

In Europe, business-to-business opportunities are also very important. *The Business of Heritage,* the official publication of

The Houston International Festival, which honors a different country at its event each April, matches important diplomatic figures with sponsors who want to do business with those countries. *Photo courtesy of Ellis Veneer.*

CEREC, recently said. "For cultural events, it is often very important for the business to know that you are solvent. But it is also important for businesses to know that the public sector supports the project. Show business that you can deliver public sector contacts. After all, one of the main audiences for the business world is the public sector."

SUCCESS STORY

U.K. RETAILER CREATES ADDED VALUE IN SEVERAL AREAS

In November 1995 international spirits and food retailer Allied Domecq became the principal sponsor of Britain's Royal Shakespeare Company (RSC) for a fee of £5.5 million (British pounds) for five years—the largest single arts sponsorship in the United Kingdom.

Because of the sponsorship, the RSC increased its overseas touring program dramatically, from only 10 weeks in the 1993 season to 35 weeks in 1996. Allied Domecq has actively supported tours in the United States, Japan, Hong Kong, Mexico, Australia, New Zealand, South America, and South Africa. Meanwhile, this sponsor achieved many goals:

- **Business-to-Business Opportunities**— The principal goal achieved by Allied Domecq was that it enhanced the corporate image of the company as a major international retailer among its predominately city-based audience investors, analysts, business media, and politicians. To celebrate the end of a 20-week tour of the United States, the company sponsored a high-profile event in New York attended by diplomats, politicians, and senior management.

- **Activating Sponsorship**—The company also integrated its sponsorship with marketing activity in support of individual brands and outlets. Pub scratch card promotions, direct mail that targeted students, and a Beefeater Gin promotion offering a weekend in Stratford, England, illustrate the breadth of the activity.

- **Employee Benefits**—The sponsorship also extends to the company's employees, who enjoy the benefits of the deep-rooted partnership; employees are the recipients of complimentary tickets. The RSC also holds workshops for employees in company offices, teaching them skills to inspire and motivate them in their work.

Target audience research has confirmed that the sponsorship is reaching its key objectives. Eighty percent of respondents were aware of the sponsorship, 84 percent thought that it improved the company's image, and 70 percent said that the sponsorship improved their opinion of Allied Domecq. The company says that the partnership has positioned Allied Domecq as a major international company with a world-class portfolio of brands and as a provider of world-class entertainment.

Exclusivity

One of the real powers event managers hold in the sponsorship arena is their ability to make a company the lone sponsor in its category. This allows the sponsor to differentiate itself from its competitors.

When you can segment the audience and your demographics match the demographics of your sponsor's customers, you have achieved the right fit and created an extremely important benefit.

DEMOGRAPHICS

SunFest in West Palm Beach, Florida, was able to persuade the state of Florida to sponsor its Youth Day. Organizers presented the state with the age statistics of the event's attendees and were able to obtain antitobacco partnership money targeting children ages 10 to 14.

For the University of California's athletic department, Carolyn Pendergast segmented the university's fan base according to seating sections. If a local lumber company wanted to distribute coupons on the seats of the alumni/Bear Backers, she could target specific sections. If someone wanted to reach students, companies could sponsor pom-poms for the student section. She also segmented the family section and young alumni sections in order to match sponsors with the demographic audiences they wanted to reach.

GUINNESS AND PUB THEATRE

In 1995, Guinness and London's Royal National Theatre brainstormed ideas for an innovative sponsorship in which the National's expertise and commitment to the theater world could be used to its best advantage and Guinness's support would have a direct and natural link with its brand and target audience.

The brewer sought to find an area to support where it would have that link. It found it in pub theatres, where owners of traditional pubs set aside space in their bars for stage productions and benefit from the increased drink orders from the audience before, during and, after the performance.

These pub theatres were invited to apply for cash prizes of £10,000 (British pounds) given for productions of new or established works with an emphasis on innovation and creativity. The first year in London was so successful that it extended the scheme nationwide.

This created a win-win situation. British pub theatres received new support, and Guinness reached its target audience.

"Guinness's business has always been rooted in the enjoyment of our customers and so the combination of the best traditions of the British pub and stimulating new work in the theatre is particularly good for us and, we hope, good for pub theatre, too," said Guinness Chairman Tony Greener.

In Las Vegas, the Web site of the *Las Vegas Review Journal* newspaper, *lasvegas.com,* wanted to reach a national and international audience. The small company did not have the budget to buy television advertising on such a large scale, but it achieved its objectives by sponsoring the World Cup equestrian championships.

Attendance for the event was almost entirely made up of people from outside the state of Nevada, 25 percent being from outside the United States. In addition, Las Vegas Events, the organization that brought the event to Las Vegas, provided *lasvegas.com* with 30-second television spot commercials on ESPN2.

The Houston International Festival has a very strong educational program. Organizers prepare text and other educational materials on their featured country each year and provide them to school districts in Texas. The program stimulates student interest, which in turn leads kids to bring their parents to the festival, greatly increasing the event's family demographics. For many sponsors, this adds value, especially for those who might be turned off by a rowdy audience.

SUCCESS STORY

USING DEMOGRAPHICS AT CHERRY CREEK

The Cherry Creek Arts Festival found that demographics were key to selling its sponsorship. "We demonstrated," said Bill Charney, "that while our event attendance included the full spectrum of income categories, we were the only large-scale public event that included big numbers on the affluent end of the spectrum."

In fact, the Festival demonstrated that its average attendee had a higher income than the average visitor to the Cherry Creek Shopping Center, which is one of the nation's premier upscale shopping malls.

Much of the Festival audience also had a college or higher-level education. Using this fact, along with the financial demographics, the event managers were able to establish that the Festival's audience also contained a large number of active voters. This led to an unprecedented sponsorship deal with Denver's Rapid Transit District.

TRUE NUMBERS

Cherry Creek also achieved what it did because it gave accurate attendance figures to sponsors. Event managers are famous for exaggerating attendance figures. In fact, many are afraid to do audience surveys because of what they might reveal. It is only a matter of time before the media will crack down on inaccurate event-attendance figures. And savvy sponsors know audience figures estimated by organizers of free events can often be greatly reduced.

Cherry Creek is one event that did not exaggerate its attendance figures. Instead of bragging about how its attendance grew in physically impossible proportions, event managers were vigilantly honest.

Even when the police said that 500,000 people were in attendance, event managers told sponsors that only a little more than one-third of a million people attended the event. "We would also tell them that, to be really honest, we had probably 240,000 individuals, because surveys showed that 25 percent of our attendees came more than one day," said Bill Charney.

This also helped sponsors to realize that sponsoring a sporting event like Denver Bronco football games was not really reaching 75,000 people (the capacity of the stadium) times eight games, because most were season ticket holders who attended every contest.

Cherry Creek used demographics to its advantage and built a sense that the Festival managers were being forthright and not trying to fool anyone with exaggerated attendance figures. "I sincerely think our industry would be in better shape if this were the norm," Charney says.

Hospitality

We mentioned earlier that providing opportunities for sponsors to entertain key clients is an important way an event can add value to sponsorships.

The National Cherry Festival's Chuck O'Connor believes that hospitality is based on excitement. The Festival sets up VIP hosting venues related to the event's major music shows, air shows, parade, golf tournament, and fireworks finale.

"They're so successful because the event revolves around exciting and/or interactive activities conducive to networking and socializing," says O'Connor. "Providing sponsoring companies the opportunity to host their key clients, prospects, and employees in this setting creates an extremely valuable sponsorship asset."

Each year the Festival offers VIP concert hosting packages. First, planners bring in top-name entertainment to a relatively small market—the Beach Boys, Christina Aguilera, Bonnie Raitt, Tim McGraw, the Neville Brothers, and other stars.

For $100 per guest (minimum of eight), companies can bring VIP guests, customers, prospects, vendors, or employees for one or more of each year's concert performances. For the fee, the Festival provides them with food and beverage, seating, hosting, VIP parking, and most important, *VIP treatment that no one else can get.*

Sporting event properties like the Fiesta Bowl can and should offer maximum hospitality. Americans in particular are hero worshipers, and even when their sporting heroes let them down with an off-field incident, they are quick to forgive.

Sporting events enjoy an advantage over other events by having winners and losers, and when teams and individuals win, many fans are not only loyal to their teams and the players (even if they do embarrassing things at times), but also to the team's sponsors.

In the major metropolitan Bay Area market, the University of California separated itself not only from other events, but also from other sporting entities. The Bay Area has two major league baseball teams, two NFL teams, an NBA franchise, and an NHL team, not to mention another major college competitor across the Bay (Stanford).

"We invited sponsors to barbecues at the athletic director's house and had our coaches there," said Carolyn Pendergast, former director of marketing for the university's athletic department. "We also invited them to tailgate parties with key alums and business leaders [more business-to-business opportunities]. In a major market like the Bay Area, the personal touch went a long way."

There are many other outstanding examples of sponsor hospitality. SEAFAIR in Seattle, which hosts the largest unlimited hydroplane race in the United States, brings sponsors by helicopter to the race from Boeing Field. The Las Vegas Rodeo takes sponsors behind the scenes, down by the bucking shoots and into locker rooms.

Despite not having the advantage of sporting properties, several events have created outstanding hospitality areas for sponsors. Sunfest in West Palm Beach, Florida, a music festival that features several big-name acts each year, has a VIP tent that is "a festival within a festival." Organizers provide lunch and dinner,

Seattle SEAFAIR helps sponsors pay for their sponsor fees by allowing them pass-through rights. *Photo courtesy of Seattle SEAFAIR.*

open bar, private restrooms (very important at a festival with many attendees), and a view of the main stage from an on-the-water location.

The Wildflower! Festival in the Dallas suburb of Richardson, Texas, does the same. "It used to be that we couldn't get people to go into the VIP tent," says director Sandra Risk. "So we created a party within a party, and the tent has become the hot spot. Now we can't keep people out."

Activating Sponsorship

Beyond signage, media impressions, and hospitality, activating sponsorship is what can take sponsorship to the next level.

It can be as simple as doing the duck-in-the-truck contest mentioned in Chapter 3, during which people were invited to the Toyota dealer's showroom to guess how many ducks were in a truck and were then given a free entry (normally $5) in the raffle-like duck race if they test-drove a vehicle. That met the two chief goals of an automobile sponsor—to get people into the showroom and to get them behind the wheel of a car—greatly enhancing a dealer's chances of selling a vehicle.

Another example of sponsorship activation is for event managers to set up sponsorship booths, as mentioned in Chapter 2. SunFest, located in West Palm Beach, Florida, set up booths with games so that marketing partners of the event could interact with attendees face-to-face.

Milwaukee's Summerfest, the largest music festival in the country, does this with Best Buy. As a major sponsor, the company is allowed to sell CDs and tapes of acts performing at the festival.

Another great example is found at the Freightliner/G.I. Joe's 200 presented by the Texaco automobile race, held in conjunction with the Portland Rose Festival. G.I. Joe's is a major Northwest sports and auto retailer. The festival's agreement with the company allows it to receive a credit toward its title sponsorship fee for helping promote the race in its Sunday newspaper circular. This, in turn, brings vendors from its store into the event's sponsorship mix. In an attempt to attract a younger fan base, the race is seeking vendors with tie-ins to products that will attract youth to the event.

Seattle's SEAFAIR has been very successful in working with convenience store retailers like Texaco, 76, and 7-Eleven. SEAFAIR makes the stores headquarters for its event and provides discount ticket offers, radio remotes, and cross promotions, whereby sponsors promote each other. It has also allowed pass-through rights for its sponsors' vendors to help pay for the sponsorship, which helps them offset the price.

Major Value

A final step can add tremendous value to what you provide for all your sponsors. Make sure that you educate everyone on your staff, and if yours is a nonprofit event, all your volunteers, on the importance of your sponsors. Write about them in your newsletters. If Coke is your sponsor, make sure that people never see a Pepsi can when they come into your office. Encourage people to purchase cars from your automobile sponsors (and make sure you drive one too). If Coors is a sponsor, serve Coors beer at your wedding (as Bill Charney did when he was at Cherry Creek). Do everything possible to establish the fact that you love your sponsors' products.

Tell your sponsors constantly how much you appreciate them. No one does this better than Carolyn Crayton of the Macon, Georgia, International Cherry Blossom Festival. She treats them with respect, makes them feel important 365 days a year, and even sends them cards on special occasions.

Help Sponsors Create Benefits

It is imperative that you, as an event manager, give benefits, benefits, benefits, because many sponsors are not sophisticated enough to think of what they really want by themselves. Many of them are, after all, grocers, auto dealers, and insurance executives—not special event marketing professionals.

"Be prepared to assist the potential sponsor with determining objectives his or her company should meet through sponsor participation," Steve Schmader and Robert Jackson say in their book,

Special Events: Inside and Out. "Surprisingly, too many companies frequently do not know what they really want or how they can benefit from such programs."

Five Keys to Developing Added Value

To develop added value for sponsors:

1. Brainstorm with your sponsors and other event managers on how you can develop as many additional benefits for sponsors as possible.
2. Analyze and research your event, so that you can provide demographic information that will be helpful to your sponsors.
3. Use the power of exclusivity to your advantage, separating your sponsors from the clutter that they find in other forms of advertising.
4. Create several situations to get your sponsors together, and generate business-to-business opportunities.
5. Be creative with your hospitality efforts—do not just provide food and drink, make the experience unique for your sponsors.

Sponsorship Activities

1. Visit *www.onlinesports.com* and look for ways to create added value for your sponsorships.
2. Visit *www.bonham.com* and find the pressroom section; look for articles on how you can add value to your sponsorships.
3. Read the section "Why Companies Sponsor" in *IEG's Complete Guide to Sponsorship.*
4. List the ways in which you can create added value for your sponsors in your proposed event.

Sponsorship Tool

Ukman, Lesa. (1998). *IEG's Complete Guide to Sponsorship.* Chicago, IL: IEG.

Web Sites

www.onlinesports.com
www.bonham.com

CHAPTER 6

Creating the Proper Image in the Eyes of Your Sponsors

An idea is a feat of association.

ROBERT FROST, *POET*

IN THIS CHAPTER YOU WILL LEARN:

- How to work with the news side of the media to develop a positive image of your event
- How to develop effective promotions to give people a positive perception
- How to create impressive collateral materials that will give a good first impression
- How to make your cause-related marketing more effective

Perception is reality. This is a phrase heard often in the world of marketing, and nothing can be truer in the events industry. That is because what the public and sponsors think of your event—often before they even attend it—becomes reality to them. Therefore, it is extremely important that a potential sponsor has a good impression of your event before you set foot in the door to sell sponsorship.

First impressions are everything. Sponsors see all sorts of collateral materials for events and meet with event professionals on a daily basis. It is important that all of your materials contain high-quality graphics and copy. Remember that potential sponsors are comparing you with the person who came in before you to pitch a sale, and the person who will come in next.

If you are not a good salesperson, make sure you have someone on staff who is. A lack of good salesmanship is often the No. 1 reason that some events are not successful at selling sponsorship, no matter how hard they try.

As mentioned earlier, media sponsorship is very important. That and your ability to work with the news side of the media are perhaps the most essential assets in creating the proper image.

For this reason, one of the most important positions on an event's staff is that of public relations (PR) director. But even more important than the PR person is the CEO. He or she must also work long and hard with the news side of the media.

What Makes the Media Tick

Most people do not understand how the media operate. Clearly, reporters, editors, and broadcasters are people like everyone else. If they have trust in you and your event, most of the time they will write and say good things about it. But they need to be treated the same way you would treat a good sponsor.

Just as the sponsorship sales process never ends, working with managing and city editors, reporters, and people who decide where the story on your event will be placed, never ends either.

The media are an intermediary between your event and the many audiences that are important to you—your sponsors, potential sponsors, your volunteers, community leaders, government officials, and others who read or hear about you in the newspapers, on radio and television, and now on the Web.

There is one very important thing to remember: News copy is generally perceived to be unbiased. Therefore, people will pay much more attention to news stories than to your ads and other marketing devices.

What members of the media write and say about you will directly influence the public's perception of you and therefore help sponsors decide whether your event is worth sponsoring.

Positive, or at a minimum, fair-minded press coverage can increase the public's awareness of your event, lead to a better understanding of your operations, and, ultimately, to better support of your organization.

Dealing with the media is no sophomore experience. It takes time, patience, inquisitiveness, and gumption. Remember, the members of the media are people working in a greatly underpaid profession. Thus, they are often young and not interested in getting involved in the community; often they could not care less about what your event does for your city.

The challenge is to make them work for you (see Figures 6-1 and 6-2).

- **Reach current attendees and sponsors with a reinforcing message that this is the event they should support.** Headlines like "Introducing the Cultural Highlight of the Year" (Galway Arts Festival in Ireland) and "It's a Wrap: Festival Ends on Sunny Note as Attendance Figures Climb" (Houston International Festival) are worth their weight in gold. But, once again, you have to build relationships with the media before you can expect headlines like these about your event.
- **Create a positive first impression with prospective sponsors even before you come face-to-face with them.** If a potential sponsor has seen headlines like "Fantastic Food Fair" (Red River Valley Street Fair in Fargo, North Dakota) or "London Gets a Giant Parade" (England), he or she is going to be very impressed with your event and more apt to become a sponsor.

Figure 6-1
Skinner's Secrets on What Good Media Relations and Publicity Can Do for Your Event

- **Complement your other marketing and advertising programs.** This is where a newspaper might do a special section on your event just prior to its opening. Because the editorial section will be perceived to be unbiased, it will be even more effective than your other marketing pieces.
- **Keep your current sponsors**—especially if you can get sponsors' names in headlines and in stories like "Stars Are Born: Tonight, the Riverbend sounds of Susan Werner, Bryndle, and Ain't Yo Mama can be heard from the NationsBank and Provident Stages" (Riverbend in Chattanooga, Tennessee).
- **Expand Your Organization's Reputation for Expertise.** The *Indianapolis Business Journal* ran a series of stories on the most influential women in Indianapolis, one of which was a piece on the president and CEO of Indy Festivals, Inc. (producers of the Indy 500 Festival and other events), Elizabeth Kraft-Meek. Imagine a potential sponsor's impression of Kraft-Meek when he or she read the first two paragraphs of the story:

    "There's a family story that helps explain why Elizabeth Kraft-Meek's marketing abilities are so legendary. More than once, as relatives headed home after a visit to Meek's house when she was just a child, her youngest cousins would turn to their parents and ask, 'How come Liz is the boss at her house?'

    "She has always been able to convince people of the wisdom of her ideas, Meek admits. Wherever people are gathered, she tends to step forward to explain her vision. In the process, she is often chosen for, and happy to provide, leadership."

    If a potential sponsor has read that story prior to her walking in the door, the sale is almost a lock if the prospect is a good one.
- **Provide You with Excellent Materials in the Form of Article Reprints.** Headlines and stories like "Miracle on Oxford Street" (London Christmas Parade) can provide you with great materials for your sponsorship sales packages.

Figure 6-1
(Continued)

The media can help you:

- Reach current attendees and sponsors with a reinforcing message.
- Create a positive first impression with prospective sponsors.
- Complement your marketing and advertising programs.
- Keep your current sponsors.
- Expand your organization's reputation for expertise.
- Establish your image with excellent materials in the form of article reprints.

Figure 6-2
How the Media Can Help an Event

How to Grab the Editor's Attention

Getting good media coverage is work. You do not expect sponsors to come knocking at your door, and you should not expect the media to automatically write good things about your event.

Here are a few things to remember about the ideas you pitch for news stories:

- **They must be news and unique.** Reporters are interested in new interpretations, angles, services, and personalities; almost everything must be new, *not the same old thing as last year.*
- **They must be timely.** Members of the media dread writing old news. Every good story has to have a "time hook."
- **They should focus on people.** Most newspapers are not interested in theory; they want to interest readers by writing about real people doing real things (including your sponsors).
- **They must be about something that many people want to know about.** Stories must have relatively broad appeal. Reporters sometimes think of themselves as talking to the masses, no matter how small the community.

Besides working with the news side of media, event managers can employ other strategies to develop a positive public image (see Figures 6-3 and 6-4).

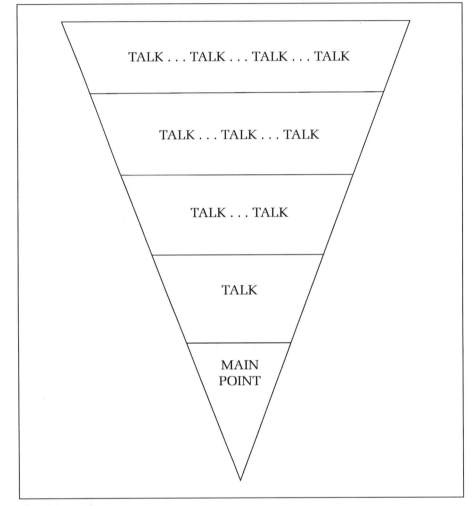

Figure 6-3
How Not to Talk to a Reporter

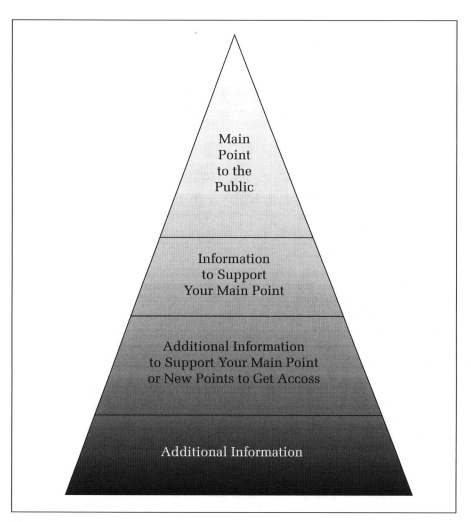

Figure 6-4
How to Talk to a Reporter

Promotion

PIN PROGRAMS

Pins and buttons are often sold for people to wear to promote an event. One of the best was developed by the Kentucky Derby Festival, which annually sells an incredible 500,000 pins at $2.00 each for its ten-day event.

Obviously, that makes a lot of money for the Festival, and it seems as though everyone in the city has one on, but what makes the promotion work really well is that it generates a lot of publicity and a good image of the event long before it happens. The media usually cover actual events very well, but sometimes it is difficult to obtain pre-event coverage, which you often need more than publicity after the event.

The pin program starts six weeks prior to the Festival. The Festival aligns itself with media partners, who promote the program.

The reason the program is so successful is that everyone is a winner when he or she purchases a pin. Each person who purchases a pin receives an envelope accompanied by a coupon redeemable for merchandise worth at least $2.00 (the cost of the pin). The prizes, provided by sponsors, include fast food, beverages, movie rentals, and lottery tickets. If the pin purchased turns out to be a gold one, the purchaser receives another instant prize at the next level, which includes $10 gift certificates, fragrance gifts, official Derby posters, and other prizes.

The gold pin purchasers also become eligible for bigger prizes, including a Cadillac, trips to Las Vegas and Disney World, or shopping sprees.

And while disc jockeys, television stations, and print media are hyping the pin program, they are also promoting the event by giving out pertinent Festival information.

"The constant promotion, and the fact that you see people wearing Kentucky Derby Festival pins seemingly all the time, create an image indicating to companies that this is a first-class event and that they need to be sponsors of it," says the Derby Festival's Bridget Sherrill.

BANNERS FOR SPONSORS

The International Festival of Lent in Maribor, Slovenia, also conducts a promotion that provides a good image for the Festival and its sponsors.

It gives sponsors yellow stickers and banners to mark the doors of their shops in the center of town. The city becomes yellow (the Festival's theme color) long before the event occurs. It tells current and potential sponsors that the people of Maribor support the Festival.

THE FIRST IMPRESSION: COLLATERAL MATERIALS

Collateral materials are extremely important. Their quality determines the image and perceived value of your event in the eyes of a potential sponsor.

Many events incur costs in the five-figure range for the development and printing of elaborate brochures. Some event managers think that this is much too expensive, *but remember, all you need to do is to sell one more good sponsorship, and the brochure is more than paid for.*

Typically, these brochures include a page of Festival facts, giving a short description of the event, dates, location, attendance, mission statement, organizational structure, and a list of sponsors. Information on the key benefits of sponsorship is also included: hospitality opportunities, tickets to the event, and sampling possibilities, as well as sponsorship levels and categories.

Some brochures go even further. The Virginia Beach Neptune Festival mentions in its high-quality brochure that 93 percent of its sponsors ranked their sponsorship experience as excellent compared with that of other similar events.

Others take these sponsorship solicitation packages to the next level. The Sylvania Alamo Bowl's brochure has a cover with the texture of a football.

The Memphis in May International Festival in Tennessee sends potential sponsors a box of items with a label that reads: "The Super Bowl of Swine." Inside the box are an event polo shirt, a T-shirt, seasoning salts, barbecue sauce, a coffee cup, and a video on the Festival.

It is also important to remember that a solicitation package does not replace your proposal. Although solicitation packages are critical when it comes to perception and first impressions, they do not address an individual sponsor's needs. Benefits in your package will interest some sponsors but not others.

The Portland Rose Festival

The Portland Rose Festival combines all the elements needed for a high-quality sponsorship solicitation package.

First, it gives highlights of the event, including a few key elements:

- Most highly rated festival in the Northwest
- Recognized as one of the top ten festivals in the world; parade voted among the top five in the United States

This photo showing a large number of runners immediately develops a good image for the Indy 500 Festival's Mini-Marathon event in Indianapolis. *Photo courtesy of Indy 500 Festival.*

- Excellent, diverse events—parade, air show, CART race, arts and crafts, rose show, waterfront festival, and many more
- Economic impact information that shows the value of the Festival to the community

Second, the Festival's presentation folder is of high quality and contains exciting, four-color art. But what really makes the kit work is that in addition to the general Festival information mentioned here, it customizes the presentation for each sponsor.

Outstanding graphics, such as those developed by the Singapore Food Festival, give a great first impression for an event. *Photo courtesy of Singapore Tourism Board.*

VIDEO

A professionally produced video presentation can be a great sales tool for your event. First secure an in-kind sponsorship from a local television station or video company to produce it for you gratis.

Most important, get an announcer to do the narration for you, a person whom the sponsor will recognize as an on-air talent. This strategy can have a great subtle effect, as local news anchors are perceived to be unbiased and are more readily believed.

Cause-Related Marketing

Cause-related marketing is one of the fastest growing areas in the event marketing field. Eight percent of all sponsorship is cause-related, according to the International Events Group (IEG), the Chicago-based company that analyzes and tracks sponsorship.

This type of marketing often involves a company's making a donation to a nonprofit in exchange for each sale of its product or service in the United States. At the very least, the sponsorship is not necessarily linked with sales, but sponsors do expect benefits in return, such as branding or hospitality.

According to the *Cone/Roper Cause-Related Trends Report,* 65 percent of U.S. adults said they would be likely to switch brands and 61 percent said they would very likely switch retailers to support a product that associated with a cause they cared about.

Cause marketing had the strongest impact on people whom Roper classifies as "influentials." This group is composed of leaders who believe in supporting companies involved in cause marketing: Sixty-eight percent said they would support a company if it was associated with a cause.

Dr. Joe Goldblatt states in his book, *Special Events,* "Increasingly sponsors are more interested in becoming involved in a new phenomenon entitled *cause-related marketing.* This provides sponsors with the added value of demonstrating that they are good corporate citizens. As more and more groups form around specific causes such as the environment, children's concerns, peace, crime prevention and other important issues, sponsors are looking for natural linkages that will strengthen the loyalty that they desire from their consumers."

Many European companies engage in cause-related marketing. HBOS (formerly known as The Bank of Scotland) has an extensive arts sponsorship program that supports organizations throughout the country. These include the Scottish Chamber Orchestra, the National Youth Orchestra of Scotland, and the Traverse Theatre.

In particular, the bank supports the development of young talent in the areas of writing and music. It believes that support at the grassroots level will help the arts flourish in Scotland into the next century.

But in contrast to its approach 25 years ago, the bank does not just expect to be listed in a program; it has marketing objectives in mind. As well as benefiting from corporate hospitality at the events it sponsors, the bank gains from branding on collateral materials and is linked with some of Scotland's most outstanding artistic endeavors.

A NOT-SO-SUCCESSFUL STORY

A BAD DAY WITH THE MEDIA

The media have the power to help your event and sponsors. But they also have the power to harm, as a Denver venue and its sponsor discovered. In a story entitled "What's in a Name," the *Denver Post* said it would call it like it sees it.

The *Post* said, on August 8, 2001, that it would refer to the then Broncos's new home as "Mile High Stadium" instead of its official name, "Invesco Field at Mile High." "The community thinks of this as Mile High, new Mile High, or the new stadium," said editor Glenn Guzzo.

Officials at Invesco, a mutual funds group that paid $120 million for naming rights, were disappointed. "It's unfortunate that the *Denver Post* has decided to not accurately report the name," an Invesco statement said.

Five Keys to Developing a Good Image for Your Event

To develop a good image:

1. Make sure your graphic materials are of high quality, because first impressions are everything. Use professional graphic designers (you can get them to become in-kind sponsors and donate this service to you).
2. Treat the media as you would a good sponsor. Building relationships here is very important. What the media write and say about you is what potential and current sponsors believe.
3. Develop effective promotions like the Kentucky Derby Festival's pin program. This will also enhance your image.
4. Get your local television station to develop a highlight video

on your event for you. Get the station to do it gratis as an in-kind sponsor.

5. Be aware that cause-related marketing is growing and that sponsors like to support good causes.

Sponsorship Activities

1. Read *The Marketer's Guide to Public Relations* by Thomas Harris.
2. Read Chapter 6, "Tell 'Em About It," in *Special Events: Inside and Out,* by Steven Wood Schmader and Robert Jackson.
3. Develop a plan to approach the media for your event.

Sponsorship Tool Kit

Finn, David, and Judith A. Jedlicka. (1998). *The Art of Leadership: Building Business-Arts Alliances.* New York: Abbeville Press.

Goldblatt, Dr. Joe. (2002). *Special Events: Twenty-First Century Global Event Management.* New York: John Wiley & Sons, Inc.

Harris, Thomas. (1991). *The Marketers Guide to Public Relations.* New York: John Wiley & Sons, Inc.

Schmader, Steven Wood, and Robert Jackson. (1997). *Special Events: Inside and Out.* Champaign, IL: Sagamore Publishing.

Schmitt, Bernd. (1999). *Experiential Marketing: How to Get Customers to Sense, Feel, Think, Act and Relate to Your Company and Brands.* New York: Free Press.

CHAPTER 7

The Creative Approach to Sponsorship

You see things; and you say, "Why?" But I dream things that never were; and I say, "Why not?"

GEORGE BERNARD SHAW, IRISH DRAMATIST

IN THIS CHAPTER YOU WILL LEARN:

- Why your creativity is very important to sponsors
- The importance of balancing tradition and change
- How an event can use a community's character-defining qualities
- The importance of working with local representatives to reach regional/national sponsors
- How an event can develop a creative partnership with its sponsors

In both 1995 and 1996, the opening keynote speaker for the annual convention of the International Festivals and Events Association

(IFEA) stressed one of the most important concepts in the special events industry: Event managers need to think outside the box and be creative in order to achieve maximum results in the sale of sponsorship.

Chic Thompson, gave the opening keynote speech, *If It Ain't Broke, Break It,* for IFEA's Vancouver, British Columbia, convention in 1995. Thompson emphasized that event managers should always seek to discover how they can do things better the next time.

Dick Nunis, chairman of Walt Disney attractions, was the keynoter during IFEA's 1996 Orlando convention and said that the Walt Disney Company is about both tradition *and* change.

The Walt Disney Company (producer of perhaps the ultimate event) has kept its traditions—there will always be Mickey Mouse, Donald Duck, Pluto, and the other familiar characters. But from the first Disneyland in Anaheim in 1955, we have also witnessed many changes. Disney now has Epcot and all of its attractions; the World Entertainment Showcase; Space Mountain; *Honey, I Shrunk the Kids;* and many other things that were not even dreamed of in 1955.

Being able to change is what separates the very best event managers from the others. They retain their best programming from year to year, but they also *change.* Events that do not change face a fickle public that will eventually say, "We don't have to go to that event, because it's the same old event as last year." It is also the event that a sponsor reconsiders before sponsoring it again.

"Too often . . . the very best ideas are never allowed to surface," Dr. Joe Goldblatt says in his book *Special Events.* "The process of shooting down ideas before they are allowed to be fully developed is a tragic occurrence in many organizations."

Creating—More Than
Just Developing Ideas

The word "creativity" comes from the Latin *creare,* which means "to cause to exist." Many event managers are great at coming up with ideas. "But it's not enough to dream, one must also *act,*" says Goldblatt. "Creativity must be encouraged and supported by event managers because ultimately the product you will offer is a creative act."

In the world of sponsorship, creativity is important in two areas: First, it can help you to be special and original in the presentation of your event, and second, it can transform your approach to how you develop your sponsorship packages.

MAKING SURE AN EVENT IS CREATIVE

Norm Langill of One Reel in Seattle, the producer of several events, including the Bumbershoot Festival on Labor Day weekend at Seattle Center, is extremely creative.

SUCCESS STORY

CREATIVITY UNLEASHED AT BUMBERSHOOT

In 1995, when organizers hired Mel Torme to open for the Ramones and Mudhoney, the since-deceased jazz singer began to fret as he looked out over the sea of rock fans in leather jackets and ripped jeans—definitely not his type of audience.

"But he didn't have to worry . . . when he began crooning, there was no booing or cursing, or shouts of 'Get off the stage!' The punks loved it," wrote Thor Christensen, pop music critic of the *Dallas Morning News*.

"It was a defining moment for a 30-year-old event that's quietly grown into one of the most vibrant pop festivals in the country. Bumbershoot has become a musical melting pot where acts accustomed to playing to club-size audiences suddenly find themselves performing for up to 20,000 adoring fans," he continued.

"[Torme] came offstage with tears in his eyes, saying it was one of the most exciting shows he'd ever done," remembers festival producer Sheila Hughes.

During the event's brainstorming sessions, there are no bad ideas to begin with. In fact, some of the most outrageous ideas turn into incredible parts of the festival. In 1995, Festival producer Norm Langill suggested at one of these staff meetings that Bumbershoot should have a wedding stage, where people could actually come to the festival and get married. "We thought Norm had finally lost it," joked former One Reel staffer Beth Knox, now president/CEO of the Boise River Festival in Idaho.

But people did come to get married, and atop a 30-foot, three-tier wedding cake, Father Guido Sarducci performed the ceremonies. Organizers burned the cake to the ground to close the Festival.

Bumbershoot is exciting, original, creative, and "outside the box," and because of that, sponsors want to be attached to the event. They are looking for something to sponsor that is different, that enables them to separate themselves from their competitors.

Each year Langill and his One Reel staff set aside creative time, get away from the day-to-day office activity, and brainstorm on how to make Bumbershoot, one of the top-performing arts festivals in the world, different.

In fact, people attend Bumbershoot each year because they want to see what new and exciting things will happen at the festival. It is self-described as being wacky, wonderful, artful, and outrageous.

Music is central, with more than 410 acts on 18 stages—everything from pop to hip hop, jazz to African vocal groups, folk to heavy metal, and many other forms of entertainment.

DOING SOMETHING THAT NO ONE ELSE DOES

Several events have also succeeded with sponsors because they have something that no one else has.

Gilroy, California, located 30 miles south of San Jose, puts on one of the top festivals in the country—the Gilroy Garlic Festival. Event managers there are uniquely qualified to produce this festival because 90 percent of the garlic in the United States is processed in Gilroy. The event features fabulous food, ranging from garlic shrimp, found in the event's Gourmet Alley, to garlic ice cream.

Consider another example: Event organizers in Bellingham, Washington, decided to organize an athletic event 25 years ago. However, instead of the usual 10K, or marathon, or bike race, they developed an event using the geography of the area.

Entrants in the Bellingham Ski to Sea Race, held on the Sunday of Memorial Day weekend, participate in a relay race. The first member of the team skis cross-country, followed by a downhill skier, who first must climb in ski boots (carrying his or her skis) up a 1,000-foot ice pack on 10,775-foot Mt. Baker. The next leg is a 10K run. A 42-mile road bike run is next, and then canoeists race down the Nisqually River. A mountain bike leg is next, and the race concludes in Bellingham Bay with a sea kayak leg.

The event is unique and therefore attractive to sponsors like AT&T, because there are very few places in the world that have a glacier mountain, good roads, and an ocean and a river in close enough proximity for such a race.

It's important to be creative when you develop an event. Instead of doing a normal 10K or similar event, participants in the Bellingham, Wash., Ski to Sea hike, downhill ski, cross country ski, run, road bike, canoe, mountain bike, and kayak. Event managers used the local terrain, the likes of which are found in very few places in the world, to develop the events for the race. *Photo courtesy of Tore Oftness Photography.*

Creativity—to Help Your Sponsors

Original ideas can be of great benefit to a sponsor. A very creative one was the Photo of the Century presented by Kodak. Philadelphia had "a Kodak moment" in front of Independence Hall on July 4, 1999 when a photo was taken of 112 Americans born on July 4—one born each year from 1900 to 1999, representing all 50 states.

The photo included a 99-year-old Florida woman and a 3½-hour-old Philadelphia baby (weighing in at a perfect 7 pounds, 4 ounces) and was taken by *New York Times* photographer Paul Hosefros, who was born July 4, 1947.

The event's objective was to generate national coverage for Kodak and the City of Philadelphia and was the kickoff to the city's 18-month millennium celebration.

It worked. The event did not spend any money on advertising, but received a lot of exposure, according to the project's logistical coordinator, Ira Rosen of Entertainment on Location. The photo story was picked up by the Associated Press and Reuters news wires, generating newspaper and magazine coverage in every state (in Philadelphia alone more than 1250 print clips), amounting to more than 105 million impressions.

Beyond the print media, the photo was also featured on Internet sites like MSNBC, CNN *Interactive,* and Fox *Newswire* and was televised on 250 shows nationwide, including *Good Morning America, CBS's This Morning* and *Evening News, CNN Headline News, The Today Show,* and ABC's *World News Now.*

The event hit the airwaves with more than 35 radio programs across the country on stations including ABC, CBS, and FOX radio affiliates, AP Radio, NPR, BBC, and the Australian Broadcasting Network.

ATLANTA: TRIVIA AND THE CHICKEN DANCE

In Atlanta, a music event used ticket giveaways tied to sponsor trivia. The successful promotion had Kraft Foods and a local radio station giving away tickets to the event by asking product-related questions: "The first caller to identify the main ingredient listed on the Kraft mayonnaise labels wins two tickets to see. . . ."

Also in Atlanta, an event with a poultry-producer sponsor provided children's entertainment throughout the day by having a "chicken dance" contest using the sponsor's jingle. Three times a day, children were invited up on stage, where they were all given sponsor T-shirts and a chance to perform their best chicken dance.

HELPING AN UNKNOWN PRODUCT

SEAFAIR got creative with Sparkletts water. As part of its sponsorship, Sparkletts ran an enter-to-win promotion for six weeks with its product at retail. Winners got to enjoy an elevated viewing area at the annual event, complete with a couch, lamps, food, and, of course, Sparkletts water. The publicity that surrounded this promotion had great public relations value for the bottled water company, which more than paid for the sponsorship.

The promotion was particularly beneficial because Sparkletts was an unknown company in a highly competitive category. It was able to heighten the visibility of its product exponentially and stand out from its competitors.

RACING WIENER DOGS

The Holiday Bowl in San Diego was extremely creative when it developed a program for Wienerschnitzel. The Bowl wanted to hold an event prior to its parade, and the fast-food chain wanted to increase its brand awareness.

Together they created the Wiener Dog Race, held just prior to the parade in 1996. In 2000 they had 232 dachshunds race on Dog Beach in San Diego. The event has appeared on *America's Funniest Home Videos,* the *Jay Leno Show,* and in many local media outlets.

"It is more fun to watch the owners at the finish line," says the Bowl's former executive director John Reid. "They'll do almost anything to get their dog to run faster."

"One owner feeds his dog chili dogs, and brings them to the finish line in order to entice his pet to travel faster," says Mark Neville, the Bowl's assistant executive director.

CHOPPING DOWN CHERRY TREES

The National Cherry Festival did a publicity stunt as part of its partnership with its regional ABC affiliate. The station helped bring in network weatherman Spencer Christian to do his national weather broadcast from the Festival. Event volunteers cut down a cherry tree in the middle of the night and transported it to the Festival's main venue.

During his forecast, Spencer ran the shaker equipment to shake the cherries off the tree in front of millions of national viewers. ABC in New York was inundated with inquiries about the Cherry Festival and cherries. Most viewers had no idea that cherries are the only fruit that is harvested in a matter of seconds by violently shaking the ripe fruit off the tree.

It was a great promotion for the festival and the regional ABC affiliate, as well as the cherry industry, which led to national publicity for all parties as part of the national weather forecast.

Using Creativity to Get Outside the Market

Selling sponsorship in a city of 4000 people can be extremely difficult, because marketing budgets of local small businesses are miniscule. One event that did this with unparalleled success was the Sequim, Washington, Irrigation Festival. The event celebrated its 100th anniversary in 1996, and event organizers wanted to increase its sponsorship level from the meager $4000 of the previous year.

Organizers knew they had to get very creative. They were faced with a situation in which $250 was a lot of money for any local business to spend on anything, whether it was for an event sponsorship or a donation to United Way.

They wanted to sell a $5000 sponsorship package to Seafirst Bank (now Bank of America), but knew they could not do so locally—the branch manager had authority to spend only $250 on any one project.

The organizers also knew that they could not chance going over the head of the local manager and approaching the marketing department in Seattle. The manager would feel slighted, and the marketing department would probably call the manager once it received the proposal anyway, to see what she thought of the event. If the manager was not already on board, at best she would be unenthusiastic.

Instead, Irrigation Festival officials went to the local branch manager and told her that they did not want money out of her budget, but rather her support of a sponsorship proposal that they wanted to send to the vice president of marketing in Seattle.

The manager enthusiastically agreed. The Festival even wrote the letter for her to mail to the Seattle marketing executive (see Figure 7-1), asking for a $5000 sponsorship package. Because marketing departments are driven to make branch managers happy, the sponsorship went through. Once again, if the Festival had gone to the regional office without contacting the local manager, it would have been dead in the water.

Once the organizers got one bank on board, the same strategy worked with other financial institutions—the others could not afford *not* to be a part of the Festival. And even though five banks were involved, the event still offered exclusivity to each institution by making each a sponsor of a particular part of the Festival. Washington Mutual donated space in one of its branches to sell merchandise and to house the Festival office.

Yet creativity did not end there. The organizers also knew that the local hospital—even though it did not sponsor anything—could afford to be a sponsor. Sequim has a large senior retirement population, the perfect demographic for any medical care facility.

The largest event in the history of the Olympic Peninsula will be held in May in Sequim, and I think that we should be a major sponsor of it.

The Sequim Irrigation Festival will celebrate its 100th anniversary May 5 through 14, with a ten-day event that will include a major fireworks show, name entertainment, the largest parade on the North Olympic Peninsula, and several events for family and kids. More than 30,000 people are expected to attend the Festival and all of its events.

I am hopeful that we can become a Gold Sponsor for the festival at the $5000 level. For that amount, we can become a title sponsor of the main stage, the name entertainment (the Shirelles and Fabian), the fireworks show, or other major areas of the event.

In addition, we would receive the following:

- Mention on banners spread throughout the North Olympic Peninsula area promoting the festival
- Recognition on 500 event posters
- An ad in the Festival program
- Mention on 100 radio spots on Radio Station KONP
- Public address recognition at the event
- Event signage

Sponsorship at this level would be for one year only, as this is a special celebration because of the 100th anniversary. We want to support the event as much as we can, but, of course, we need your help to reach the Gold level.

We think that this sponsorship makes great marketing sense for us. Instead of being part of the advertising clutter of print and broadcast, this would put us in a position to be part of a small group of sponsors that will receive major recognition.

I will give you a call in the near future so that representatives of the Festival can come and meet with you.

Sincerely,

Figure 7-1
Suggested Letter to SeaFirst Vice President of Marketing

By getting people involved who had leverage with the hospital, they were able to sell a major sponsorship to it.

The organizers also went to the then recently opened Seven Cedars Casino, during a time when gambling was quite controversial in the state of Washington. Because the casino wanted a favorable local image, it became a sponsor. It also brought four of its vendors to the table and sponsored the "Taste of Sequim" as part of the Festival.

When all was said and done, Irrigation Festival managers had sold $185,000 in sponsorship, an incredible success story for a community of 4000 people.

We mention throughout this book that we think sponsorship is best sold by professional staff. Sequim was an exception—the Festival's sponsorship was sold by a volunteer, but by someone who acted like a professional staff member. Before beginning his sales efforts, Rand Thomas took a year off from his lumber business and

SUCCESS STORY

SIEMENS MOBILE WAP PROGRAM

In September 2000, Siemens Mobile demonstrated that with every new technological advancement, there are also opportunities to be creative in the event world. The company launched the world's biggest wireless application protocol (WAP) service, which provides match results and news for football fans across Europe.

WAP is an open, global specification that empowers mobile users with wireless devices to easily access and interact with information and services instantly.

The WAP program is part of a $100 million sponsorship agreement with 23 of Europe's leading football clubs, one national football team, and two national football leagues. Football fans with WAP phones can access the latest information on their favorite football clubs at wap.siemens-sportal.com.

The three-year exclusive agreement paves the way for using the potential of third-generation services such as live video screening of games and real-time interaction between football fans and clubs.

In addition, the football clubs and Siemens will team up to offer fans officially branded mobile phones in their clubs' colors and logos, providing a new consumer base for Siemens Mobile.

"This is an inspiring moment, both for Siemens and for football fans across Europe," said Peter Zapf, president of Siemens. "Beginning with WAP, Siemens put real-time information directly into the hands of fans."

went to several conferences put on by the International Festivals and Events Association to learn how to sell sponsorship. In addition, Rochelle McHugh, a local real estate salesperson, did the same.

Linking with Creativity

Especially in Europe, sponsors like to link themselves with creative projects.

Audi, a major sponsor of the Salzburg Music Festival in Austria, provides support for selected innovative projects that seek to treat new themes and expand dramatic creativity in the areas of opera, concert, and theater.

Siemens is among the high-tech companies that also like to sponsor arts and culture; its corporate slogan is "Be Inspired."

Using Creativity to Meet a Sponsor's Needs

It often happens that an event has to be very creative to sell a sponsorship, and this is usually done by listening very carefully to a sponsor.

For its 50th anniversary, SEAFAIR wanted to bring back an event that had been popular in its early days—the Aqua Follies. It was originally held in an outdoor setting on Green Lake in Seattle and featured top national divers, synchronized swimmers, and other water acts.

SEAFAIR worked very hard to find a sponsor, but organizers were reaching a lot of dead ends. So they went to Key Bank, an institution that understands risk management, and asked its marketing executives to have the bank share the risk with the festival.

"We told them that if we sold a certain amount of tickets, they would pay nothing for their sponsorship," said festival CEO Beth Wojick. "If the event was a flop, they would cover the ticket goal. They ended up paying about $7,000 for a $55,000 sponsorship package."

The Fiesta Bowl did its homework when it researched the needs of Insight Enterprises, a manufacturer of computers and computer accessories. The company had been struggling with the question of how it could quickly convert its sales efforts with phones to focus on on-line equipment.

It became the first dot-com sponsor of any sport; now, of course, there are many. And most important, the company successfully reached its goal of increased on-line sales.

Falling Out of the Box

Certainly, we can sometimes get too creative. The *New York Times* reported in its September 6, 2001, edition that one of the scenes in British writer Fay Weldon's novel *The Bulgari Connection* takes place in the Bulgari jewelry store on Sloane Street in London. It further reported that "Bulgari, the Italian jewelry company, paid Ms. Weldon an undisclosed sum for a prominent place in the book."

The arrangement, believed to be a first for the book industry, brought a scathing commentary from *Times* reviewer Melvin Jules Bukiet who wrote, ". . . product placement has long provided significant revenue for motion pictures, but books . . . books! As a writer, I'm shocked."

He continued, ". . . there is a difference between art and advertising. Sadly, Ms. Weldon seems to have chosen the latter."

It is extremely important that sponsors and event managers do not create situations in which sponsorship can backfire on them. If a consumer is offended by the sponsorship, it is bad for both event and sponsor alike.

Events = Creativity

In their book, *Special Events: Inside and Out,* Steve Schmader and Bob Jackson write that there is no shortage of creativity. "But too little of it is used, especially in the special events field, which by its very nature should epitomize the highest levels of creative application.

"If the event is to be a real stand-out in the national—or even regional—event picture, it must be different from and better than others."

And it is definitely time to heed Chic Thompson's words mentioned in the opening of this chapter. *It's time to break it!*

SUCCESS STORY

THINKING ON YOUR FEET

Creativity sometimes needs to be instantaneous.

Jim and Kathi Austin (the Houston International Festival's CEO and vice president of marketing, respectively) called on a major airline executive who was responsible for $250,000 worth of annual sponsorship for the event. A new marketing executive had just come on board and wanted title sponsorship of the event—something that the Festival was not willing to sell.

Upon meeting with him, the Festival's representatives discovered what his real objective was. He did not understand why individual area sponsors, who were in effect title sponsors of those areas, received bigger signage than the airline. He asked Kathi, who was the lead contact with the potential client, why his sponsorship signs had to be smaller and how people could be expected to know the prominence of his company's sponsorship. Kathi drew a blank.

However, Jim looked the executive right in the eye and quickly replied, "Why, microphone signage, of course." He told him that if his signs were small, but placed on event microphones, he would receive more TV time than the area title sponsors. Their signs were placed up high and were certainly too large to be part of a news story, which usually focused on the entertainers at the microphones. The executive was sold.

"Kathi and I walked out of his office, got on the elevator, and after a big 'Whew'," Jim remembers, "Kathi asked, 'How did you come up with that?' "

Jim was not sure how, but it was creativity at its instantaneous best. The sponsor was happy with the answer, and the partnership continued.

Four Keys to Becoming More Creative

For the creative approach to sponsorship:

1. Brainstorm! Schedule meetings with your colleagues and/or volunteers to discuss how you can take your event to the next level.

2. Do not copy—make your event original. Too many times we duplicate an event that is held somewhere else, and it becomes a second-rate imitation.
3. Find something in your community that is unique to your area, and create an event around it.
4. Be very creative with your sponsors. This will bring them more than the contract promises, which will mean that they will be back the following year.

Sponsorship Activities

1. Read Roger von Oech's Book, *A Whack on the Side of the Head,* to enhance your creative abilities.
2. Read "The Creative Process in Event Management" section in Dr. Joe Goldblatt's book, *Special Events: Twenty-first Century Global Event Management.*
3. Read Chapter 4, "A Matter of Quality," in Steven Wood Schmader and Robert Jackson's book, *Special Events: Inside and Out.*
4. List the ways in which you can make your event different from all others that are part of the special event landscape.

Sponsorship Tool Kit

Goldblatt, Dr. Joe. (1997). *Special Events: Twenty-first Century Global Event Management.* New York: John Wiley & Sons, Inc.

Salzman, Marian L. (1999). *Next: A Spectacular Vision of Trends for the Near Future.* Woodstock, NY: Overlook Press.

Schmader, Steven Wood, and Robert Jackson. (1997). *Special Events: Inside and Out.* Champaign, IL: Sagamore Publishing.

Spolin, Viola. (1999). *Improvisation for the Theater.* 3rd ed. Evanston, IL: Northwestern University Press.

von Oech, Roger. (1983). *A Whack on the Side of the Head.* New York: Warner Books.

CHAPTER 8

The Keys to Successful Sponsorship Sales

All thing being equal, people will buy from a friend. All things being not quite so equal, people will still buy from a friend.

MARK MCCORMACK, CHAIRMAN AND CHIEF EXECUTIVE OFFICER,

INTERNATIONAL MANAGEMENT GROUP

IN THIS CHAPTER YOU WILL LEARN:

- How to meet a potential sponsor in person
- How to use board members, sponsors, and others as door openers
- How to leverage retailers
- How to price your sponsorship
- How to sell to in-town and out-of-town sponsors
- The importance of asking for the check

Unfortunately, many event organizers start the sales process before they have completed the steps found in the first seven chapters of this book, and their chances for success are thus greatly diminished.

They do not know the value of their event and have not made it the best it can be. They have done very little, if any, research and do not know why sponsors sponsor what they do, let alone the goals and objectives of the sponsor whom they are soliciting. They have not created a positive image and, in many cases, do not even know what their image is.

They have created a generic proposal that is not unique to their event and, in fact, have even fired it off to several competing properties simultaneously, hoping to strike it rich. They will not get an in-person interview with the potential sponsor, making their chances for success almost nil. They may also be using age-old tactics from the "contributions" days, sending out event volunteers to do the selling, such as someone who may have a personal relationship with the sponsor, but little knowledge about the complex world of sponsorship selling.

Selling sponsorship is not like selling long-distance telephone service. It is much more complex, much more difficult than selling other forms of advertising. That is why the first seven chapters of this book are so important—you need to do your homework.

The First Sponsors to Approach

When selling, you first want to approach the sponsors that you think you have the best chance to sell to. These are usually the companies that, through your research, you have found to fit your event for some reason or another. Once again, the subjects covered in the earlier chapters of this book are extremely important before you reach this point. They provide you with the necessary information to help you find that perfect fit.

In 1996, the 40th London Film Festival found that fit when it targeted Visa International, because of the natural synergy between a credit card and a major film event reliant on telephone and postal bookings.

Visa agreed to become a principal sponsor of the Festival. The sponsorship formed a year-long marketing campaign for Visa known as "London Welcomes Visa." Overseas visitors in particular were encouraged to come to London to visit different attractions and were offered various incentives to pay with their Visa cards.

Visa also undertook its own promotional campaign in support of the sponsorship, with a series of competitions. Participants in the London Welcomes Visa campaign were rewarded with tickets to films at the Festival and invitations to the Visa Mid-Term Gala.

Visa was also promoted as the payment system for the Festival with all booking forms and box office sites and by staff. A series of inducements for people to make multiple ticket purchases by Visa (such as cinema tickets and T-shirts) were introduced and offered in a London-wide advertising campaign.

The promotions resulted in a staggering 69 percent of all tickets for the festival being purchased by Visa payments (in previous years they accounted for just 30 percent).

The company's role as principal sponsor was promoted in all festival publications, replicated on a London underground poster and in a London bus campaign, and the logo appeared on the festival trailer, a short film screened before every film at the festival.

Timing

The persons described in the opening paragraphs of this chapter have also likely made the fatal error of sending out their proposals one month prior to their events. They should have contacted the sponsor 6 to 18 months earlier, depending on the sponsor's own internal processes and budgeting cycles.

"Timing is very important; don't expect much if you approach someone 30 days out," says Denver's Bruce Erley of the Creative Strategies Group. "Strategic selling occurs 9 to 14 months out, tactical selling 4 to 9 months out—'combat' sales are 1 to 3 months out, and that's when you start taking casualties."

Sponsorship is complicated and needs to be developed—you do not want to be in a situation where it is urgent for you and not for them. In that case, you probably will not sell the sponsorship because you are immediately seen as disorganized, and even if you do, it will be for much less money than the sponsorship is worth.

Face-to-Face

As we said earlier, sponsorship is about relationship building—people buy from people. Before you approach potential sponsors, you should get to know them—not only should you know the background of a company, but you should also have a good professional relationship with the person sitting across the table from you.

A salesperson who has established relationships with customers will have a much better chance of selling a product than one who has not. Through relationship building, trust and ties are developed that, even in the worst of times, will be difficult to break.

To develop those ties, you need to meet with your prospects in person. That can be extremely difficult to do with so many persons out peddling sponsorship packages. However, the No. 1 priority in selling a sponsorship is to meet with someone in the company face-to-face, a person at as high a level as possible. You have a much better chance of selling the product if decision makers see your presentation in person, rather than on a printed page, which may be one of many they receive each day.

Of course, even the most savvy of sponsorship salespeople cannot be expected to have this type of relationship with every sponsor, especially when sponsors are new. But it is still crucial to remember the axiom mentioned earlier: *People buy from people.* If you do not know the person you want to see, get others to help you.

ARRANGING A MEETING

You often have to work to get in the door. High-level executives are not going to see you to the exclusion of everybody else just because you have been persistent on the telephone.

Here are some ways to get closer to seemingly unreachable people:

- Create situations in which you can meet these people. Attend the meetings they attend, and participate in their volunteer activities so that you can meet them personally. Have colleagues introduce you.
- If yours is a nonprofit event, a vital link to potential sponsors is your board, as board members often can get you in the door. Phoenix's Fiesta Bowl has a 160-member Fiesta Bowl

Committee. Together, those 160 members know almost every major player in the state. If event managers want to sit down with any corporate executive in Phoenix, this committee can almost always arrange for a meeting.

A committee member sets up the meeting and accompanies the professional sponsorship event manager. The committee member typically does two things: introduces the event manager and thanks the person for seeing them. With a committee member present, a sale is almost guaranteed, *especially if the potential sponsor owes the committee member something.*

A nonprofit board that has strong executives in its mix has a distinct advantage over those that do not. Many events do not allow people on their boards unless they work themselves up through the ranks by first doing such things as emptying garbage cans at the event or moving barricades.

Unfortunately, many corporate players do not have the time or inclination to be involved in the trenches, but we need them just as much as, if not more than, those who have worked their way up the ladder. They not only can help you sell sponsorship, they also can provide vision and will not micromanage.

How to Use the Board

Although events still use board members to help raise money, the board's role has changed drastically in the last 20 years.

In the days when we used to go to a company's donations department for funds, a board member could make the sales call just as easily as the professional staff person. In fact, board members were probably more effective, as they had leverage over the person to be contacted and had developed a personal relationship.

That all changed when we started going to marketing departments. Experienced marketing people want to deal with experienced event professionals, not volunteers. Sponsorship is much more complex because of such activities as cross-promoting, packaging benefits, and the like, and the average volunteer does not understand these nuances.

Volunteers, however, can still help you get in the door and make the sale. One of the best examples of this occurred prior to the first annual Cherry Creek Arts Festival. Festival managers had met several times with the Coors Brewing Company, its headquarters located close by in Golden, and had been turned down.

One of the Festival's board members gave a party at his house and asked Festival CEO Bill Charney to make a presentation to his invited guests, one of whom just happened to be Pete Coors. After the presentation, Coors asked Charney to be in his office Monday morning. The result? Nine consecutive years of very successful major sponsorship.

The University of California's athletic department developed a marketing committee composed of marketing and advertising professionals in the Bay Area, who were also involved in the "Bear Backers" donor/alumni organization.

All of these people had strong contacts in the Bay Area and a deep and sincere love for Cal athletics—a perfect combination for opening doors for athletic department marketing staff and developing new sponsorship business.

Board members of nonprofit events have also opened the door to potential sponsors many times. Members of the Fiesta Bowl Committee are asked to "claim" potential sponsors each year. They are matched with marketing staff and team together with them to sell the sponsorship.

Existing Sponsors

Several events use existing sponsors to help them sell. Chuck O'Connor of Traverse City's National Cherry Festival constantly asks satisfied sponsors whether they have business relationships with companies that they think might benefit from a partnership with the Festival.

SUCCESS STORY

USING YOUR BOARD

When the Alamo Bowl was concerned about replacing its title sponsor, Builders Square, the Bowl struck it rich when one of its board members happened to play golf with an executive from Sylvania. The board member was trying to make sure that Sylvania came back as the sponsor of the Bowl's gala. During the course of the golf outing, the Sylvania representative not only said that the company would be back, but asked, "Why don't we become the title sponsor?" The rest, of course, is history.

"Several good things can result from this approach," says O'Connor. "Because these ideas come from existing partners, it increases their buy-in for your event. Because you approach the new prospect with your existing sponsor, you will have trusted personal testimony supporting your proposal. Additionally, it almost always generates leveraging or business-to-business opportunities."

Dianna Craven at SunFest in West Palm Beach has made many close friends of people in the media. "They're normally not willing to share, as they don't want you to take business away from them," she says. "But I try very hard to accommodate our media sponsors so that they can return the favor by providing contacts later in the year."

In-Town Sponsors

There are two types of sponsors: in-town and out-of-town, better known as local and regional/national. It is much easier to sell local than national sponsorship because local companies want to give back to the community that has supported them.

In Des Moines, Iowa, Pioneer Hi-Bred International sponsored a program to provide free bus service for attendees to the Des Moines Arts Festival. To get that sponsorship, Festival executive director Mo Dana first looked at what other programs Pioneer Hi-Bred International, the world's largest seed corn supplier, was sponsoring in the area. Most of them were programs for youth, senior citizens, and disadvantaged groups.

"I thought many of them might not come to the arts festival because they didn't have cars," Dana said. "Or they couldn't drive or weren't comfortable driving downtown."

She thought a free shuttle service might resolve those concerns and give more people a chance to experience the Festival. Pioneer Hi-Bred paid the Festival $50,000 to provide the Outreach Shuttle Service beginning in 1998. The service stops at about 20 locations within a 25-mile radius of the event.

Patrons express their gratitude for the sponsor's support by painting a giant "thank you" mural on a city bus, giving the sponsor year-round exposure.

In Atlanta in 2000, citizens faced a holiday season without two cherished downtown traditions: an ice-skating rink and a light display in Centennial Olympic Park. Both attractions had lost their sponsors. Because it receives no tax funding, the public park could not produce the rink or the light display without sponsor support.

Brian Hill, assistant general manager of the park, searched for a way to rescue them. He found one in BellSouth.net, later known as BellSouth Internet Service. It turned out that the Georgia Internet service provider had wanted to support the community through a seasonal event for some time.

In both the Des Moines and Atlanta examples, the primary motivation for the sponsors was to support a local effort. And although local sponsors also sponsor events for the same reasons listed in Chapter 2, they have an additional motivation—to give something back to the community where they are located. Even large national companies are much more apt to sponsor an event in the community where they are headquartered.

Local sponsorship is the ultimate grassroots level of cause-related marketing. Once again, companies used to give "donations" to local causes. Now they "sponsor" at higher monetary levels, but they also expect more exposure in return.

Out-of-Town Sponsors: Leveraging

Many people have asked us, "How can I sell sponsorship regionally or nationally? I have sold all that I can at the local level."

One way to get to these sponsors is to get local companies to sell for you by leveraging their vendors (see Figure 8-1). *The key is to have someone involved who is actually working with product suppliers and doing the buying.* In Phoenix, the Fiesta Bowl produced a hot air balloon race. Fry's Food Store was the title sponsor for the event. It was great that Fry's paid to be the title sponsor, but it was even better that the store's buyers went to 50 of their vendors and sold individual hot air balloon sponsorships at $1,500 each. Not only did that bring in another $75,000, but they did all the work, and we at the bowl were able to reach the regional and national headquarters that normally would not pay attention to the event.

Fry's used its leveraging power. Because products are constantly fighting for shelf space, more shelf space, end aisle dis-

- You can develop a close, personal relationship with contacts.
- Local relationships will help you leverage other potential sponsors.
- These organizations already sponsor events locally; it is just a question of whether they will sponsor yours or someone else's.
- Local companies want to support the local community and enhance its quality of life.

Figure 8-1
Local Sponsorship—Easier to Sell

plays, and so on, vendors almost had no choice but to say yes to Fry's.

This can also happen on a much smaller scale. A Rotary Club in the town of Sequim, Washington, is involved in a duck race. The general manager of Sequim Super Valu went to 70 of his vendors and sold corporate ducks at $250 each (instead of $5) to them. For a town of 4000 people, another $17,500 is substantial.

The Fiesta Bowl not only sold Fry's Food Stores on the idea of sponsoring its hot air balloon race, but also got them to sell other sponsorships for the event to companies that had products in their stores. *Photo courtesy of Fiesta Bowl.*

The Sylvania Alamo Bowl uses its board members to open doors to the upper levels of business for staff members to sell sponsorship. *Photo courtesy of Tommy Hultgren.*

There are many other examples of how events have leveraged retailers, some of them already mentioned earlier in this book (such as that of Sylvania's Alamo Bowl found in Chapter 2 and the Portland Rose Festival/G.I. Joe's in Chapter 5).

The Michigan Thanksgiving Day Parade solicited the help of its largest sponsor, Art Van Furniture, in this manner too. Store representatives went with the parade managers to meet with Sealy and La-Z-Boy, both of whom became float sponsors for the holiday event.

The Kentucky Derby Festival in Louisville has had a different fragrance sponsor every year. Organizers work with a major retailer, which in turn goes to Georgio, Estee Lauder, Ralph Lauren, and others to design a special perfume for the festival.

"It works well, because the fragrance company has lots of advertising and promotional money to spend," says the Festival's Bridget Sherrill. "And the retailer has exclusivity to the perfume's introduction, although it may be sold elsewhere after the Festival," she said.

The Festival's role is to present the official fragrance and to provide sampling opportunities at the Festival and at local hotels. "We offer sampling at selected Festival events and include samples in the Derby packages we put together for hotels. We also suggest that the fragrance retailer include a card in the package with a phone number for ordering the perfume," Sherrill said.

Pricing

Of course, part of the selling piece involves how much you want to charge (see Figure 8-2). This can vary greatly depending on the size of the community. The same sponsorship (attendance, benefits, etc.) in a town of 4,000 people will generally go for much less to a local sponsor than in one of 500,000 people, because of the size of local marketing budgets in each of those communities. Figure 8-3 offers some tips to help you with pricing.

For example, a title sponsorship for a local event in a market of 3,000,000 people like Phoenix, Arizona, will typically go for $10,000 to $200,000. In a smaller market like Port Angeles, Washington (18,000 people), the same title will go for about $1,000 to $2,000.

Both numbers can be increased if the local sponsor is able to approach the regional or national headquarters for more money, as explained earlier.

- Help you reach seemingly unreachable sponsors.
- Save you a lot of sales work, since the retailer does it for you.
- Bring more money to your bottom line.

Figure 8-2
What a Retailer's Leverage Can Do for You

> - Find out what other events in your market are charging.
> - Determine how much it costs to purchase a full-page advertisement in the local newspaper. This will give you an idea of how much money a sponsor spends for traditional advertising, and how much that sponsor might spend with you.

Figure 8-3
Tips to Help You with Pricing

Ask for the Check

There is a final piece of the puzzle in the sales process: Always make sure you ask for the check. We have been to many sales presentations where the salesperson makes a wonderful pitch, but never asks the question, "Can we count on you to be our sponsor this year?" *Never make a presentation without asking for a decision.*

Six Keys to Selling Sponsorship

For effective sponsorship selling:

1. Before you begin the sales process, make sure you complete all the steps presented in the previous chapters of this book.
2. Develop a plan for getting in to see a potential sponsor face-to-face.
3. Make a list of local buyers who might help you sell sponsorship to their vendors.
4. Determine how you can leverage local companies to help you sell national sponsorship.
5. Establish price parameters.
6. Always ask for the check!

Sponsorship Activities
1. Read Tom Hopkins's books, *How to Master the Art of Selling* and *Selling with Dummies*.
2. Read Brian Tracy's, *Advanced Selling Strategies: The Proven System of Sales Ideas, Methods, and Techniques Used by Top Salespeople Everywhere.*

3. Read "Relationship Marketing: The Key," in Chapter 2 of Philip Kotler's book, *Marketing Management: The Millenium Edition.*
4. Visit *www.event-solutions.com* and read step 8 in "10 Steps to Sponsorship Success."
5. Visit *www.aedme.org,* the Website for CEREC, the European Committee for Business, Arts and Culture and read information on sponsorship.
6. List the networks that you would establish to help you get in the door of potential sponsors.

Sponsorship Tool Kit

European Committee for Business, Arts and Culture (CEREC), www.aedme.org

Hopkins, Tom. (1982). *How to Master the Art of Selling.* Edited by Warren Jamison. New York: Warner Books.

Hopkins, Tom. (2000). *Selling for Dummies.* Indianapolis, IN: Hungry Minds, Inc.

Kotler, Philip. (2000). *Marketing Management: The Millennium Edition.* Upper Saddle River, NJ: Prentice-Hall.

Tracy, Brian. (1995). *Advanced Selling Strategies: The Proven System of Sales Ideas, Methods, and Techniques Used by Top Salespeople Everywhere.* New York: Simon & Schuster.

Web Sites

www.aedme.org; Telephone: 34 93 237 26 82; Fax 34 93 237 22 84; e-mail: contact@cerec.org

www.event-solutions.com

CHAPTER 9

The Legal Issues in Event Sponsorship

Well, I don't know as I want a lawyer to tell me what I cannot do. I hire him to tell me how to do what I want to do.

JOHN PIERPONT MORGAN, AMERICAN FINANCIER

IN THIS CHAPTER YOU WILL LEARN:

- The importance of the Taxpayers Relief Act of 1997 in regard to sponsorships
- Why a confirmation letter, a letter of agreement, and a formal contract are similar as well as different documents
- How to draft a sponsorship agreement
- The five basic purposes of a sponsorship agreement
- How to develop a multiyear agreement

From a legal standpoint, August 5, 1997, was probably the single most important day in the history of corporate sponsorship in the United States. It was on this day that many producers of nonprofit events breathed a sigh of relief when President Bill Clinton signed the Taxpayers Relief Act of 1997, a law that protects events from taxation of most corporate sponsorship income.

The Taxpayers Relief Act is known by most Americans for the significant changes it offers to tax law governing IRAs, deductions for dependents, capital gains, and a host of other tax issues.

But for events, this piece of legislation has special meaning. The bill contains language that many event organizers had been fighting for since 1991. Twice this measure had made it to the president's desk, only to find its host or vehicle bill vetoed.

The Taxpayers Relief Act of 1997 effectively exempts most sponsor income from a 33 percent unrelated business income tax (UBIT) that 501 (c) (3) nonprofit organizations might otherwise be forced to pay.

The IRS had raised the anxiety of event producers when it ruled that the organizers of two popular college football bowl games, the Mobil Cotton Bowl and the John Hancock Bowl, had to pay tax on millions of sponsorship dollars. Almost immediately, several members of Congress introduced legislation to reverse the ruling, which was finally passed in 1997.

Zia Gipson was the legislative coordinator for the International Festivals and Events Association during this fight. She outlined a few highlights in *Festivals: The How-To of Festivals and Events,* the official publication of the International Festivals and Events Association (IFEA).

- The bill creates distinctions between sponsor activities that provide recognition (nontaxable) versus advertising (taxable).
- For example, from the bill, section 796: "Qualified sponsorship payments" are defined as any payments made by a person engaged in a trade or business with respect to which the person will receive no substantial return benefit other than the use or acknowledgment of the name or logo (or product lines) of the person's trade or business in connection with the organization's activities. Such a use or acknowledgment does not include advertising of such person's products or services, meaning qualitative or comparative language, price information or other indications of savings, or value or an endorsement or other inducement to purchase, sell or use such products or services.

Thus, for example, if in return for receiving a sponsorship payment an organization promises to use the sponsor's name or logo in acknowledging the sponsor's support for an educational or fund-raising event conducted by the organization, such a payment will not be subject to UBIT. In contrast, if the organization provides advertising of a sponsor's products, the payment made to the organization by the sponsor in order to receive such advertising will be subject to UBIT.

- The bill's language is identical in effect to the proposed IRS regulations (January, 1993—Proposed Rulemaking (EE-74-92) Taxation of Tax-Exempt Organizations' Income from Corporate Sponsorship) with one very important difference: The Taxpayers Relief Act does not allow the IRS to "taint" one otherwise nontaxable sponsor payment if a separate sponsor activity is deemed taxable.

  For example, if the sponsorship agreement provides (taxable) advertising support for the sponsor as well as nontaxable recognition such as posting of simple sponsor logos on festival banners, each sponsor activity and income stream will be evaluated separately to determine whether a tax is due.

- The bill is effective for sponsor payments received or solicited after the end of calendar year 1997.

According to the IRS, taxable unrelated business income (UBIT) is the income from a nonprofit trade or business that is regularly carried on by an exempt organization that is not substantially related to the performance by the organization of its exempt purpose or function, except that the organization uses the profits derived from this activity.

As opposed to the preceding sponsorship regulations, advertising in a periodical of a nonprofit (exempt) organization that contains editorial material related to the festival or event is an unrelated business that exploits an exempt activity, the circulation, and readership of the periodical. Therefore, it is taxable.

Sponsorship Contracts

Although the Taxpayers Relief Act of 1997 was very important to event managers, other event sponsorship issues are similarly important to explore. No one knows this better than Eric L. Martin of Bands of America in Schaumburg, Illinois, who has a very special background. Not only is he an outstanding event producer, he is also a graduate of the University of Michigan Law School and thus understands legal issues from both sides of the fence.

According to Martin, there are three types of sponsorship documentation:

1. The Confirming Letter
2. The Letter of Agreement
3. The Formal Contract

THE CONFIRMING LETTER

Martin says that the confirming letter is not, in and of itself, a contract. "Without the signature and the written commitment of both parties, it is merely one party's statement of what the oral contract involves," Martin says. "However, just because there is no confirming contract does not mean that one [a contract] does not exist."

The actions and promises (oral or written) of one party and the reasonable reliance of another is often enough to sustain the existence of a contract in court.

Oral agreements are valid particularly where one party has acted to its detriment or relied on the word or oral promises of another. The confirming letter (when not disallowed in a timely fashion) provides evidence of the parties' intent and is often relied upon in cases of dispute.

LETTER OF AGREEMENT

The letter of agreement, according to Martin, is just that. It is—when fully executed—a contract. It is simply less formal, less expensive, and often less intimidating than a formal contract.

A formal contract, usually more detailed and more intimidating, is no more enforceable than a letter of agreement. It does, however, call the parties to a higher level of attention.

In fact, in the early 1980s at the Fiesta Bowl in Phoenix, we sold a $75,000 sponsorship to Greyhound Bus Lines and submitted a letter of agreement. The company fell on hard times and asked whether the sponsorship could be reduced. If we had signed a formal contract, the company probably would not have asked.

Martin has also developed a checklist for drafting an agreement. "Drafting an agreement should be direct, tell a story, and answer the reader's basic questions," he says. "More important, unless you're a highly paid lawyer, with a need to defend the value of years of legal training and experience, it ought to be simple."

Eric Martin's Checklist for Drafting Sponsorship Agreements

Martin warns against getting bogged down in form. It matters not that an agreement be in perfect form. It just needs to be clear and cover all the necessary points of agreement. When preparing an agreement, he seeks to answer certain questions, which are found in Martin's Checklist (Figure 9-1).

DRAFTING A SPONSORSHIP CONTRACT

Now that you have gotten an overview of content, how do you get down to the business of drafting? Martin says to begin by plagiarizing.

Who—The parties to the agreement; the specific persons, organizations, or the types or qualifications of persons who must perform.

What—Name of the agreement, i.e., "This is a contract for . . ."

Recitals—Intent of the parties, why we have come together (e.g., offer and acceptance).

Specifications—Who does what for whom? (e.g., subject matter).

When—Dates for performance, payment, and the term of the agreement (do not forget to "date" the agreement).

Where—Place of performance and place of governing law and litigation where notices, payment, and other communications must go.

How—Specific methods of performance (where necessary and important, state how the parties must do what they are committing to do; (e.g., consideration).

How Much—Who gets what, when, and how much?

Signatures—The essence of an agreement, written in concurrence with terms (don't forget to get the agreement fully executed and delivered to each party).

Match these questions and considerations with the appropriate answers, and you have a contract. Good drafting uses the present tense and active voice; e.g., "Joe and I agree that Joe shall do 'X' on 'Y' date, and I shall pay Joe 'Z' dollars on 'A' date in exchange therefore."

Figure 9-1
Eric Martin's Checklist for Drafting an Agreement

He always starts with a good form. It can be his own "tried and tested" creation or that of another individual or lawyer. "When I use another's form, training and writer's pride always makes me improve (change) it," he says. "However, I'm never too proud to use another's good work."

Be sure to evaluate the perspective of a form. Make sure that it was prepared by a party or person viewing life from your perspective. Martin recommends that you never start with a "sponsor's form," unless you have made a concentrated, detailed effort to examine it and to remove much of the pro-investment sponsor language.

"You should do what most good lawyers do," he says. "Build your own forms file. Keep a copy of every contract you ever come across. In addition to your regular files, maintain a file of contracts by type. Go to your local law library. I do not highly recommend over-the-counter/general bookstore forms. However, forms that accompany a good law treatise or forms produced by a good association, like IFEA or IEG [International Events Group], are usually worth their weight in gold (or savings in legal fees)."

Mary Hutchings Reed, author of the *IEG Legal Guide to Cause Marketing,* says in her book that "part of the reason why sponsorship contracts are important is that the terms *sponsor, title sponsor, presenter* and *official supplier* have no standard meaning in the industry. They mean only what the parties agree they mean.

---

1. To clarify the rights the sponsor is getting and the rights the event owner is retaining
2. To preserve the value of the sponsor's exclusivity by avoiding possible conflicts with other presenters and other problems likely to arise
3. To protect both parties from unwanted liability for personal injury, property damage, and other problems likely to arise
4. To protect each party's trademarks and official symbols and logos
5. To protect the owner's and sponsor's respective proprietary interests in the event

Source: Courtesy IEG.

Figure 9-2
Mary Hutchings Reed's Five Basic Purposes for a Contract

A written agreement is the best way to prove what the parties intended by those terms when they began their relationship."

She says that a sponsorship contract can serve five basic purposes (see Figure 9-2). Note that she says, in No. 3, that both parties have to be protected in the contract, which most commonly appears in a contract under the heading "Hold Harmless and Indemnification."

Sylvia Allen and C. Scott Amman, in their book, *How to Be Successful in Sponsorship Sales,* explain that indemnification is the protection of each party's rights for a mistake or negligent act committed by the sponsors and/or event, and who is responsible for that protection.

Reed says that "the contract should address liability and indemnification, and should specifically address the amounts and types of insurance the organization will obtain (naming the sponsor as an insured) to back up the indemnity."

Allen also gives a Sponsor Contract Checklist in her book, which specifically addresses event issues that should be covered (see Figure 9-3).

Sponsorship Rights

1. Sponsor's Official Status
   - As only sponsor?
   - As only sponsor in a category?
   - Right to veto other sponsors for reasons of incompatibility?
   - Any conflicts with official suppliers?
   - What about sponsorships at other sites or related events?
2. Signs at the Event
   - How many?
   - What is the size and placement of sponsor's name relative to others?
   - Who pays?
   - Distance from others' signs?
   - Sign on curtain?
   - Billing on marquees?
   - Signs on vehicles (sound trucks, courtesy cars, etc.)?
   - Any conflicts with permanent signage or arena suppliers?

Figure 9-3
Sylvia Allen's Sponsor Contract Checklist

3. Advertising Credits
   - On stationery?
   - In name of event?
   - On program cover?
   - In program advertisement?
   - In all advertising?
   - In all print advertising only?
   - In television billboards?
   - On souvenirs (T-shirts, bumper stickers, etc.)?
   - In press releases?
4. Sponsorship Fee
   - How paid?
   - When paid?
   - Secured by letter of credit or escrow?
   - Refundable if television ratings are poor?
   - Exclusivity?
5. Trademarks
   - Sponsor's quality control
   - Promoter's quality control
   - Ownership of special logos
   - License/royalties/merchandising
6. Liabilities
   - To observers
   - To participants
   - To the site
   - To innocent bystanders
   - For infringement of trademarks
   - For contractual commitments in the event of rain, broadcast interruption, force majeure events
7. Miscellaneous Topics
   - Term
   - Confidentiality
   - Insurance
   - Arbitration/court
   - Best efforts clause
   - Modifications/amendments
   - Ambush
   - Boilerplate clauses

Figure 9-3
(Continued)

8. Merchandising Rights
   - Can the sponsor sell T-shirts, mugs, similar souvenirs?
   - Can the sponsor manufacture its own souvenirs or buy from the promoter at cost?
   - Who gets the profit on merchandising efforts?
9. Ownership of Television Rights
   - Who owns and controls?
   - If the promoter owns, does the sponsor have right of first refusal on available spots?
   - Is there an estimated rating and/or a rebate for low ratings?
   - Does the sponsor get opening/closing credits or billboards?
   - Does the sponsor have rights to use footage of the event for current and/or future advertising?
   - Will the promoter get all rights necessary from participants to allow use of clips in commercials without further compensation?
10. Public Relations and Personal Appearances
    - Can the promoter commit key personnel or talent to personal appearances on behalf of the sponsor?
    - Can the promoter commit its spokespersons to mention the sponsor's name whenever possible?
    - Does the sponsor have the right to erect a courtesy tent?
    - Can the promoter commit the key personnel participating in an event to attending post-event parties in their honor?
    - Does the sponsor get free tickets (for key customers, tie-in contests, etc.)?
11. Future Options
    - Does the sponsor have the right to renew its sponsorship on the same terms and conditions (plus a fixed increase in the price)?
    - Does the sponsor have the right of first refusal for subsequent years?

Source: Courtesy of Sylvia Allen and C. Scott Amman.

Figure 9-3
(Continued)

SAMPLES OF A SPONSORSHIP AGREEMENT

Figure 9-4 is an example of a sponsorship agreement currently used by the Fiesta Bowl. Figure 9-5 is a sample of a multiyear sponsorship agreement.

_____ , 2002

Re: Sponsorship of_____

Dear _____ :

This letter will set forth the terms and conditions under which _____ ("_____") and the Fiesta Events, Inc., an Arizona nonprofit corporation ("Fiesta Events") agree to stage_____(hereinafter sometimes referred to as the "2002 Event"). Fiesta Events and [Sponsor] hereby agree to jointly sponsor, promote, and stage the Parade under the following terms and conditions:

1. _Description of the Event._ The 2002 Event shall be the annual Parade to be held in the City of _____,_____, on _____ , 2002.

2. _Sponsorship Fee._ [Sponsor] agrees to pay Fiesta Events a nonrefundable fee equal to _____ No/100 Dollars ($_____). [Sponsor] shall pay this nonrefundable sponsorship fee in accordance with the following schedule:
   (a) On or before_____, [Sponsor] shall pay Fiesta Events one-half of the nonrefundable sponsorship fee, $_____.
   (b) On or before _____, [Sponsor] shall pay Fiesta Events the remaining one-half of the nonrefundable sponsorship fee, $_____.

3. _Responsibilities of Fiesta Events._ Fiesta Events shall be responsible for the overall planning, staging, and promotion of the 2002 Event. All final decisions concerning the staging, planning, and promotion of the 2002 Event shall be made by Fiesta Events, in consultation with [Sponsor], or other agents or committees designated by those organizations.

Figure 9-4
Letter of Agreement

4. *Sponsorship Activities.* Fiesta Events agrees to provide the following services, benefits, and publicity to [Sponsor]:
   [Examples of sample benefits that are specific to Event]
   (a) Fiesta Events shall use the official title of the 2002 Event, "[Sponsor] Fiesta Bowl Parade," in all of Fiesta Events' publicity, press releases, public announcements, and surrounding publicity. Fiesta Events shall refer to [Sponsor] as the 2002 Event's title sponsor. Fiesta Events agrees to use its best efforts to promote the official title of the 2002 Event with all national and local media and participants.
   (b) Fiesta Events shall provide [Sponsor] with a start and finish line banner, made to the specifications and approval of [Sponsor].
   (c) Fiesta Events shall provide markers at each mile interval during the 2002 Event, which designate [Sponsor] status as the official race sponsor of the 2002 Event.
   (d) Fiesta Events shall print at least_____race brochures and distribute these brochures throughout the Metropolitan Phoenix Area, at Fiesta Events' expense. Brochures shall include the 2002 Event's official title, including graphics identifying [Sponsor] as the 2002 Event's official race sponsor.
   (e) Fiesta Events agrees that [Sponsor] shall have the exclusive right to the official title of the 2002 Event, the "_____ ."
   (f) Fiesta Events shall provide up to eight (8) invitations, to designated [Sponsor] customers or employees, to attend a special prerace sponsors brunch on the day of the 2002 Event.
   (g) Fiesta Events will recognize [Sponsor] as the title sponsor of the 2002 Event in all Fiesta Events publications, including (1) the Fiesta Bowl Game Program, which has an approximate circulation of 24,000 readers, (2) the Fiesta Bowl Program, (3) the Fiesta Bowl Media Guide, which has an approximate circulation of 3000 readers, (4) the Fiesta Bowl Team Manual, which has an approximate circulation of 500 readers, (5) the Fiesta Bowl Pocket Calendar, which has an approximate circulation of 25,000 readers, and (6) the Fiesta Bowl News Release Letterhead, which has an approximate circulation of 30,000 readers.

Figure 9-4
(Continued)

(h) Fiesta Events shall provide, to all 2002 Event participants, a T-shirt naming [Sponsor] as the title sponsor for the 2002 Event.

(i) Fiesta Events shall periodically mention [Sponsor] as the title sponsor of the 2002 Event on the public address system located at the event site.

(j) Fiesta Events shall name [Sponsor] as the title sponsor of the 2002 Event on the scoreboard at the 2002 IBM/OS2 Fiesta Bowl Game, and also provide [Sponsor] with a scoreboard thank-you picture.

5. *Term of This Letter of Agreement.* The term of this Letter of Agreement shall expire after the 2002 Event, and [Sponsor]'s sponsorship of the 2002 Event shall be on the same terms and conditions as herein set forth, except that the nonrefundable sponsorship fee for the 2002 Event shall be $_____ .

6. *Additional Sponsorship.* Fiesta Events may solicit and obtain other sponsors and sponsorship support for the 2002 Event, provided any such additional sponsorships do not in any way conflict with the terms and conditions of this Letter of Agreement.

7. *Force Majeure.* Fiesta Events shall not be liable for any failure to perform hereunder resulting from unforeseen events or circumstances beyond its control including, but not limited to, any delay, postponement, or cancellation due to adverse weather or other conditions. In the event that Fiesta Events is unable to perform because of any such unforeseen events or circumstances, [Sponsor] shall remain responsible for all costs and expenses incurred in an amount not to exceed the sponsorship fee. In the event Fiesta Events is unable to provide [Sponsor] with each benefit specifically described in paragraph 4 hereof, the parties agree that [Sponsor] may substitute other comparable benefits of equal or greater value.

8. *Nonrefundable Fee.* All sponsorship fees paid by [Sponsor] hereunder are nonrefundable, and [Sponsor] shall be responsible for all costs incurred in excess of agreed-upon sponsorship fee, or if the 2002 Event is held without Fiesta Events consent.

Figure 9-4
(Continued)

9. *Indemnity.* [Sponsor] and Fiesta Events agree to indemnify, defend, and hold harmless one another, their directors, committee persons, officers, agents, employees and volunteers, and any successors and assigns of both parties from, for, and against any and all losses, costs, damages, and expenses, including without limitation all claims, actions, suits, judgments, and attorney's fees relating to or resulting from the death of any person or damage or injury to any person or property of any person, all of which results from or arises out of the 2002 Event or successor event, as applicable.

10. *Miscellaneous.* This Letter of Agreement shall be construed and enforced in accordance with the laws of the State of Arizona. This Letter of Agreement shall succeed and inure to the benefit of the respective successors and assigns of both Fiesta Events and [Sponsor]. This Letter of Agreement may not be amended or assigned without the prior written consent of both Fiesta Events and [Sponsor].

If the foregoing accurately sets forth our agreement, please indicate by signing the two copies of this Letter of Agreement in the space provided below and return one copy to me. On behalf of Fiesta Events, I wish to thank you for your generous support of our activities. I look forward to a long and mutually beneficial relationship.

Very truly yours,

Fiesta Events, Inc.

ACCEPTED and agreed to

This _____ day of _____ , 2002

By: _____

Name: _____

Title: _____

Figure 9-4
(Continued)

The Houston International Festival

More than 500,000 people come together each year to enjoy the Houston International Festival, Houston's Official Celebration of the Visual and Performing Arts. Produced by the Houston Festival Foundation, a 501 (c) (3) nonprofit organization, the Festival schedules many activities and events throughout the year, making provisions for year round promotional exposure, networking forums, business development, and community-wide involvement. Each year, a specific country is spotlighted, from which the Foundation builds upon three pillars: business, art, and education.

The Houston International Festival also celebrates the region's own special flavor while showcasing other cultures of the world with the presentation of the outdoor Festival. This colorful and exciting event consists of 20 blocks that bustle with outdoor stages, a dizzying array of cafés, arts and crafts markets, food and beverage booths, children's programs, street performances, and much, much more. There are seven major entertainment areas within the outdoor Festival, referred to as Zones. They include the American, Latin, African, International, Texas, and Kid's Zones. The highlighted Zone for the year 2002 will be in honor of this year's spotlighted country, Ireland. In addition to the seven major entertainment areas, the Festival also presents the International Specialty Beer Garden, the Art Car Parade, and the International Carnival Parade.

HIF 2002—Ireland: The 2002 Festival will spotlight Ireland. From its theater, literature, music, and flourishing business environment, to its tremendous popular appeal, Irish culture is sure to afford an amazing variety of interesting subjects to discover. As board member and chairman of the Country Selection Committee, Robert Sakowitz stated, "From Oscar Wilde to the band U2, or from James Joyce to Van Morrison . . . Ireland has it all."

HIF 2003—France: Plans are under way to repeat countries spotlighted in the past. A European setting will be featured through the presentation of the unique performing and visual arts of France at the 2003 Festival.

American Heritage Zone

The American Heritage Zone is recognized as one of the more popular destination spots of the Houston International Festival. The American Heritage stage features fun and continuous, exciting, homegrown (Cajun, Zydeco, country, Blues, and jazz sounds) talent

Figure 9-5
Event Description

on stage by day, in addition to national touring performers in the late afternoon. Last year, crowds danced and tuned in to artists such as Jerry Jeff Walker, Blind Boys of Alabama, Ann Nesby, Chubby Carrier, Beau Jocque, Wayne Toups, and more. Four radio stations and one television station will partner-up to promote the American Heritage Stage. In addition to enjoying music at the American Heritage Zone, festival-goers will be able to shop for handmade expressions at the Gypsy Market, then take a break at the International Specialty Beer Garden to sample a smorgasbord of brew tastes.

SPONSORSHIP STATUS

Budweiser will be positioned as the *Official Beer* of the Houston International Festival for the 2002 and 2003 Festivals.

Budweiser will be positioned as the *Title Sponsor* of the American Heritage Stage on the weekends for the 2002 and 2003 Festivals.

SPONSORSHIP BENEFITS AND EXPOSURE

Budweiser will receive the following benefits and exposure:

(a) Logo exposure on approximately eight (8) drink booths. Exposure includes banners, coolers, and menu signage. A signage layout will be provided for banner placement for all beverages served from the drink booths. Budweiser will be ensured upper-level signage on all drink booths.

(b) Recognition in the post-Festival sponsor appreciation ad that runs in the *Houston Chronicle.*

(c) Logo recognition in select *Houston Chronicle* ads.

(d) Logo exposure on the front of the Event's Official Poster. Circulation: 7,500.

(e) Name exposure on collateral and publicity pieces promoting the Stage Line-Up for the American Music Stage.

(f) Logo exposure in the Event's Official Guide. Logo will be placed on the location map *and* the American Heritage Zone panel. Circulation: 125,000.

(g) Logo exposure (4′ × 8′ banners) on three (3) Sponsor Advertising towers located in high-traffic areas.

(h) Logo exposure on the American Music Stage title banner.

(i) Logo exposure on two (2) 4′ × 8′ banners on the American Music Stage towers.

Figure 9-5
(Continued)

(j) Audio mentions in thirty-second (:30) prerecorded spots promoting the *Budweiser* American Music Stage on the following radio stations: FM 100.3 KILT, Young Country KIKK 96.5, KMJQ Majic 102, KBXX 97.9 The Box, and KTSU Choice 90.9. Each radio station is expected to run a minimum of fifty (50) promotional spots in conjunction with the American Heritage Stage.

(k) Logo identification in thirty-second (:30) prerecorded spots promoting the *Budweiser* American Music Stage on KPRC–Channel 2 (NBC affiliate). Approximately forty (40) spots are scheduled to run over a three-week period.

(l) A minimum of four (4) scripted public address announcements per day.

TICKETS, PASSES, AND INVITATIONS

Budweiser will receive the following number of Festival passes and tickets, along with complimentary invitations to several Festival-related business-to-business activities and receptions. These events typically attract an audience of local, regional, national, and international elected or appointed representatives, media, and leading Houston business executives.

Event	Quantity	Attendance
Festival Admission Tickets—Promotional admission tickets, good for any of the four weekend festival days for use as employee and/or client incentives	500 per year	500,000 per person
Sponsor Hospitality—On-site sponsor hospitality passes for weekend festival days for use in client entertaining and/or VIP exposure	20 per year	300 per person daily
Sponsor Wristbands—Allow free admission to the Festival for company employees working on-site	50 per year	NA
Parking Passes—Allow sponsors to park free of charge	6 per year	NA

Figure 9-5
(Continued)

SPONSORSHIP REQUESTS

(a) Budweiser agrees to pay a cash sponsorship amount of $50,000 (fifty thousand dollars) for sponsorship of the Year 2002 Festival, $53,500 (fifty-three thousand five hundred dollars) for sponsorship of the Year 2003 Festival, and a $58,500 (fifty-eight thousand dollars five hundred) for sponsorship of the Year 2004 Festival.

Due on or before January 15, 2003
Due on or before January 15, 2004

Please make check payable to the Houston International Festival

The Houston International Festival is a 501 (c) (3) nonprofit organization.

(b) Budweiser agrees to an in-kind donation of the I-45 Billboard at the Pierce Elevated. The Festival is responsible for expenses related to production and design.

(c) Budweiser agrees to an in-kind donation of an attraction per year (such as what is outlined for the Year 2002—Budweiser Clydesdales for the first weekend / Bud World Exhibit for a minimum of one weekend and possibly a second weekend).

(d) Budweiser agrees to provide media tags about the Festival on planned Budweiser media, when possible.

(e) Budweiser agrees to an in-kind donation of product and cups to be provided for the following venues and events:
- On-Site Sponsor Hospitality (1200 people/four days)
- On-Site Volunteer Rest Area (300 people/four days)
- Two VIP Events (500 people per event)

PLEASE NOTE: The *Budweiser* logo will be used for multiple applications and sent to various vendors in order to produce signage, invitations, and printed promotional materials. *Please provide us with the current Budweiser logo in both a color and a black-and-white version in either a minimum of 3 logo slicks or on an IBM disk in .tiff format on or before August 31 of each year, sent to the address below.*

Figure 9-5
(Continued)

Should the above elements meet your approval, please indicate your acceptance by signing in the appropriate space below and returning this signed agreement along with the completed Sponsor Contact Form to the following address:

Wendy Paynter
The Houston International Festival
1915 Commonwealth Suite 102
Houston, TX 77006
Fax: 713-522-5766

---------------------------------   ---------------------------------

Authorized Signature for   Authorized Signature for the
Budweiser/Silver Eagle   Houston International Festival
Distributing

Date: _____   Date: _____

For information regarding sponsorship elements and opportunities, please call Wendy Paynter at 713-522-9723, ext. 227.

Source: Courtesy Houston International Festival.

Figure 9-5
(Continued)

Three Keys to Addressing the Legal Issues of Sponsorship

To address the legal issues of sponsorship:

1. Study the Taxpayers Relief Act of 1997 and determine how it can affect your event.
2. Decide whether you should use a confirming letter, a letter of agreement, or a formal contract. At the very least, a letter of agreement should be signed by all sponsors.
3. When drafting an agreement or contract, you can follow the checklists found in this chapter, hire an attorney, or, better

yet, get an attorney to prepare one for you gratis. You can also copy the contracts of other events, like those found in this chapter.

Sponsorship Activities

1. For the best basic event legal guide, read Eric Martin's *Festival and Event Legal Issues.*
2. Read Mary Hutchings Reed's *IEG Legal Guide to Cause Marketing* for a more in-depth look.
3. Prepare a statement explaining the importance of the Taxpayer's Relief Act of 1997 to U.S. event managers.
4. List the key components of a sponsorship contract.

Sponsorship Tool Kit

Black, Henry Campbell. (2001). *Black's Law Dictionary.* St Paul, MN: West Group.

Burnham, Scott. (1987). *Drafting Contracts.* Charlottesville, VA: Michie Company.

Howell, John C. (1980). *The Complete Guide to Business Contracts.* Englewood Cliffs, NJ: Prentice-Hall.

Martin, Eric. *Festival and Event Legal Issues.* Available from IFEA Library, 2601 Eastover Terrace, Boise, ID.

McGonagle, John J. (1982). *Business Agreements.* Randor, PA: Chilton Book Company.

Neibert, Christopher, and Jack Withaim Jr. (1980). *How to Handle Your Own Contracts.* New York: Greenwich House.

Reed, Mary Hutchings. (2001). *IEG Legal Guide to Cause Marketing.* Chicago, IL. Contact IEG at 1-800-834-4850.

CHAPTER 10

The Staff—Sponsor-Client Relationship

The sale merely consummates the courtship. Then the marriage begins. How good the marriage is depends on how well the relationship is managed by the seller.

THEODORE LEVITT, AMERICAN EDUCATOR AND AUTHOR

IN THIS CHAPTER YOU WILL LEARN:

- How corporate sponsorship has increased the number of event managers
- Why it is imperative to have good professional managers on your staff
- The qualities of a good sponsorship event manager
- The makeup of a good staff for an event
- How to create a sponsorship manager job description

The International Festivals and Events Association's (IFEA) staff compensation survey in 1981 noted that the average staff size for an event with a budget of more than $1 million was two event managers. And most other events with that budget did not have any staff, because they were run by all-volunteer organizations.

Twenty years later, a subsequent survey showed the average staff size of larger-budget events had increased to *17!* And many more events, some with relatively miniscule budgets, have at least one manager on staff.

What is the motivating factor behind this increase? Corporate sponsorship.

As you have seen in the earlier chapters of this book, the selling of corporate sponsorship is very complicated. Many of the sponsors to whom you are pitching do not understand the process. This complexity, coupled with events' increased need for corporate support, has driven organizations in the industry to hire more specialized event managers.

Volunteers discovered that they had neither the time nor the knowledge to effectively sell and, most important, service sponsors. Not only have events' sponsorship sales staff increased (in most cases, they have been created, because most events did not sell sponsorship in 1980), but the number of other event manager positions has also risen.

Corporate sponsors have provided events with revenue, but they expect even more than increased sales in return. *They expect better events, too.* And because of that, events have added staff in all areas to make their organizations more successful.

"It's extremely important for an event to have good staff," says Dennis Boese, the corporate manager of fair and festival marketing for the Miller Brewing Company. "Without them, it makes my job twice as difficult.

"Events like Summerfest in Milwaukee and the Kentucky Derby Festival have really sharp people. They not only sell you the sponsorship, but they act like your agent within the festival. They're constantly staying in touch, calling, updating, and letting us know what is happening."

Dennis Bash, vice president and western region manager of corporate sponsorship for U.S. Bank in Portland, looks to creative, professional event staff to bring new ideas to the table. "In many markets our brand is well established so branding is a secondary

Many sponsors won't consider sponsoring an event unless they can work with competent staff, like that found at the Kentucky Derby Festival. "They not only sell you the sponsorship, but they act like your agent within the festival," says Dennis Boese, the Corporate Manager of Fair and Festival Marketing for the Miller Brewing Co. *Photo courtesy of Kentucky Derby Festival, Inc.*

or tertiary concern. But we do need to achieve ROI [return on investment] on our sponsorships, and we do that in part by selling product. It's a huge help to us when an event's staff comes to us with ideas on how we can sell product. That speaks volumes of their commitment to us as a sponsor."

"You can tell when an event is run by an event professional," says the Colorado Lottery's Laura Stitt. "There's more return on investment."

As we have said before, it is much more important now to have professional staff than it was 20 years ago, when a volunteer could visit an acquaintance in the business world and ask him or her for a donation. Companies expected very little in return—a mention in an event's program would suffice. A volunteer could easily do that job; contacts in the business world were much more important than content delivered.

When the Fiesta Bowl became the first festival to hire a full-time staff person (current Bowl president and CEO John Junker) in 1984, it was easy for it to differentiate itself from other events and nonprofit organizations.

A common sales pitch was, "Do you want to be a sponsor of the Fiesta Bowl and receive signage, mentions in the brochure, advertising, and other benefits, or do you want to donate to another nonprofit and receive only a program listing?"

That, of course, has all changed. Most events and nonprofits now have professional staff who deliver packages of benefits to sponsors. There are two reasons that it is difficult for a volunteer to deliver the same results as a professional event manager:

1. The selling of sponsorship takes more time than most volunteers have to give. Instead of the one meeting that it took to get a donation from a business, it now takes several meetings. The sponsorship sales process never ends, and staff are needed to keep in continual touch with the sponsor. The volunteer board member can still open doors, but it is necessary to have good event managers in place in order to follow up with sponsors.

2. Like anything else in the marketing world, the selling and retention of sponsors requires expertise, which has been outlined in the earlier chapters of this book. It requires someone who has knowledge, not only of marketing, but of event marketing. He or she must know how to research a company and provide the proper fit for a sponsor. Event managers must take care of a myriad of details. "When it comes time to make sure my logo is in the right PMS color and that there is proper seating for our CEO next to the mayor, I want to make sure I have professional staff to work with," says Carolyn Pendergast, marketing and communications director of the Arizona Biltmore Resort Hotel in Phoenix.

The reason many events do not evaluate sponsorship is that it is difficult and very time-consuming. "It's also very subjective," says Pendergast, who is also the former director of marketing for the University of California's athletic department. "But more and more, sponsors are needing it in order to justify costs, and sometimes in order to bill specific departments."

Anniversary Opportunity

The National Cherry Festival's Chuck O'Connor demonstrates an especially effective sponsor–client relationship strategy.

The festival has taken advantage of milestone anniversaries by working with potential sponsors on special creative promotions that result in big public relations and return-on-investment hits.

These take a lot of time and expertise, but they turn out to be extremely worthwhile. With the Festival set to celebrate its 75th anniversary in 2001, event managers looked for likely partners who could benefit from making a big splash. After deciding on creating the world's longest cherry ice cream sundae during the Festival's opening ceremonies, the event's marketing department sat down with likely partners.

Both Country Fresh Ice Cream and the cherry industry loved the idea, realizing the value of the media attention the event would draw. They underwrote the whole production. Submitting the feat—the creation of a 320-foot-long cherry ice cream sundae—to Guinness World Records (the publication's new name in 2001) topped off this very creative promotion and set the stage for increased sponsor involvement for the next year.

O'Connor used the anniversary idea again in the same year when he observed that the Festival's official airline, Northwest Airlines, was celebrating its 75th anniversary at the same time. That led to an in-flight magazine article on the Cherry Festival. "You can set up a meeting with other organizations or sponsors that may be celebrating the same anniversary," O'Connor said. "Then you can brainstorm on a special promotional celebration that uses your event as the springboard."

There are several other examples of event managers creatively courting a sponsor, again something that a volunteer does not have the time or expertise to do.

SUCCESS STORY

BENDING OVER BACKWARDS—THE INTERNATIONAL FESTIVAL OF LENT

Sometimes it is the little things a professional staff person can do that can produce big results. One year at the International Festival of Lent in Maribor, Slovenia, a storm surprised everyone and toppled a hot air balloon of one of the event's major sponsors, Adriatic Insurance Company, and blew it into the River Drava.

At the time, two of the event's staff were talking to the director of the company. They immediately jumped in the river and chased the balloon for a half hour, finally saving it and bringing it back to shore.

The Adriatic director thanked the staff profusely, to which they replied, " 'Anything for a sponsor' is our motto!" The act led to the immediate renewal of the sponsorship for the following year, and at an increase in monies.

SunFest: Relationship Building

Dianna Craven at SunFest in West Palm Beach has made a lot of close friends with people in the media. "They're not normally willing to share, as they don't want you to take business away from them," she says. "But I try very hard to accommodate our media sponsors so that they can return the favor by providing contacts later in the year."

Alamo Bowl: Hospitality at Its Best

Derrick Fox, executive director of the Sylvania Alamo Bowl in San Antonio, works with sponsors in many different ways, one of which is to provide the best in hospitality.

Fox and his staff heavily involve themselves with executives at Sylvania to ensure customer satisfaction and to make sure the Bowl's title sponsor gets the very best price and quality it can.

"We live in San Antonio and they are headquartered in Boston," Fox said. "We want to make sure that they are not treated as a one-time-a-year out-of-town customer, but rather as a multiyear,

SunFest builds relationships with key marketing personnel throughout the year, which leads to more sponsor contacts. *Photo courtesy of SunFest of Palm Beach County, Inc.*

multimillion-dollar sponsor that makes this event a reality for San Antonio."

The Bowl's staff provides the best possible experience for Sylvania and its guests, knowing that if the sponsor and guests are happy, the sponsorship will last. "It is easy to pass off these extra responsibilities, but I would rather incur the extra work to ensure customer satisfaction," Fox says. "We would rather not pass that responsibility off to a third, fourth, or fifth party who does not have Sylvania as its No. 1 priority."

If you have reached the point at which you are seeking to hire someone who has the qualities of this professional, then you need to develop a job description. See Figure 10-1 for the qualities of the ideal sponsorship event manager. See Figure 10-2 for a description of the sponsorship manager's position at SunFest of Palm Beach County.

Finding the right person to sell sponsorship for an event is extremely difficult. There are very few people who have the expertise.
Here are qualities to look for:

- A good salesperson. However, he or she must meet many more qualifications than an advertising salesperson.
- A good sponsorship event manager should know the market in which the event is held and some of its players. CEREC, the European Committee for Business, Arts and Culture, instructs its network to build relationships. The organization writes, "People give to people. Keep them informed before, during and after events. Have someone, even part-time, dedicated to this 'socializing' task."
- He or she should have a good knowledge of the events industry. Events are varied, and you have to understand the industry before you can sell.
- Most important, a sponsorship manager should know how to communicate with potential sponsors and understand their needs. This requires research and the ability to learn as much about a sponsor's business as possible.
- Writing skills are important, because there will be many proposals to write.
- A manager should be able to develop and coordinate sponsor hospitality programs.
- If the salesperson is working for a nonprofit organization, it is imperative that he or she is capable of working with volunteers. This includes not only getting along with them, but also knowing how to use them to open doors.
- A manager should be a good listener. Sylvia Allen, who along with C. Scott Amman wrote *How to Be Successful at Sponsorship Sales,* says in their book, "Potential sponsors will quickly tell you what their marketing objectives are and how your program will or won't fit into their marketing program. If you agree it's not a good fit, move on to the next one. Don't waste time arguing or attempting to fit a square peg into a round hole. Conversely, you may need to reposition your proposal to better comply with the potential sponsor's needs before giving up completely."
- An event manager has to be innovative and prepared to seize the moment. Bill Charney demonstrated this when he was at the Cherry Creek Arts Festival in Denver. In the initial year of the Festival,

Figure 10-1
Skinner's Description of the Perfect Sponsorship Event Manager

Coors Brewing Company had signed on as a three-year sponsor. Surprisingly, at a time when Coors was shrinking its portfolio, it called Charney six months before the deal was to elapse and said that it wanted to meet to extend the contract by five years. When the details had been worked out with Coors vice president Swede Johnson, Charney asked, "Why the long-term renewal when you're cutting back on sponsorships?" Johnson replied that Coors had renewed because the Festival was a great property and that it was strategically important for the company to be involved with a major event where it did not have competition. "And," Johnson said, "you sent me a Christmas card. No other event did."

Figure 10-1
(Continued)

Title: Sponsorship Manager

Position Purpose: To develop, implement, and manage
                            sponsorship programs for the organization

Position Status: Full-time, year-round

Education/Experience Requirements:

- BA or BS in Marketing or related field
- Minimum of five years' experience in marketing/sponsorship/ fund-raising
- Excellent organizational, written, and verbal skills
- Proficient computer skills in Microsoft Word and Excel
- Experience with special events and/or nonprofit organizations

Reports to: Executive Director

Directly Supervises: Sponsorship Coordinator
                            Sponsorship Assistant (part-time/seasonal)

Position Duties:

- Meet established sponsorship sales goals.
- Identify and solicit potential national and local cash sponsors.
- Create sales promotional and collateral materials for proposals.

Figure 10-2
SunFest of Palm Beach County, Inc.—Job Description

- Develop, negotiate sale and administer sponsor contracts for the festival and other SunFest events.
- Coordinate electronic and print media sponsorships with Marketing Manager.
- Maintain detailed documentation of all sponsorships.
- Oversee the coordination of sponsor servicing and distribution of benefits, i.e., media exposure, signage, booth space, tickets, etc.
- Develop and coordinate Sponsor and Hospitality Committees and assist with other committees as needed.
- Develop and administer related budgets and expenditures.
- Perform other duties in support of the organization as needed.

Figure 10-2
(Continued)

The Modern-Day Event Staff

In today's world of events, the most important component of staff expertise is the ability to sell and retain sponsors. This is because most events fall into one of two categories:

1. Festivals or events with break-even budgets. If an event's sponsorship income drops, then there is a good chance that the event will not survive, as it no longer breaks even. We have seen a number of events with high-quality operations whose administrative event managers fail because they do not have the necessary sponsorship sales expertise.
2. Cause-related events. These events are designed to make as much money as possible, but usually do not have to worry about whether they are going to make money; it is a question of how much money. However, if the sale of sponsorship fails, the event will not comply with the charity's budgeting plans for the year.

THE ONE-PERSON STAFF

It is very important that an event manager who is the lone staff member be able to sell sponsorship. Obviously, if he or she does not, no one else will, because even the best of volunteer salespeople lack the time and expertise.

- **One event manager**—This person needs to be able to sell sponsorship and handle administrative duties.
- **Two event managers**—One person needs to be adept at selling sponsorship, the other able to handle administrative, finance, and operations duties.
- **Three event managers**—First manager handles sponsorship; second, administrative, finance, and operations; third, public relations, promotions, and marketing.
- **Four event managers**—First manager handles sponsorship; second, administrative and finance; third, operations; fourth, public relations, promotions, and marketing.
- **Five event managers**—First manager handles sponsorship; second, administrative and finance; third, operations; fourth and fifth, a mixture of public relations, promotions, marketing, and sponsorship sales shared between the two people.
- **Six event managers**—Here is where you start to grow the staff within the preceding categories, especially in the sponsorship area.

Figure 10-3
The Modern Event Staff

SUCCESS STORY

THE GATOR BOWL BOAT LIGHT PARADE

Pat Craig Corda joined with the City of Jacksonville to create the Gator Bowl Boat Light Parade in 1987. For years she sent written proposals to Mazda (already the event's title sponsor) to try to get the company to provide a car for a prize to be awarded to the parade's best-decorated boat.

She was unsuccessful until she was invited to play in a golf tournament at Amelia Island, where she arranged to be included in a foursome with the vice president of marketing for Mazda. One of his employees remarked to him that Corda had been trying to get Mazda to give a car for the grand prize for the parade.

When she returned home, she had a message that Mazda would like to give her an RX7 for the prize. "Persistence does pay off," Corda said. "Mazda ended up giving us the RX7 for five years." To show her appreciation, Corda purchased the same vehicle for her personal use—a gesture that can go a long way to impress a sponsor.

Likewise, in a two-person staff situation, if the No. 1 person is not adept at selling sponsorship, then the No. 2 person must be. One of these people must handle sponsorship mostly full-time. And, obviously, that expertise is essential as a staff starts to grow (see Figure 10-3).

Events and their personnel differ, so you do not have to follow the model in Figure 10-3 exactly, but it gives you a good example of a staff that emphasizes the sale and attention to sponsors.

Five Keys to Developing Good Sponsorship Event Managers

To develop good sponsorship event managers:

1. First, it is important to have as many sponsorship managers on staff in relation to the size of your event. Sponsors want to talk to staff people, and not volunteers.
2. Keep in mind that a good sponsor-client relationship has managers working with sponsors on a year-round basis. A staff person needs to use new and creative ideas to enhance a sponsor's experience with an event.
3. Use the criteria found in this chapter in hiring sponsorship managers.
4. Develop a staff model for your event, using the criteria found in Figure 10-3.
5. Develop a job description for your sponsorship manager, using the sample job description found in Figure 10-2.

Sponsorship Activities

1. Read *Organizational Behavior: A Book of Readings,* compiled by Keith Davis.
2. Read Chapter 56, "Twelve Reasons Why Salespeople Don't Succeed," in *How to Be Successful at Sponsorship Sales,* by Sylvia Allen and C. Scott Amann.
3. For a good European perspective, check out the Web site of the European Committee for Business, Arts and Culture (CEREC).
4. Make a graphic depiction of the staffing structure for your event, listing the duties of your event managers.

Sponsorship Tool Kit

Allen, Sylvia, and C. Scott Amann. (1998). *How to Be Successful at Sponsorship Sales.* Holmdel, NJ: Allen Consulting.

Davis, Keith. (1977). *Organizational Behavior: A Book of Readings.* New York: McGraw-Hill.

European Committee for Business, Arts and Culture (CEREC). *www.aedme.org*

CHAPTER 11

The Law of Return: How to Keep Sponsors Coming Back

The absolute fundamental aim is to make money out of satisfying customers.

SIR JOHN EGAN, JAGUAR

IN THIS CHAPTER, YOU WILL LEARN:

- How to retain sponsors year after year
- How to give sponsors a sense of ownership in your event
- How to involve sponsors' employees and get them to be highly supportive of your event and their company's sponsorship
- How to keep in touch with sponsors and make sure the sales process never ends
- How to under-promise and over-deliver benefits to sponsors
- How to make sure that sponsors have a positive experience
- How to make the sponsorship process easier for your sponsors

Corporate sponsorship has spread rapidly throughout the world. Just 20 years ago sponsorship was limited to golf, tennis, and automobile racing, but now events of all types, concert tours, festivals, arenas, shopping centers, and many other venues have embraced sponsors as a way to benefit events and venues.

However, one of the authors of this book was still taken aback upon entering Flavian's Amphitheater in Rome, better known as the Roman Coliseum, to find that the arena had a corporate sponsor. The restoration of the facility was being sponsored by Banco di Roma.

This probably was not what the Caesars and the ancient Roman Republic had in mind. Though the sponsorship was tastefully evidenced, no visitor can enter this two-centuries-old facility and not know that Banco di Roma is the exclusive corporate sponsor of the restoration project. Banco di Roma's sponsorship of the Coliseum is a tremendous example of one thing that can keep sponsors coming back each year—the bank definitely feels ownership in the success of the restoration project; it knows that its sponsorship is doing something good not only for the city of Rome, but for this most impressive stadium facility that has had no equal for almost 2000 years.

Turning Sponsors into Owners

If a sponsor feels ownership in your event, chances are it will continue to sponsor your event year after year.

Sunkist executive Ray Cole felt such ownership when he landed in Phoenix in 1985 and was immediately greeted with Sunkist Fiesta Bowl banners at Sky Harbor Airport. Not only did he feel as though Sunkist owned the event, he felt "like we owned the city."

In the International Festivals and Events Association's (IFEA) *Official Guide to Sponsorship,* Bill Charney writes that building an association between the sponsors and the specific components of an event is not enough. Charney says, "You must ensure that your audience makes that association.

"The sponsor's image shouldn't just appear on a wall of logos. Sponsor contacts and corporate executives attending the event

Bank One imprinted their logo and the "Proud to Be an Official Sponsor" designation on its customer receipts in conjunction with the Cherry Creek Arts Festival, further developing a feeling of ownership. *Photo courtesy of Joel Silverman and the Cherry Creek Arts Festival.*

need to see how they're part of something big, and how their particular component offers something tangible to enjoy, associate with, and boast about. If it works, when it comes time to discuss renewal, they won't want to imagine their competitor's name associated with their element of the event."

Charney cites the Cherry Creek Arts Festival's sponsorship arrangement with Bank One of Colorado in the Festival's inaugural year in 1991. Festival managers worked with the bank and came up with an idea to produce an insert to go along with the bank's monthly statement, promoting the efforts of Bank One (then Affiliated Banks of Colorado) in helping to establish the Arts Festival as a tradition for Denver.

"It was apparently well received," said Charney, "because in the weeks before the event, the bank imprinted our logo and the 'Proud to Be an Official Sponsor' designation on the receipts they gave customers making deposits."

It was a great promotion for the arts festival, and also gave the bank ownership of the event.

Working with Employees

Another key way to establish ownership is through employee involvement. Companies spend a great deal of time trying to make employees happy. If your event can help a sponsor do that, you should have very little difficulty retaining that sponsor.

For years, parades like the Kentucky Derby Festival Parade in Louisville and the Pro Football Hall of Fame Parade in Canton, Ohio have encouraged the entry of privately built floats. These entries are constructed and decorated by employees, who take great pride in their floats and, therefore, their company and the event.

SUCCESS STORY

EMPLOYEE INVOLVEMENT IN THE UNITED KINGDOM

American Express has always believed that its employees should be positively involved in the communities in which they live and work. To this end, American Express has begun an innovative sponsorship program in the United Kingdom, giving its employees an incentive card that allows them free or discounted access to certain participating arts and heritage venues.

The Culture Card gives the company an opportunity to provide grassroots support to a wide range of great arts institutions in the United Kingdom, while providing benefits to the workforce, which is so vital to its continued success in business.

In use with about 20 arts organizations, including the Tower of London, the National Trust, the Science Museum, Shakespeare's Globe Theatre, and the Brighton Dome, the Culture Card allows employees free or reduced admission to many of the Southeast region's top cultural venues.

Getting Senior Management Involved

Some events recruit key management from sponsors or potential sponsors to become involved in their organizational structure.

When Citibank relocated its western U.S. headquarters to Phoenix in the mid-1980s, the Fiesta Bowl immediately put the president of the regional headquarters on its board. He had fun being involved in the Bowl, and, to the Bowl's benefit, the bank, now Citicorp, became a major sponsor, as he and the bank felt ownership of the event.

The Houston International Festival strives to include a sponsor's highest-ranking decision maker on its board. "This ensures that he or she has firsthand knowledge of the worthiness of the product and feels that his or her company is being consulted," said Festival president and CEO Jim Austin.

The Fiesta Bowl does everything it can to get its sponsors fully integrated into the Bowl organization. It invites sponsors to serve on the prestigious Fiesta Bowl Committee (the top movers and shakers in Arizona) and takes them on incentive trips, assists them with charitable needs, and extends invitations to management to become involved with different events, along with their families.

"We try to make their relationship with us a part of their lives, not just part of their job," says the Bowl's Doug Blouin. "This, in turn, makes us a priority to them and ensures that if we continue to do our job, they will continue to support us through good times and bad."

The Importance of Sponsorship Renewal

Any event manager will tell you that it is far easier to renew a sponsor than to go searching for a new one. You already know the company's hot buttons, you have created relationships with its management and marketing personnel, and, most likely, you have helped them achieve some of their goals.

However, many event managers fall short in their quest to bring sponsors back the following year. They sell the sponsorship to a company and then "take the money and run." They pay little attention to the sponsor after receiving the check, other than maybe sending a thank-you letter after the event is over. In such cases the key ingredients that create an effective partnership are missing. Not only has the event manager not provided the ownership ingredient, but he or she has also failed to do the many other things necessary to ensure that the sponsor will continue with the event.

The Alamo Bowl's Derrick Fox continually meets with sponsors, both before and after a sponsorship is sold. He works with each one of his sponsors to develop a program that best meets its goals and objectives.

"At the end of the year, we send every sponsor a survey asking it how we did and to outline its priorities for the next year," Fox said. "This enables us to get an early read on our sponsors' interests for the following year."

The National Cherry Festival's Chuck O'Connor says that it is necessary to constantly listen to sponsors and respond to change.

"I think it would be fair to say that few of the benefits that were listed in the contracts with our long-standing sponsors like Pepsi, CenturyTel, Country Fresh, and Pontiac-GMC resemble what they started out to be," he said. "What has really worked for us is letting the returning sponsor help design the new partnership from year to year, even if it's a multiyear deal. The best deals always come from brainstorming together."

The Sponsorship Sales Process—Never Ending

Sue Twyford was the executive director of the outstanding West Palm Beach music and art festival, SunFest, for 11 years. She says that one of the keys to retaining sponsors is staying in touch.

"When the contract is signed, it can be tempting to file it away and keep selling," she says. "However, it's important to take the time to make a plan for staying in touch:"

In the International Festival and Events Association's (IFEA) *Official Guide to Sponsorship,* she tells us how to do that (see Figure 11-1).

By staying in touch, you have a better chance of making a sponsor look good. "It's important to help the sponsor[s] get the most out of their investment," Twyford says.

- Follow up with a phone call and a note, thanking the sponsor.
- Meet again to discuss the sponsor's goals, concerns, and needs and follow up as needed.
- Put the sponsor on a mailing list for newsletters, flyers, and updates.
- Call or fax the sponsor when something big is being released to the media so that it will have the news before it hits the paper the next morning.
- Stay current with the news and trends affecting the sponsor or its industry.
- Use advertising tags to reinforce the name association (provide camera-ready art with the event logo and "official sponsor" type).
- Outfit select workers or volunteers in logo attire provided by the sponsor.

Source: Courtesy of Twyford Groupline, Inc.

Figure 11-1
How to Keep in Touch with Your Sponsors

Kirk Hendrix, formerly with Las Vegas Events, has always made it a point to contact all of his major sponsors the week prior to the event. First of all, they are extremely impressed by his calling, as they know that this is a very busy time for him. Second, it enables him to make sure that he has taken care of his sponsors' needs—learning about a problem after the event may be too late.

Under-Promising and Over-Delivering

Many event managers do not provide what they promised a sponsor.

However, if you under-promise and then give the sponsor more—that is, over-deliver—you have a sponsor that will be coming back to you year after year.

"The key to renewing your sponsors is to promise them the moon, then deliver them the universe," said Howard Freeman, producer of the Quick Chek New Jersey Festival of Ballooning.

For this balloon event's title sponsor Quick Chek, he delivered $1.8 million in nonpromised, unexpected media coverage. Not only did the sponsor get billboard, newspaper, and television coverage, Quick Chek signage was prominently displayed on a 16-by 30-foot banner, positioned across the chest of a 125-foot American eagle hot air balloon.

"The next morning, every newspaper in New Jersey had a picture of that on their front page," said Freeman.

The Festival's presenting sponsor, Prudential Health Care, had signage adorning a purple dragon, which made an appearance on the *Regis and Kathie Lee Show.* Freeman estimated that Prudential received a half million dollars in total media coverage surrounding the event.

Freeman said that the average Festival attendee spends seven and a half hours at the event, so sponsors not only know that their signage will be noticed, but they can sample and demonstrate products, run contests to generate mailing lists, and distribute bounce-back coupons as well.

"Make sure you have a way to quantify the results," he said. "Then start the renewal process the second they say yes to the sponsorship."

The Portland Rose Festival is another event that over-delivers. In 2001 event managers produced a first-ever Spanish broadcast of its Grand Floral Parade, which benefited title sponsor Southwest Airlines' marketing strategy to promote its service to the Hispanic population.

Event managers have also used the airline's Web site and its increasing traffic to point to promotions tied to sponsors and to display links to sponsors' Web sites.

When Bill Charney was at the Cherry Creek Arts Festival, "Under-promise and over-deliver" was the event's working motto. "Don't let there ever be any question about whether you've provided something you promised prior to signing a contract. If you plan to put a sponsor's name/logo on six signs, talk about two in your negotiations. Then produce the six signs and let them know you were able to provide them something extra."

When he was with the Michigan Thanksgiving Day Parade in Detroit, Kirk Hendrix adapted this philosophy a little differently.

"With some sponsors, I actually cut their price in subsequent years," he said. "When we were in financial debt, we asked a few people to pony up more money to help us keep afloat. As we started accumulating capital, I actually lowered their sponsorship prices, or gave them new floats at used float prices to show my appreciation. They were stunned."

Another time he had an event that was an utter failure. "I returned about 40 percent of the sponsor's money," he said. "I basically sent them a letter with a check and said that I didn't think that they got what they paid for and I wasn't comfortable with it. They became a long-time supporter after that."

GIVING KEY SPONSORS UNSOLD ITEMS

The International Festival of Lent in Maribor, Slovenia, gave unsold sponsorship items to its key sponsors. That led some of them to increase their sponsorship the following year. In addition, because the event's producer, The Cultural Center in Maribor, produces more events and festivals during the year, event managers are able to surprise sponsors and list them as sponsors for other events.

Steven Schmader, currently the president of IFEA, was the president of the Boise River Festival for 11 years. He also used unsold sponsorship to add value to existing major sponsorships. "For example, if one of our sponsorships went unsold for any particular year for the festival, I would give it to one of our existing bigger sponsors as an extra benefit," he said. "Many times that would lead them to increase their sponsorship the following year."

"Give them unexpected perks and benefits," says SEAFAIR's Beth Wojick. "One year we gave General Motors the center spread in our magazine along with additional display space."

MAKING SURE YOUR SPONSOR HAS FUN

As opposed to other traditional forms of advertising, events are fun. It is important to make sure your sponsors have more fun than anyone else, and that will keep them involved for years (see Figure 11-2).

Carolyn Crayton of the Macon Cherry Blossom Festival in Georgia makes sure her sponsors have fun. She allows her balloon sponsor to ride in a balloon, to appear live on television and radio, and to be featured in the newspaper.

"As such, we do more than just fulfill our written obligations; we stroke egos and make people feel important, even famous, if even for just a short while," she says. "Most people love to be in the spotlight."

- If you have celebrities in for your event, make sure your sponsors get to rub shoulders with them—even play golf with them or introduce them at an event.
- Give sponsors access to occasions, such as private parties, that others cannot attend.
- Set up an intimate sponsor appreciation party before an event for your biggest sponsors.
- Invite sponsors to press conferences and introduce them.
- Hold a brunch at an elegant location for sponsors and their spouses.
- Let sponsors be the first to see the new poster or pin.
- Make sure sponsors' parking spaces are convenient.
- Create a sponsor hospitality club with preferred seating and complimentary hors d'oeuvres and drinks.
- Introduce sponsors to board members, and have board members visit them during the event to tell them how much they are appreciated.
- Recognize sponsors with a colorful keepsake of the festival, such as a framed poster, to hang in the office or home. Make sure that this is something no one else can get. (The Fiesta Bowl used to give major sponsors a team watch.)
- Write and call after the event to say thank you.

Figure 11-2
How to Have Fun with Your Sponsors

Sandra Risk at the Wildflower! Festival does this when she gets executives to put together bands representing their companies and play as part of the Battle of the Bands at the Festival. "The company gets its exposure, the executives have fun with their five minutes of fame, and the families and co-workers crowd in to cheer on 'their' band."

MAKING LIFE EASY FOR SPONSORS

Believe it or not, many sponsors are ignorant of the ways in which they can maximize their event sponsorship. Therefore, it is imperative that event managers work hard to help that happen.

"An effective sponsorship association can mean a lot of hard work for a sponsor," says Sue Twyford. "Take the time to make it easier on the sponsor" (see Figure 11-3).

- Create a sponsor handbook with fact sheets, maps, and answers to commonly asked questions.
- Meet with the sponsor once more before the event to go over the handbook. Give clear instructions on parking, credentials, loading, equipment, and other frequently overlooked areas.
- During the event, take photographs of the sponsor's signs, banners, booths, and displays. Take pictures of the sponsor's employees working and having fun.
- Set up a sponsor servicing desk at the event where the sponsor can always find a knowledgeable, caring person to answer questions and provide assistance.

Source: Courtesy of Twyford Groupline, Inc.

Figure 11-3
Making the Sponsorship Easy for the Sponsor

SUCCESS STORY

HELPING TO RETAIN JOBS

Nova KBM Bank is the major sponsor of the International Festival of Lent in Maribor, Slovenia. The board of the bank wanted to change management when the bank got into financial trouble in the late 1990s, but the Festival was able to save management's jobs.

The Festival persuaded the media to write about the bank's exemplary sponsorship of the Festival and produced the clear message that the bank was good for society. The bank came out as a champion because the public knew that the Festival would not exist without the bank's support. Management stayed on and increased sponsorship of the Festival by 20 percent the following year.

The Follow-up Report

Providing a follow-up report can be a crucial part of getting your sponsor back for another year. In the second year of Sunkist's sponsorship of the Fiesta Bowl in 1986, the Bowl subscribed to a national clipping service. Because the game featured Penn State versus Miami for the national championship of college football, thousands of clippings were amassed, all of which were piled on top of two extremely large conference tables—mounds of evidence that the name Sunkist was used many times. It cost $27,000 for the service, but for a multimillion dollar sponsor, it was well worth it.

Of course, we realize that not every event can do this. However, it is important that you create a comprehensive final report documenting sponsorship values. Put the results in notebook form and include photographs, copies of media affidavits, tear sheets, press releases, and articles, and show where you have exceeded the contract.

Your sponsor cannot possibly listen to every radio and television broadcast or read every newspaper, so even they will be surprised by how much publicity they have received.

Sponsor servicing takes time, but if you act on the ideas in this chapter, you will receive many multiyear contracts, which, of course, is another way to help sponsor retention.

Multiyear Contracts

There are a number of reasons that a sponsor will agree to a multiyear deal, including:

- The sponsor can lock out its competitors for a longer period of time. Budweiser, Coca-Cola, and Ozarka all went to multiyear deals with the Houston International Festival for this reason.
- The sponsor can also lock in a sponsorship price and know that its fees will not increase dramatically during the life of the sponsorship. For example, Luther's Bar B-Q signed a two-year deal with 1st Power of Houston so that it could have the same price each year and be guaranteed an annual event.
- If you have a good event, the sponsor wants to be involved on a multiyear basis. "When national companies first get involved with SEAFAIR," said the festival's president and CEO, Beth Wojick, "they aren't quite sure how their sponsorships will work out. But once we get them in the house, they recognize that we have a lot to offer. Texaco, General Motors,

and Southwest Airlines all started out as one-year sponsors and signed subsequent multiyear deals."

- If your event has a multiyear plan, sponsors often want to help you meet those long-term goals. When the Michigan Thanksgiving Day Parade wanted to increase its national television network, it got Chrysler to agree to a three-year contract to help grow the network. "It made sense because as we grew the network, the value of media and exposure and sponsorship to Chrysler grew with it," said former president and CEO Kirk Hendrix.

Eight Keys to Retaining Sponsors

To keep sponsors coming back:

1. Make your sponsors feel as though they own your event. Get their employees involved, and it will be difficult for them to give up their sponsorship.
2. Integrate sponsors into your organization. Put a company's major executives on your board or committee.
3. Work with sponsors to develop the sponsorship, so that they feel that they are part of the process.
4. Keep in touch all year long. Send sponsors thank-you notes—for record earnings and the like.
5. Under-promise and then over-deliver. Give sponsors more than they asked for.
6. Give sponsors something when they least suspect it.
7. Make sure sponsors have fun.
8. Sign multiyear agreements with sponsors.

Sponsorship Activities
1. Read Chapter 10, "Sponsor Renewal: How to Keep Them Coming Back," in *IFEA's Official Guide to Sponsorship.*
2. List the ways you can keep your sponsors coming back in the future.

Sponsorship Tool Kit
IFEA's Official Guide to Sponsorship. (1997) Boise, ID: IFEA.

CHAPTER 12

The Sponsorship Evaluation Process

In an era of relationship marketing, sales excellence is demonstrated by the number of customers who make a second purchase.

LOUIS E. BOONE, AMERICAN EDUCATOR AND BUSINESS WRITER

IN THIS CHAPTER YOU WILL LEARN:

- The importance of a post-event report
- How to develop a post-event report
- How to measure tangible and intangible results
- How to match the evaluation process with a sponsor's goals and objectives

---

Sponsorship evaluation is one of the most overlooked steps in the sponsorship process. Most events do not compile post-event evaluation reports for their sponsors, and even those that do often offer merely a recap of the event rather than a report that values an individual sponsor's participation.

As the level of sophistication in sponsorship continues to increase, however, so does the need for more sophisticated post-event sponsorship evaluations.

When it used to be good enough just to have sponsor signs and to mention sponsors on posters and brochures, it was very easy for sponsors to see what they received. Virtually all they had to do was to attend the event and see the signage. Then by watching television, listening to the radio, and reading the newspaper, they were able to ascertain what their total benefit package was.

But in the modern era of pass-through rights, tangible and intangible benefits, cost-benefit ratios, the ability to involve retailers, and so forth, it's up to event managers to make sure sponsors know what they receive in return for their investment (ROI).

At the very least, managers need to develop a post-event report. A good report lists everything a sponsor received before, during, and after an event—mentions on brochures, quantity and location of signs, photos of the event and of the sponsor's participation in the event, media impressions, tickets, and so forth.

SUCCESS STORY

THE PITTSBURGH THREE RIVERS REGATTA EVALUATION REPORT

Ida D'Errico, executive vice president of the Shop 'n Save Three Rivers Regatta, prepares excellent post event evaluation reports.

More than 1.5 million people attend the event, held the first week in August, that annually celebrates Pittsburgh's three rivers. The celebration includes children's events, concerts, fireworks, and powerboat racing for the air, land, and water event.

Figure 12-3 shows how event managers evaluated the participation of Pontiac-GMC during the 2000 Regatta. It gives advertising and publicity values for television commercials and promotions, as well as for radio

and print coverage, signage, tent/display space, and miscellaneous components. All told, the report values the sponsor's participation at almost $1.5 million.

The report also features:

- Copies of print clips that include mentions of Pontiac-GMC and photographs of the company's signage
- Documentation of radio and television mentions
- Event-produced photographs of the company's signage
- Proof of Web site identification
- Event-produced printed materials with sponsor mention

The best post-event report goes beyond the contract. It tells sponsors that you provided them with all of the items that were listed in the contract, and *more*.

The Increasing Importance of Evaluation

The reason many events do not evaluate sponsorship is that it is difficult and very time-consuming to do so. "It's also very subjective," says Carolyn Pendergast, former director of sponsorship for the University of California's athletic department. "But more and more, sponsors are needing it in order to justify costs, and sometimes in order to bill specific departments."

The National Cherry Festival's Chuck O'Connor keeps a separate set of files for each sponsor, dedicated to ROI materials. Whenever there is a Cherry Festival event or activity that generates any exposure for any one of his sponsors, he documents and files that exposure.

After the event during the fall and winter months, he meets with each interested sponsor to go through a post-event report and an accompanying notebook, which includes everything from the file.

"I consider this meeting to be one of the most important functions of the sponsorship process," says O'Connor. "Together, we value the sponsorship's success. It allows the partners to recap whether predetermined objectives were met and accomplished. It also identifies and addresses problem areas, helps to generate new ideas reflecting changing marketing objectives, and introduces new people to the process.

"But most important, it often locks up a renewal budget. I attribute the Cherry Festival's low sponsor attrition track record to these very important off-season meetings."

Event managers at the International Festival of Lent in Maribor, Slovenia, also provide post-event follow-up reports to sponsors. Not only do they provide them with the number of newspaper and other media mentions, they also hire PR Plus, a research and marketing company, to compile an evaluation report for them. The 150-page document has two parts: The first deals with attendees' comments on the Festival itself (programming, safety, catering,

Questions asked festival attendees:

▪ Did you notice sponsors at the festival?	94.3% said yes
▪ Who was the main sponsor?	65% had recall
▪ Are sponsors important to the festival?	95.5% said yes; 0.5% said no
▪ Will you buy products or use services of sponsors because they are connected to the festival?	64% said yes; 31.5% maybe; 4.5% didn't know

Figure 12-1
International Festival of Lent Evaluation Report

etc.), and the second covers opinions regarding sponsors (see Figure 12-1).

Because of the favorable comments, the managers of the event are able to prove to sponsors that their sponsorship was worthwhile. They also have vital information they can use to help sell new sponsorships the following year.

THE CHERRY CREEK ARTS FESTIVAL

Bill Charney, founding president/CEO of the Cherry Creek Arts Festival in Denver, also notes that event evaluation is one of the most underperforming areas in the sponsorship process.

While he was at Cherry Creek, Charney's sponsor evaluation reports consistently won awards in the annual IFEA Pinnacle Awards Contest.

Charney's award-winning reports were divided into five areas:

1. Overall event success
2. Event demographics—sponsor retention statistics, economic impact, etc.
3. Documentation of all specific sponsor recognition—on-site, media, collateral, etc.
4. Documentation of all media coverage, electronic and print, both with and without the individual sponsor's identification
5. Photographs of specific sponsor recognition at event and related activities

The reports also contained extensive consumer research that is beneficial to a sponsor. One year's report showed the following:

- Several demographics that would be of interest to a sponsor.
  - More than 70 percent of the event's attendees have a college degree.
  - Almost 60 percent of attendees have a household income of more than $50,000, 28.5 percent of which are earning $90,000 or more.
  - More than 70 percent of the audience are between the ages of 25 and 54.
  - Three out of four attendees said they owned a home, and two out of three said they had a cell phone.
- The event had become the sixth largest cultural attraction in the city of Denver, *even though it lasts for only three days.* All others are year-round institutions (the museum of natural history, zoological gardens, library, center for the performing arts, and botanic gardens). It outdraws the Denver Art Museum.
- Statistics indicating that one in three attendees say that they would be more likely to buy a company's products knowing the company had sponsored the Festival, with 70.6 percent saying they thought having corporate sponsors enhanced the Festival.
- The Festival had contributed $15.5 million in direct and indirect economic value to the local area, 55 percent of which (more than $8.5 million) was considered new business to the city and county of Denver.

All of these figures can be used to retain present sponsors and entice new sponsors. The last figure was also pivotal in garnering civic support, as it documented tangible economic benefit and tax revenues to the city of Denver.

Giving information on festival attendees stimulates the sponsorship interest of companies seeking very high demographics.

Tracking Sales

Although still rare but increasing in popularity, some companies have begun tracking sales as a result of their sponsorship.

As reported in *Sports News (www.onlinesports.com/sportstrust/ sports13.html),* the following are examples of sponsorships that have driven sales:

- In 1992, Visa, an Olympic sponsor, advertised that it would donate a percentage of each card transaction to the U.S.

Olympic team. Transactions increased by 17 percent. Up until that point, Visa had never gotten more than a 3% increase from any advertising or promotional campaign it ran.

- NationsBank used its 1996 Olympic sponsorship not only to enhance its image, but also to generate new business. The number of new checking and savings accounts increased 20 percent over the year before. An Olympic-themed giveaway (which required opening a new account or applying for a loan) and other Olympic promotions were considered the primary reason for the change.
- A few years ago Country Time lemonade used its sponsorship of a NASCAR team as a promotional tie-in. A race car simulator exhibit was taken to retail locations around the country. Each consumer who presented a Country Time label could try out the simulator. In the Southeast, where NASCAR is especially popular, product sales increased 66 percent.

The Bonham Group, a national sports/entertainment marketing firm based in Denver, is regarded as one of the foremost companies in understanding the value of sponsorships. The company focuses on three areas when evaluating sponsorships:

1. The impressions on behalf of sponsors, and the value of the impressions.
2. Brand awareness and brand understanding. "You might be aware that 3Com has the naming rights to a sports facility and you might be aware of the brand, but you might not understand what the company does," says Bonham chairman and CEO Dean Bonham.
3. Bottom line impact, to the extent that it can be measured. "We represented a consumer products company that was involved with NASCAR," says Bonham. "We were able to track that the sales of products in grocery stores and other locations increased as a result of the relationship."

IEG Sponsorship Valuation

The most sophisticated sponsorship valuation service has been developed by the International Events Group (IEG). Not only does the service determine values for tangible assets like signage, identification on event collateral materials, advertising, and the like, it also determines value for intangible assets, such as prestige of the property and protection from ambush by competitors.

IEG created its industry standards by analyzing patterns of the relationship between the rights-fees sponsors pay and the benefits they receive. More than 150 leading sponsors endorse the IEG Valuation Service.

IEG values a property's tangible assets in seven different areas. For each, analysts multiply the reach (attendance or people participating) by a formulated amount, which varies for each category. Here are some of the areas the company's evaluators consider, all of which are given a dollar value:

Guaranteed Sponsor ID in Nonmeasured Media

Sponsor ID in Publications and Collateral
- ID on tickets
- ID on program book
- ID on event schedule

On-Site Signage or Mentions
- Banners
- Electronic logos
- Jumbotron ads
- Public address announcements

Visibility on Property's Web Site
- Banner ad on homepage
- Co-branded area
- Editorial feature on sponsor page
- Use of site's e-mail list

Guaranteed Sponsor ID in Measured Media
- ID in property's buy
- ID visible on event broadcasts

Mailing Lists
- Insert in mailing to audience

Sampling
- Product sampling

Tickets and Hospitality (face value or estimated value)
- Tickets to event

- Facility usage for sponsor function
- VIP gift packages

Advertising In Measured Media
- Program book advertising

IEG's Valuation Service goes further than just analyzing these intangible benefits. It also values the intangible benefits of a property.

- Prestige of property—A property can create value by building equity in its own brand.
- Recognizability and awareness—Focus on increasing the likelihood that placement of a property's marks and logos on packaging or in sponsor promotions will move product.
- Audience loyalty—Demonstrate that your audience's affinity for the property is high.
- Category exclusivity—More value is added if a sponsor is the only one of its type associated with the event.
- Protection from ambush—Ensure that nonsponsors cannot get the spotlight and look like sponsors.
- Degree of sponsor clutter—Keep value as clean as possible so that each sponsor gets noticed.
- Ability to activate—Deliver turnkey promotions that allow sponsors to engage the audience.
- Networking opportunities—Offer opportunities to sponsors to cross-promote and/or identify new distribution channels.
- Media coverage potential—Drive media to cover your event.
- Established track record—Work toward a high sponsor renewal rate. Fulfill everything that was promised and over-deliver.

Hometown Sponsor Evaluation Service

Sylvia Allen, who runs Hometown Sponsor Evaluation Service (HTSES), offers a simplified evaluation service. An event completes a form listing values, as shown in Figure 12-2. Once the event completes the form, Allen values the event and suggests sponsorship pricing, as shown in Figure 12-3.

Hometown Sponsor Evaluation Service (HTSES)

NAME OF EVENT: _____

DATES OF EVENT: _____

TOTAL ATTENDANCE: _____

MARKETING MATERIALS (IF NOT APPROPRIATE TO YOUR EVENT, JUST WRITE "NA" IN THE APPROPRIATE PLACE):

- Radio (list quantity, type—:60, :30, :10, station[s])

  _____

- Television (same as above)

  _____

- Newspaper (name of newspaper[s], number of ads, size of ads, frequency, other benefits [advertorial, program book, etc.], circulation)

  _____

- Magazine (name of magazine[s], number of ads, size of ads, frequency, other benefits, circulation)

  _____

- Internet (site, how many links, how many hits total, etc.)

  _____

- Brochures (quantity, size, distribution channels)

  _____

- Posters (quantity, size, distribution, length of time they are up, daily traffic by those posters)

  _____

- Flyers (quantity, size, where distributed, how distributed)

  _____

Figure 12-2
Sample Evaluation Form

- Horizontal banners (size, location, number of days hanging, daily traffic count)

  _____

- Vertical banners (same as above)

  _____

- Payroll stuffers (quantity, size, distribution channels)

  _____

- Bag stuffers (quantity, size, distribution channels)

  _____

- Bill inserts (quantity, size, distribution channels)

  _____

LIST OTHER MARKETING ELEMENTS HERE SPECIFIC TO YOUR EVENT

- Logo exposure on _____ (Please be very precise in describing the marketing vehicle, the quantity, and the number of people who were exposed to it.)

- _____

- _____

- _____

ON-SITE BENEFITS (IF NOT APPROPRIATE TO YOUR EVENT, JUST WRITE "NA" IN THE APPROPRIATE PLACE):

- On-site signage (how many, where, size)

  _____

- Sampling opportunities (booth size, number sampled)

  _____

Figure 12-2
(Continued)

- Product sales (booth size)

  _____

- Tickets (quantity printed, sponsor exposure)

  _____

- Audio announcements (quantity, length)

  _____

LIST OTHER ON-SITE ELEMENTS
SPECIFIC TO YOUR EVENT

- _____
- _____
- _____
- _____

HOSPITALITY BENEFITS (IF NOT APPLICABLE
TO YOUR EVENT, JUST WRITE "NA" IN THE
APPROPRIATE PLACE)

- Tickets (for paid/gated events: quantity, retail value)

  _____

- VIP parking (quantity)

  _____

- VIP hospitality (define—hotel, airfare, food, etc.—be specific)

  _____

- Priority viewing (for free events—how many?)

  _____

LIST OTHER HOSPITALITY ELEMENTS
SPECIFIC TO YOUR EVENT

- _____

Figure 12-2
(Continued)

- _____
- _____
- _____
- _____

OTHER BENEFITS (LIST ANYTHING THAT WAS NOT COVERED BEFORE)

- Retail partner benefits (bag stuffers, on-bag promotions, in-store announcements, weekly flyers, etc.—quantity, size, distribution channels)

- _____
- _____
- _____
- _____

CURRENT SPONSORSHIP OFFERINGS:

TITLE: $_____

PRESENTING: $_____

Source: Allen Consulting Inc.

Figure 12-2
(Continued)

Pontiac-GMC
Sponsor Benefits Report

TELEVISION
PUBLICITY

- Inclusion within the "Ya Gotta Regatta" Preview Show airing on KDKA-TV2, Friday, July 26, 2002, at 7:30 P.M.
    - 1:05 Feature segment including an interview with Pontiac-GMC's Regional Division Marketing Manager, John Konkel.

    Ad Value: $2,400.00
    Publicity Value: $12,000.00

- Pontiac-GMC banner inclusion within a 6:35 segment in the "Roar Before the Thunder" Preview Show airing on WCWB WB22 on Sunday, July 28, 2002, at 10:30 P.M.

    Ad Value: $2,600.00
    Publicity Value: $13,000.00

- Pontiac-GMC Balloon inclusion within the 2:31 WPXI-TV 5:00 P.M. News Broadcast Clip airing June 20, 2002.

    Ad Value: $3,750.00
    Publicity Value: $18,750.00

- GMC Banner inclusion within the 2:51 WPGH-TV 10:00 P.M. News Broadcast Clip airing on June 20, 2002.

    Ad Value: $2,400.00
    Publicity Value: $12,000.00

- GMC Banner inclusion within the 3:40 WPGH-TV 10:00 P.M. News Broadcast Clip airing on July 31, 2002.

    Ad Value: $3,000.00
    Publicity Value: $15,000.00

- Pontiac-GMC Banner inclusion within the 4:18 KDKA-TV 6:00 P.M. News Broadcast Clip airing on August 1, 2002.

    Ad Value: $10,940.00
    Publicity Value: $54,700.00

- GMC Banner inclusion within the 2:16 WPGH-TV 10:00 P.M. News Broadcast Clip airing on August 1, 2002.

    Ad Value: $1,860.00
    Publicity Value: $9,300.00

Figure 12-3
Example of Sponsorship Valuation

- GMC Banner inclusion within the 3:46 WTAE-TV 11:00 P.M. News Broadcast Clip airing on August 3, 2002.

Ad Value: $14,725.00
Publicity Value: $73,625.00

- GMC Logo inclusion within the :44 WTAE-TV 6:00 P.M. News Broadcast Clip airing on August 4, 2002.

Ad Value: $1,495.00
Publicity Value: $7,475.00

TOTAL AD VALUE: $43,170.00

TOTAL PUBLICITY VALUE: $214,850.000

COMMERCIALS

- 15 :30 Dedicated Pontiac Fixed News Promos airing on KDKA-TV.

Value: $9,695.00

- 15 :30 Dedicated GMC Fixed News Promos airing on KDKA-TV.

Value: $7,285.00

- 28 :30 Dedicated Pontiac Rotator Promos airing on KDKA-TV.

Value: $10,500.00

- 26 :30 Dedicated GMC Rotator Promos airing on KDKA-TV.

Value: $6,785.00

- 29 :30 Dedicated Pontiac-GMC Promos airing on WPGH FOX53.

Value: $1,360.00

- 24 :30 Dedicated Pontiac-GMC Promos airing on WCWB WB22.

Value: $1,000.00

TOTAL FIXED NEWS COMMERCIALS: 30 :30

TOTAL COMMERCIALS: 107 :30

TOTAL BONUS COMMERCIALS: 7 :30

TOTAL COMMERCIAL VALUE: $36,625.00

PROMOS

- 20 :60 Presented by Pontiac-GMC Logo-Tagged Sponsor Promos airing on KDKA-TV.

Value: $11,850.00

Figure 12-3
(Continued)

- 16 :60 Presented by Pontiac-GMC Logo-Tagged Sponsor Promos airing on WPGH FOX53.

  Value: $9,990.00

- 15 :60 Presented by Pontiac-GMC Logo-Tagged Sponsor Promos airing on WCWB WB22.

  Value: $680.00

- 167 :30 Presented by Pontiac-GMC Logo-Tagged Sponsor Promos airing on KDKA-TV.

  Value: $76,190.00

- 65 :30 Presented by Pontiac-GMC Logo-Tagged Sponsor Promos airing on WPGH FOX53.

  Value: $5,230.00

- 73 :30 Presented by Pontiac-GMC Logo-Tagged Sponsor Promos airing on WCWB WB22.

  Value: $3,560.00

- 142 :15 Presented by Pontiac-GMC Logo-Tagged Sponsor Promos airing on KDKA-TV.

  Value: $52,320.00

- 51 :15 Presented by Pontiac-GMC Logo-Tagged Sponsor Promos airing on WPGH FOX53.

  Value: $3,350.75

- 34 :15 Presented by Pontiac-GMC Logo-Tagged Sponsor Promos airing on WCWB WB22.

  Value: $1,683.50

- 92 :10 Presented by Pontiac-GMC Logo-Tagged Thank-You Spots airing on WPGH FOX53.

  Value: $6,907.50

- 129 :10 Presented by Pontiac-GMC Logo-Tagged Thank-You Spots airing on WCWB WB22.

  Value: $4,765.00

TOTAL PROMOS: 804

51 :60
305 :30
227 :15
221 :10

Figure 12-3
(Continued)

TOTAL BONUS PROMOS: 554

51 :60
55 :30
227 :15
221 :10

TOTAL PROMO VALUE: $176,526.75

TOTAL TELEVISION VALUE: $429,001.75

RADIO

COMMERCIALS

- 17 :60 Dedicated Pontiac-GMC Promos airing on WISH 99.7 FM.
  Value: $1,690.00

- 18 :60 Dedicated Pontiac-GMC Promos airing on 1320 WJAS.
  Value: $800.00

- 13 :60 Dedicated Pontiac-GMC Promos airing on 1360 WPTT.
  Value: $350.00

- 35 :60 Dedicated Pontiac Promos airing on WLTJ 92.9 Lite FM and Channel 97 WRRK.
  Value: $5,060.00

- 24 :60 Dedicated GMC Promos airing on WLTJ 92.9 Lite FM and Channel 97 WRRK.
  Value: $2,725.00

TOTAL COMMERCIALS: 107 :60

TOTAL BONUS COMMERCIALS: 37 :60

TOTAL COMMERCIAL VALUE: $10,625.00

PROMOS

- 200 :60 Presented by Pontiac-GMC Tagged Sponsor Promos airing on 106 JAMZ WAMO.
  Value: $30,795.00

- 201 :30 Presented by Pontiac-GMC Tagged Sponsor Promos airing on 106 JAMZ WAMO.
  Value: $26,990.00

- 142 :60 Presented by Pontiac-GMC Tagged Sponsor Promos airing on WISH 99.7 FM.
  Value: $13,360.00

Figure 12-3
(Continued)

- 165 :30 Presented by Pontiac-GMC Tagged Sponsor Promos airing on WISH 99.7 FM.

  Value: $13,980.00

- 133 :60 Presented by Pontiac-GMC Tagged Sponsor Promos airing on 1320 WJAS.

  Value: $6,810.00

- 173 :30 Presented by Pontiac-GMC Tagged Sponsor Promos airing on 1320 WJAS.

  Value: $8,360.00

- 150 :60 Presented by Pontiac-GMC Tagged Sponsor Promos airing on 1360 WPTT.

  Value: $5,250.00

- 200 :30 Presented by Pontiac-GMC Tagged Sponsor Promos airing on 1360 WPTT.

  Value: $7,000.00

- 140 :60 Presented by Pontiac-GMC Tagged Sponsor Promos airing on WLTJ 92.9 Lite FM and Channel 97 WRRK.

  Value: $18,885.00

- 379 :30 Presented by Pontiac-GMC Tagged Sponsor Promos airing on WLTJ 92.9 Lite FM and Channel 97 WRRK.

  Value: $53,340.00

TOTAL PROMOS: 1,883

765 :60
1,118 :30

TOTAL PROMO VALUE: $184,770.00

TOTAL RADIO VALUE: $195,395.00

PRINT RECAP

- 150,000 Regatta Schedule of Events Flyers distributed in sponsor locations, downtown areas, and Point State Park. Pontiac-GMC logo inclusion and Presenting Sponsor listing.

  Value: $5,000.00

- Regatta Newspaper Supplement, 431,172 distribution via *Pittsburgh Post-Gazette* (Sunday edition).

Figure 12-3
(Continued)

- Pontiac-GMC logo inclusion on the front cover.

  Value: $14,720.50
- Pontiac-GMC Presenting Sponsor listing.

  Value: $4,246.20
- Pontiac-GMC location listing on the Point State Park Site Map.

  Value: $14,720.50
- Pontiac-GMC received two (2) full-page color ads.

  Value: $20,408.00
- Pontiac-GMC received one-quarter (1/4)-page editorial.

  Value: $1,516.50

- Pontiac-GMC inclusion within nine (9) Regatta print clips. (See Print Clip Report)

  Editorial Value: $174,689.10

- Regatta Press Kit (1000 distributed)—Pontiac-GMC feature release and inclusion within all other press releases.

- Pontiac-GMC Presenting Sponsor listing in the Regatta Anchor Awards Gala Program honoring Duquesne University President, Dr. John Murray, and Pittsburgh Steelers President, Mr. Dan Rooney.

TOTAL PRINT VALUE: $235,300.80

SIGNAGE

- Twenty-five (25) City Billboard locations with event logo, event dates, and Pontiac-GMC logos for a four-week, three-day period.

  Value: $281,250.00

- One-hundred (100) 4′ × 6′ City Street Pole Arm Banners with Event logo, Event dates, and Pontiac-GMC logos, for a total of 600 feet of signage for a seven-week, five-day period.

  Value: $1,925,000.00

- Ten (10) 3′ × 24′ Overhead Street Banners with Event logo, Event dates, and Pontiac-GMC logos, for a total of 240 feet of signage for a seven-week period.

  Value: $175,000.00

- Five (5) 2′ × 6′ Pontiac Pole Arm Banners displayed throughout Point State Park, for a total of 30 feet of signage.

  Value: $7,500.00

Figure 12-3
(Continued)

- Five (5) 2' × 6' GMC Pole Arm Banners displayed throughout Point State Park, for a total of 30 feet of signage.

  Value: $7,500.00

- Five (5) 3' × 10' Pontiac Banners displayed on the Roberto Clemente Bridge for the Regatta Bridge Party, July 31, 2002.

  Value: $31.25

- Five (5) 3' × 10' GMC Banners displayed on the Roberto Clemente Bridge for the Regatta Bridge Party, July 31, 2002.

  Value: $31.25

- Thirty-eight (38) 3' × 10' Pontiac banners displayed throughout Point State Park and the North Shore, for a total of 380 feet of signage.

  Value: $57,000.00

- Thirty-eight (38) 3' × 10' GMC banners displayed throughout Point State Park and the North Shore, for a total of 380 feet of signage.

  Value: $57,000.00

- One (1) 8' × 40' Portal Bridge Welcome Banner with Event logo, Event dates, and Pontiac-GMC logos.

  Value: $3,000.00

- One (1) 40' × 40' North Shore Bridge Wall Banner with Event logo, Event dates, and Pontiac-GMC logos for a five-week period.

  Value: $70,000.00

TOTAL SIGNAGE VALUE: $258,331.40

TENT/DISPLAY SPACE RECAP

- One (1) 15' × 15' high-quality modular display tent located in a high-traffic area.

  Minimum Value: $8,000.00

- Three (3) display vehicle locations throughout Point State Park with a total of 35 Pontiac-GMC vehicles.

  Minimum Value: $280,000.00

- Four (4) display vehicles on the Roberto Clemente Bridge during the Regatta Bridge Party.

  Minimum Value: $32,000.00

Figure 12-3
(Continued)

- One (1) Cold Air Inflatable and vehicles displayed on the Roberto Clemente Bridge during the Regatta Bridge Party.

    Value: $500.00

- Four (4) Cold Air Inflatable locations throughout Point State Park.

    Value: $8,000.00

TOTAL TENT/DISPLAY VALUE: $328,500.00

MISCELLANEOUS

- Inclusion within Regatta interactive Web site.

    Value: $2,500.00

- Twenty (20) V.I.P. Concert Series Seating wristbands for each of the four (4) Main Stage concerts, for a total of eighty (80) wristbands.

    Value: $2,400.00

- One (1) table for ten at the Regatta Anchor Awards Gala held at the Westin William Penn Hotel.

    Value: $750.00

- Two hundred fifty (250) Hospitality Passes for the Regatta Thunder Fireworks Party held at the Carnegie Science Center.

    Value: $12,500.00

- One hundred (100) hospitality passes for the IOGP Powerboat races aboard the Gateway Clipper Fleet's *Majestic*.

    Value: $5,000.00

TOTAL MISCELLANEOUS VALUE: $23,150.00

GRAND TOTAL VALUE: $1,469,678.90

Source: Courtesy of Portland Rose Festival Association.

Figure 12-3
(Continued)

Portland Rose Festival Sponsorship Survey

The Portland Rose Festival sends a survey form (shown in Figure 12-4) to sponsors so that they can help in the sponsorship evaluation process.

Portland Rose Festival Sponsor Survey

Please take a moment to help us serve you better by answering this questionnaire.

Company/Business: _____

Name and title of person completing questionnaire:

_____

Phone: _____

E-Mail: _____

Please rank your sponsorship objectives by using the following rate scale: 1 = very important; 2 = somewhat important; 3 = not important; 4 = not applicable.

Consumer trial/sampling _____

Sell products/services directly at events _____

Reach specifically targeted market segments _____

Differentiate product from competitors _____

Increase awareness of company and/or product _____

Entertain key clientele with VIP hospitality _____

Contribute back to the community _____

Enhance quality of life for your employees _____

Shape or reinforce public perception of company _____

Other: _____

_____

_____

The Rose Festival offers a variety of benefits in the following areas (exact benefits may be based on sponsorship category and level). Please rate them in order of importance to you, using the following rating scale: 1 = very important; 2 = somewhat important; 3 = not important; 4 = not applicable.

Sales opportunities at Rose Festival events _____

Prominent mention in printed pieces _____

Figure 12-4
Sample Survey Form

In-house promotions team _____

Identification as sponsor in print media _____

Identification as sponsor in radio media _____

Identification as sponsor in television media _____

Identification as sponsor on Rose Festival Web site _____

Personalized event recap audits _____

Personalized event recap letter _____

Sponsor promotional workshops _____

Sponsor reception _____

Event signage on-site _____

Hospitality opportunities _____

Use of Rose Festival logo _____

Event participation _____

Special sponsor tickets _____

First right of renewal options _____

Opportunities for employee volunteer involvement _____

Integrated Web site promotion _____

Other: _____

_____

_____

Are there any additional benefits that the Rose Festival might offer your company?

_____

_____

There are many areas in which to spend your sponsorship dollars. Why do you support the Portland Rose Festival? (Please check as many as three.)

- Community aspect _____
- Affordable sponsorship property _____
- Staff and level of service _____

Figure 12-4
(Continued)

- Sensitivity to sponsors' competitors   _____
- Return on investment   _____

Please rate the following Rose Festival Events that, in your mind, have the highest amount of sponsorship value. Think in terms of being a title or presenting sponsor (1 being the most valuable for a sponsor).

Rose Festival Air Show   _____
Jazz Band Classic   _____
Queen's Coronation   _____
Grand Floral Parade   _____
Waterfront Village   _____
Festival of Bands   _____
Showcase of Floats   _____
Portland Arts Festival   _____
CART Auto Race   _____
Junior Parade   _____
Starlight Parade   _____
Milk Carton Boat Race   _____

From where do your sponsorship dollars come?

Marketing budget: _____

Contributions budget: _____

Advertising budget: _____

Entertainment budget: _____

CEO/Management discretionary fund: _____

Other: _____

Did you spend any additional dollars in support of your Rose Festival sponsorship (i.e., for advertising, point of purchase, promotions, cross-promotions)?

_____ Yes   _____ No

If yes, can you estimate the ratio of promotional dollars to sponsorship dollars spent? (for example, 1 to 1, meaning $1 advertising for every $1 sponsorship)

How can we specifically increase the value of your sponsorship to you?

Figure 12-4
(Continued)

_____

_____

_____

Corporate Hospitality is important to a majority of sponsors.
Do you have any suggestions for improving Rose Festival sponsor hospitality programs?

_____

_____

_____

_____

In what month does your fiscal year begin, and when do you begin the budget planning for the upcoming year?

_____

Would you be interested in sponsorship of other Rose Festival events? If yes, please name them.

_____

Overall, how would you rate the services of your sponsorship by the Rose Festival?

   1   2   3   4   5   6   7   8   9   10

Lowest   Highest

Please list any suggestions on how we can improve our services to you.

_____

_____

_____

_____

Figure 12-4
(Continued)

The Keys to Developing Good Post-Event Evaluation Reports

To develop a good post-event report:

- File materials for the report on a year-round basis, always thinking of things you can do that can be presented to the sponsor after your event is over.
- Include items to show the sponsor how good the event was for the company and to sign up the sponsor for ensuing years.
- Consider using an outside evaluation service, such as the IEG Evaluation Service or the Hometown Sponsor Evaluation Service.

The Three Rivers Festival in Pittsburgh compiles extremely complete evaluation reports for its sponsors. *Photo courtesy of Three River Festival.*

Milwaukee's Summerfest is the largest music festival in the country and also gives its sponsors good reports after the event. *Photo courtesy of Milwaukee World Festival, Inc., the owner and operator of Summerfest.*

Sponsorship Activities

1. Visit *www.bonham.com,* the Web site for the Bonham Group in Denver; find the Pressroom section, and read "How Is Corporate Sponsorship Gauged?"
2. Visit *www.event-solutions.com* and read Step 10, "Post-Event Sponsorship Maintenance and Renewal," in "10 Steps to Sponsorship Success."
3. Read the section "Measuring Sponsorship Results" in the *IEG's Complete Guide to Sponsorship.*

4. List the ways in which you will evaluate the success of your sponsors in your event.

Sponsorship Tool Kit

Ukman, Lesa. (1998). *IEG's Complete Guide to Sponsorship.* Chicago: IEG.

Web Sites

www.bonham.com
www.event-solutions.com

CHAPTER 13

The Globalization of Event Sponsorship

Don't overlook the importance of worldwide thinking. A company that keeps its eye on Tom, Dick, and Harry is going to miss Pierre, Hans, and Yoshio.

AL RIES, CHAIRMAN, TROUT & RIES, INC.

IN THIS CHAPTER YOU WILL LEARN:

- About sponsorship as a means of cultural support
- The importance of understanding a sponsor's goals
- The issues to be considered in the solicitation process
- Why managers must have a good understanding of the global interests of potential sponsors

Corporate sponsorship of events in Europe has increased dramatically over the last several years.

When the phenomenon hit the United States in the mid-1980s, many European festivals were leery of tying themselves to corporate financing, but have increasingly done so after government funding sources have begun to dry up.

Much more than those in the United States, Europeans are driven to promote, protect, and preserve cultures that have survived for thousands of years. They actively do this in the staging of events such as Carnival in Nice (the first Carnival/Mardi Gras), the Edinburgh International Festival, the International Festival of Lent in Maribor, Slovenia, the Mozart Festival in Salzburg, and many others.

In the beginning, events of this type were afraid that corporate involvement might change the way those cultures were preserved. However, by carefully selecting partnerships, many events in Europe have created strong bridges with corporate cultures.

Sponsorship as a Megatrend

In the 1990s, this change in the way culture is funded was one of the megatrends of the contemporary world, and these developmental processes will continue into the twenty-first century (Naisbitt, 1990). Corporations are finding that they want to be attached to cultural events in Europe. The reasons are numerous, as shown in Figure 13-1.

It was hard to imagine a decade ago that 300,000 people would listen to operatic arias in the stadiums and parks of European and

---

- The information and telecommunications revolution has brought culture closer to ordinary people.
- Leisure time is increasing, and people are devoting more time to satisfying their cultural needs.
- There is a growing attachment to traditional cultural values as a response to modern technical universalism.
- The role of the state and corporations in financing and understanding arts and culture is changing.

Figure 13-1
Why Sponsors Want to Be Attached to Events

U.S. cities (the famous three tenors), that the Cankarjev Dom Cultural Center would attract more spectators annually than all of the football stadiums in Ljubljana, Slovenia, and that more than 8 million people a year would visit the modern cultural center George Pompidou in Paris.

A great majority of contemporary corporate executives admit that art is important for their quality of life and their business contacts. Many are convinced that art is significant to the economic development of a country and that it fosters economic projects, tourism, and other business opportunities. Individuals, companies, and states see culture as a way to increase value, promote their products, and improve their image in society.

THE DECLINE OF GOVERNMENT FINANCIAL SUPPORT

In the 1980s the contributions of corporations and individuals to culture doubled, and funding by governments decreased. Sponsorship of cultural centers, theater and opera houses, museums, exhibitions, and festivals is growing and becoming an increasingly important source of contemporary arts funding in Europe. The old philanthropic model of funding the arts has changed to a modern sponsorship model based on companies' need to accomplish business objectives while supporting the arts.

Managers in corporations compare their work to artistic creativity. Peter Drucker takes particular delight in presenting top managers as orchestra conductors. The attitude to culture and the arts has changed dramatically, with corporate executives determining funding for events, rather than the rulers or aristocratic patrons of the past.

Funding and support of the arts is a very old tradition in Europe. In the Roman period, the patronage of arts was in the hands of the rulers and army commanders. Later, the central role was played by the church, statesmen, and aristocratic patrons. They all demonstrated a strong commercial spirit and never invested money in artists or art production without clearly defining their objectives.

Shakespeare created his Royal Theatre Group. The Roman popes and other church dignitaries were clients or supporters of artists such as Michelangelo and Leonardo da Vinci. The Medici family in Florence and the Sforci family in Milan were among the most famous patron families. However, that type of patronage has slowly changed since the nineteenth century. Important rulers, church dignitaries, and aristocrats have been replaced by entrepreneurs and executives. The latter, in addition to state officials, determine the artistic trends they support and define through their commercial activities.

THE INCREASE IN CORPORATE SPONSORSHIP

Corporate decisions greatly affect modern cultural policy. The Economist Intelligence Unit (EIU, 1992) states three reasons for a better link between modern business and arts:

- Companies are becoming more socially accountable.
- Arts ensure a satisfactory ratio between invested funds and effects.
- Cultural events fit the new quality of life and higher values of the prevailing middle class.

In the past, the state has supported cultural events and institutions that are important for cultural heritage. However, especially at the national level, government no longer provides the amount of money needed by cultural events to plan for good programming. That may be a good thing, because excessive state funding of culture and the arts results in typically irrational spending by recipients—cultural institutions and numerous event organizers.

There is only one possible solution: Event managers must seek corporate sponsorship. This will mean that the state subsidy will be complementary, instead of vital.

Defining Sponsorship

As in most of the world, the definition of sponsorship is not easy. Europeans often confuse it with patronage. Tying down definitions of sponsorship resembles an attempt to shoot a butterfly in the spring breeze.

Patronage is centuries old. The goal of patronage was not to achieve a certain product, but rather to support the artist as a provider of a cultural product. It determined the artist's social status, constituted a traditional way of financing artists, and glorified the patron.

Similarly, sponsorship is not a donation for which very little

- A clear definition of goals on both sides
- The seeking and coordination of mutual benefits
- The formal identification of mutual relationships
- The long-term and global nature of business cooperation.

Figure 13-2
Sponsorship Management Issues

is expected in return. Donations are altruistic and do not constitute commercial activity.

Sponsorship is also more than advertising. Advertising is a one-way business street. We advertise products, services, and activities in order to maximize sales and profits.

Rather, sponsorship can be defined as financial aid to cultural activities, with the expectation of a return on the investment. Sponsorship is a two-way business activity, mutually beneficial to the sponsor on one hand, and to the event on the other. It combines commercial and charitable activity, providing for profit goals and nonprofit intentions at the same time.

The sponsorship market consists of cultural institutions and events as properties and corporations as providers. The greatest difficulty of sponsorship is the potential for both sides to fail to understand each other and underestimate the management problems of sponsorship.

The management of sponsorship depends on several issues, as shown in Figure 13-2.

The first condition for an effective sponsorship is a clear identification of the objectives that both parties wish to achieve. The principal long-term objective of a company is to maximize its values and profits, complemented by other factors, such as company development, market and social position, goodwill, image, and social accountability.

Understanding Goals

Although companies clearly define their commercial goals, their sponsorship objectives are much less precise. They often sponsor in a totally disorganized manner.

In sponsorship, the principles that apply are similar to those in marketing. We must know what we want to achieve through sponsorship before any contract is signed. Every sponsor should define its objectives in any given contract. In order to set objectices, there are certain issues that a sponsor must consider (see Figure 13.3):

- **Impact on the program of a cultural project:** This is a feature of long-term sponsorship contracts. Although it is controversial with event organizers, sponsors are sometimes able to influence long-term cultural policy and adjust it to their global business needs.
- **Sponsor identification in the name of the event:** Events and institutions are often named after the primary sponsor (especially sporting events). In the arts world, this does not mean that the conductor or members of an orchestra should carry the sponsor's name on their backs, but the stage, tickets, printed programs, and the venue of the event should clearly indicate who the sponsor is.
- **Tickets and other advantages for the sponsor:** Sponsors typically receive tickets for their sponsorship, which, of course, have an economic value. This also can be useful for tax reasons.
- **Advertising:** Advertising is a part of a sponsorship package and is defined in a contract. Advertising may be direct (at the event itself) or indirect (as a part of media packages).
- **Special hospitality opportunities:** A sponsor is granted certain exclusive rights within the framework of events that specifically indicate the sponsor's importance. They are of-

---

- Impact on the program of a cultural project
- Sponsor identification in the name of the event
- Tickets
- Advertising
- Special hospitality opportunities
- Promotional material
- Long-term cooperation

Figure 13-3
Issues Sponsors Must Consider Before Sponsoring

ten part of special events organized for the sponsor by the event manager (such as receptions).

- **Promotional material:** Sponsors often invest in ancillary activities and products that support the event. These products are typically promotional and are sold at the event (T-shirts, caps, umbrellas, and other items). Some of these products are given as interesting gifts, especially at outdoor summer events. Such gifts also contribute to the image of the event.
- **Long-term cooperation:** Sponsors can attain their objectives if they support the same type of event over a period of time. Long-term arrangements bring benefits to both sides. They allow arts institutions to make more extensive plans, and sponsors to benefit from the repetition of positive effects.

It is important for a company to answer the following questions when it sponsors an event:

- What are the company's objectives?
- Who is the target audience?
- What products and services of the company best suit the audience?
- What geographical territory interests the company?
- How can sponsorship affect its market position?
- How can goals be attained and mutual interests satisfied?
- How can business policies be affected (short- or long-term, local or global)?

Sponsorship policy is often divided into three business areas at a company:

1. Marketing department, covering most of a sponsorship
2. Public relations department
3. Personnel department or top management (board of directors), in the case of many major sponsorships

Most sponsorship policies of a company include the following elements:

- Identifying various sponsorship opportunities
- Establishing objectives
- Setting the budget
- Analyzing the target audience
- Identifying benefits expected from the sponsorship

- Identifying limitations of a particular sponsorship that may affect the competitive position of the company
- Developing annual sponsorship plans and ways to fulfill them
- Defining the duration and local activity of sponsorship
- Carrying out a global assessment of benefits and costs of sponsorship
- Negotiating with cultural institutions and programs
- Identifying control mechanisms to monitor the fulfillment of contractual obligations

We recognize successful companies by their effective sponsorship. Large or rapidly developing companies in Europe will soon realize that they need sponsorship as an important form of their market presence and growth.

What is particularly important here is that they develop a special policy of sponsorship and effective managerial mechanisms in sponsorship. It is crucial that they are able to distinguish the significance of managing cultural events in comparison with other activities (sports, for example) and that they identify the strategic selective goals about what, how, and whom they want to sponsor. Major companies should sponsor primarily major cultural events, high-quality projects, and established cultural institutions. Everything else should be left to minor local sponsors.

Sponsor Solicitation Process

Sponsorship is a two-way process. This means that it is important for cultural and arts institutions to understand the decision making at companies, in addition to being aware of their own needs and wishes. For this reason we have paid special attention to companies and their sponsorship proposals. Successful sponsorship is always a result of hard work, entrepreneurial imagination, and economic calculation.

When seeking sponsors, event managers should consider a number of guidelines, as shown in Figure 13-4.

In seeking sponsorship, it is crucial to set objectives and identify the services we offer to sponsors in exchange for their financial assets. The issues to be considered in seeking sponsorship are:

- Sponsorship is a special form of a company's social accountability.
- Sponsorship has to be within the limits of good taste, which is why moderate (not fully commercial), but diverse, forms of advertising are recommended.
- Sponsorship of culture affects the image of the company.
- Corporate sponsorship should be long-term.
- Sponsorship can make a strong impact internally at a company.

Figure 13-4
Sponsorship Guidelines for Event Managers

- The connection with a sponsor's products and services
- The connection with a sponsor's image
- The goals of potential sponsors
- The benefits and drawbacks of sponsorship
- Potential advertising in media
- Potential on-site advertising
- Previous sponsorships

The size of the event's total budget dependent on sponsorship is, to a great extent, contingent on an event's business plan. A cultural/arts event manager must work out a plan in which the purpose of the event is defined in more detail, and which includes the potential audience, the possibility of increased sales, the technology of the event, the venue, the number of subevents, costs, financial sources, the necessary staff, and how to connect all this for an appropriate commercial entity. The business plan (Figure 13-5) is a starting point for determining the budget for the event.

It is important to provide a potential sponsor with an investment prospectus/proposal that contains all the elements of the business plan in a shorter version. It should include:

- The program and providers
- The potential audience
- A listing of all benefits offered to sponsors
- The financial obligations of a sponsor
- A sponsorship cost-benefit analysis

The prospectus/proposal should describe an event's cultural entrepreneurship and previous sponsorships and identify the long-term objectives it wishes to attain through the sponsorship of

	Budget
Four financial sources may form a budget:	
▪ Subsidy provided by the national government	————
▪ Subsidy provided by local authorities	————
▪ Commercial sponsorship	————
▪ Other earned income (ticket sales, etc.)	————

Figure 13-5
A Typical Event Business Plan

cultural events. The corporate philosophy of sponsorship seekers is based on what can be offered for the given scope and structure of the funds available.

A manager's report should include the following:

- A clear identification of the sponsor's objectives
- The strategy of the event
- The event's business plan
- A sponsorship prospectus/proposal
- A linkage between the interests of the project and the potential interests of sponsors

The event manager can then prepare a contract, which includes a payment schedule.

Five Keys to Successful Sponsorship Programs in Europe

A successful sponsorship program in Europe requires attention to a number of considerations:

1. An event, especially a cultural or arts event, must be careful to preserve culture while selling sponsorship.
2. It must tap into a company's strong desire to sponsor events, especially arts and cultural events.

3. The event should make sure that both sides (the event and the sponsor) define the goals and objectives they want to achieve.
4. Event managers must understand the goals and objectives of a company.
5. Event managers must also develop a good business plan in order to determine how much sponsorship revenue is needed.

Sponsorship Activities

1. Go to *www.aedme.org,* the Web site for CEREC, the European Committee for Business, Arts and Culture, and look for sponsorship suggestions.
2. Read Rosanne Martorella's book, *Art and Business: An International Perspective on Sponsorship.*
3. Read Roger E. Axtell's book, *The Do's and Taboos of International Trade: A Small Business Primer.*
4. Describe the differences in selling sponsorship between Europe and the United States.

Sponsorship Tool Kit

Axtell, Roger E. (1994). *The Do's and Taboos of International Trade: A Small Business Primer.* New York: John Wiley & Sons, Inc.

Martorella, Rosanne. (1996). *Art and Business, An International Perspective on Sponsorship.* Westport, CT: Prager Publishers

Web Sites

www.aedme.org, the Web site for CEREC, the European Committee for Business, Arts and Culture.

www.eiu.com, the Web site for the Economist Intelligence Unit.

CHAPTER 14

The Importance of Networking

If you steal an idea, it's called stealing.
If you steal two or more, it's called market
research.

ANONYMOUS

IN THIS CHAPTER YOU WILL LEARN:

- The critical connections you must establish
- How trade associations facilitate the event sponsorship industry
- The significance of the International Festivals and Events Association (IFEA), International Events Group (IEG), the International Society of Special Events (ISES), and the European Committee for Business, Arts and Culture (CEREC)

Carnival in Nice, France, is probably the oldest continuing event in the world, dating back at least 1000 years. It was also the original pre-Lent carnival, of which there are now hundreds in the world, most of which culminate on Fat Tuesday (Mardi Gras).

The Battle of Flowers Parade in Nice is a great example of what networking can do—many European Carnivals, Mardi Gras in New Orleans, the Pasadena Tournament of Roses Parade and many others are an offshoot of the event. *Photo by author.*

Therefore, all carnival/Mardi Gras events, including Mardi Gras in New Orleans, have their origins in Carnival in Nice. For years, event managers borrowed ideas to begin their new events through a process known as "networking."

One of the featured events in Nice during this time is the Battle of Flowers Parade, which features floral floats that go up one side of the Promenade d' Anglais, and then turn around and go down the other side, *twice*. On the second time around, float riders throw the flowers that adorn the float into the crowd.

In 1889, when it was just a shade under 900 years old, a man from Pasadena, California, was at Carnival in Nice. He returned home and told friends, "Pasadena should have an all-floral parade like Carnival in Nice." That was, arguably, how the best parade in the world, the Pasadena Tournament of Roses Parade, was born.

Those who have been to Mardi Gras parades in New Orleans know that float riders throw plastic beads into crowds of people, many of whom fight with frenzy for the "throw." Not only did Mardi Gras come out of Carnival in Nice, but it is thought that the idea of throwing flowers, as found at the Battle of Flowers Parade, was transformed into the throwing of beads in New Orleans.

In addition to those mentioned here, hundreds of pre-Lenten carnivals (including Carnival in Rio and the Battle of Flowers Parade, which is part of Fiesta San Antonio each April), came out of Carnival in Nice.

Networking

Networking, part market research, is a very old idea in the special events business. It is made possible by two things:

- For the most part, event managers, unless they have an event the same weekend as another property's, do not compete with each other, so they are rarely territorial about "trade secrets."
- Even more important, most event managers crave peer interaction because they are underappreciated in the communities where they live. Those who produce one event a year constantly hear comments such as, "Is that a full-time job?" "What do you do the rest of the year?" "I know you work 80 hours a week, but it's fun and you don't have any stress."

Event managers are especially open to the benefits of networking. They greatly enjoy meeting with people who understand what they do and appreciate the stressful situations they have to endure.

There are many associations—those that represent the film industry, shopping centers, real estate developers, arenas, and so forth—that present conferences and hold sessions on sponsorship. But there are only three that have sponsorship as an integral part of their programs:

1. The International Festivals and Events Association (IFEA), headquartered in Boise, Idaho
2. The International Events Group (IEG), located in Chicago, which stages the largest gathering of buyers and sellers of sponsorship in the world
3. The International Special Events Society (ISES), which also has its offices in Chicago

The International Festivals and Events Association

IFEA is a trade association that has provided a myriad of benefits to members since 1956. In the area of sponsorship, it has many sessions at its annual convention on the subject and has published a book, *IFEA's Official Guide to Sponsorship*. It also presents an annual conference on sponsorship in the spring, usually held around an event, such as Mardi Gras, the Kentucky Derby Festival, Fiesta San Antonio, and many others.

It is IFEA's goal to bring the entire industry together, so it also has many members who are sponsors. For these members, IFEA offers the opportunity to network with other leaders in the sponsorship arena and a chance to create a unique dialogue and closer relationship with the world's leading event managers and with members who supply products and services to events.

There are several other reasons for an event manager to belong to IFEA:

- **Annual Convention**—Normally held in the fall, this event attracts more than 1200 of the industry's top festival and event organizers, sponsors, and suppliers. It allows industry professionals to share ideas and rub elbows. The convention also offers more than 100 sessions on how to produce events, many of which are on the topic of sponsorship.

- **Affinity Groups**—IFEA offers several affinity group sessions at its annual convention, including one on sponsorship. This allows event professionals to gather to discuss a single topic in an open forum setting and to leave with their questions answered.

- **Industry Awards**—The association believes that recognition by one's peers is the highest compliment, and each year at the convention it recognizes the top event promotional materials and innovative programs, including those on sponsorship, with its Pinnacle Awards.

- **Maximizing Assets: Profits and People Seminar**—This is the conference in the spring that IFEA usually holds in conjunction with an outstanding event. Attendees not only can attend outstanding seminars on sponsorship, but can also see it being demonstrated in action at the event. This behind-the-scenes portion combines classroom learning with field experience at the top events in the industry and allows people to hear from other event organizers as they go through the production process, providing for experiential learning at its best.

- **State and Regional Conferences and Seminars**—IFEA is affiliated with 22 state and regional chapters that represent all 50 states. In fact, when you join IFEA, you are also automatically a member of an IFEA-affiliated state or regional association. IFEA recognizes the sometimes prohibitive costs of traveling to attend a national or international convention. It was for this reason that it initiated regional and state chapters so that event managers could learn without having to bear the costs of traveling to a national conference. These chapters typically offer annual conventions themselves, which offer educational sessions on sponsorship. They also have entire seminars on the subject.

- **International Seminars**—If you want to learn about sponsorship on an international level, IFEA has several affiliated international chapters in Europe, Canada, South Africa, Singapore, and Australia. Seminars and conventions are held in these locations too, which are often held in conjunction with outstanding international events.

- **Economic Impact Assessment**—Surveys of this type, which calculate the economic impact of your event on your community, can help you sell sponsorship. Typically, these surveys are expensive to conduct, but IFEA has developed a low-cost program with several option levels.
- ***Festivals and Events Business: The Professional Mapping of the International Events Industry***—Each member receives this quarterly magazine, which has a "Profits" section on how to sell sponsorship and other money-making ideas. It also has many other specifics for the events industry in a full-color glossy format.
- ***IFEA Membership Directory***—This annual publication lists more than 3000 event, sponsor, and supplier members worldwide. Each member receives a free directory and listing.
- **Chapter Newsletter**—Each member also receives the newsletter for his or her affiliated state or regional chapter. The newsletter often includes articles on sponsorship.
- ***The IFEA Library***—This library contains many publications; most notably, it offers *IFEA's Official Guide to Sponsorship*. The book is written by many event professionals and is a nuts-and-bolts publication on how to sell sponsorship. The library also has tapes and videocassettes on the subject that you can buy, also presented by several top industry professionals.
- **Certification Program**—Members have an opportunity to become a CFE, a Certified Festival Executive. The process of achieving a CFE designation involves learning and becoming proficient in the area of sponsorship.

U.S. Associations

INTERNATIONAL SPECIAL EVENTS SOCIETY (ISES)

ISES comprises over 3000 professionals in more than a dozen countries representing special event producers (from festivals to trade shows), caterers, decorators, florists, destination management companies, rental companies, special effects experts, tent suppliers, audiovisual technicians, party and convention coordinators, balloon artists, educators, journalists, hotel sales managers, specialty entertainers, convention center managers, photographers, entertainers, and others.

As education providers, ISES is only 15 years old, but its rapid growth has put it at the forefront of the industry. It was spearheaded in 1989 by its founding president, Dr. Joe Goldblatt. The Society quickly became a leader in the special events industry under his leadership. ISES held its first professional development conference in Atlanta in the same year it was founded.

"We wanted to provide a forum for education and networking and to lay the groundwork for future certification of special event professionals," said Goldblatt, who is dean of the Alan Shawn Feinstein Graduate School at Johnson & Wales University in Providence, Rhode Island.

Prior to founding ISES, Goldblatt was the founding director of the Event Management Program at George Washington University in Washington, D.C., where he created a one-of-a-kind event management certificate program and masters concentration that have been eagerly embraced by students nationally and internationally.

The mission of ISES is to educate, advance, and promote the special events industry and its network of professionals, along with related industries. It strives to:

- Uphold the integrity of the special events profession to the general public through its Principles of Professional Conduct and Ethics
- Acquire and disseminate useful business information
- Foster a spirit of cooperation among its members and other special event professionals
- Cultivate high standards of business practice

ISES covers the area of sponsorship in several of its member benefits:

- **Local Chapter Networks**—With more than 25 chapters worldwide, ISES members are able to participate by attending local meetings and educational seminars and receive chapter newsletters with local industry and sponsorship information.
- *Eventworld*—This publication gives members the latest trends and provides practical information and creative ideas, including those on sponsorship.
- **Conference for Professional Development**—Held each August, this conference offers hands-on training and features

well-known industry speakers and educators. And, of course, networking is an important part of the conference.

- **CSEP Designation**—The process of becoming a CSEP—Certified Special Events Professional—includes training in the sponsorship arena.
- **Regional Education Conferences**—These conferences include information on how to sell sponsorship.
- **International Study of Event Management**—This profile of event management contains eight years of industry data, much of it on sponsorship.
- **Other publications, books, and reports**

INTERNATIONAL EVENTS GROUP (IEG)

IEG is the world's leading provider of independent sponsorship valuation, advice, and analysis.

It was started by Lesa Ukman, a graduate of Colorado College in 1978. Ukman went to work as a speech writer for Chicago mayor Jane Byrne and urged the mayor to use special events to improve the quality of life for people in Chicago. She started such neighborhood festivals as the Chicago Jazz Festival and the Taste of Chicago.

She recognized the potential to tie in sponsors with festivals and events on a national level. "I thought if this is good for the mayor's office, it could be for the sponsors," Ukman said. "I saw it as a win-win situation for everyone. Sponsors were getting a lot out of it, and it seemed obvious to me that other cities could do the same thing."

She left her speech writing job to start IEG in 1981. The organization, which she heads along with her brother, Jon, shows marketers how to use sports, arts, events, entertainment, and cause marketing as a strategic and cost-effective medium. IEG's products and services collectively provide comprehensive coverage of the entire sponsorship marketplace on a local, national, and global level.

The company's products include:

- *IEG Sponsorship Report*—There are other publications, such as *Advertising Age, Amusement Business,* the IFEA publication *Festivals,* and others that dedicate portions of their publications to sponsorship, but this is the only one totally dedicated to sponsorship. The *Report* is published every two weeks, and each issue has news and analysis on the latest sponsorship deals, what sponsors look for, and how you can negotiate deals.

- **IEG's Annual Event Marketing Conference**—This is by far the largest conference in the world totally dedicated to sponsorship. Every year attendees learn about new sponsorship ideas, make new business contacts, and hear new marketing perspectives. It also provides an opportunity to network with 1200 industry pros, both buyers and sellers.
- **IEG's Sponsorship Seminar Series**—Four one-day business seminars are held around the country, designed to build the knowledge of event managers in the sponsorship area. Seminars include Selling More Sponsorship, Advanced Sponsorship Sales, Sponsors Only, and Measuring Sponsorship's ROI.
- *IEG's Complete Guide to Sponsorship*—A detailed, practical book gives essential building blocks and shows you how to apply them. It includes checklists and real-life examples that illustrate principles in practice.
- *IEG Sponsorship Sourcebook*—This directory includes 4500 cash, media, and in-kind sponsors, the 300 most active sponsors, 2000 sponsorship opportunities, and more than 750 industry agencies and suppliers.
- **IEG Sponsordex**—This package includes contact information for more than 2000 top sponsorship decision makers on CD and in a hard-copy index, a prototype sponsorship proposal with sales-driven offer letter, and ready-to-use mailing labels. This can help you find the right decision makers.
- **IEG Intelligence Reports**—These give in-depth examinations of sponsorship activity in a given sector, including arenas/auditoriums, auto racing, causes, festivals/fairs, golf, international/Olympic sports, performing arts, pro sports leagues, and zoos/museums/malls/aquariums.
- **IEG Valuation Service**—This service establishes the fair market value of on-line and off-line sponsorship packages for a property. The IEG Valuation Service uses real-world standards and measures that take the guesswork out of valuing sponsorship opportunities. This service has been endorsed by more than 250 sponsors.
- **IEG Consulting**—The company utilizes its vast databases and research to help clients anticipate trends and opportunities.

- *www.sponsorship.com*—A good place to find information on the latest sponsorship activities around the world.

European Associations

INTERNATIONAL FESTIVALS AND EVENTS ASSOCIATION EUROPE

IFEA Europe is the European festival and events organization for event managers. Members are automatically members of IFEA World.

The Association offers sponsorship training as a part of its benefits to members:

- **Annual Conference**—Three- to four-day conferences are hosted by various member organizations in different cities each year. Sponsorship topics are included in the program.
- **Behind the Scenes**—The association arranges a yearly Behind the Scenes Seminar in connection with member festivals and events, and attendees can see sponsorship in action.
- **Publications**—Members receive *Festivals Europe* and an e-mail newsletter.

THE EUROPEAN COMMITTEE FOR BUSINESS, ARTS AND CULTURE

The European Committee for Business, Arts and Culture (CEREC) is an independent nongovernmental organization, constituting a network of member associations and affiliate members, which are arts organizations and sponsors. CEREC promotes partnerships across Europe between the private sector and the arts. Representatives of the network speak at numerous events and conferences each year and undertake advocacy work on a European level. The organization is extremely effective in helping arts events and venues sell sponsorship.

ARTS & BUSINESS

Arts & Business (formerly Association for Business Support of the Arts, ABSA) is the world's foremost organization in the field of arts and business partnerships and holds the presidency of CEREC. It exists to promote and encourage partnerships between businesses and the arts to their mutual benefit and to the benefit of society as a whole. Arts & Business runs its programs through a network of 18 offices nationwide and provides a wide range of services to over 350 business members as well as to arts organizations and museums through membership in the Arts & Business Development Forum.

Its services and programs are open to all not-for-profit cultural organizations, foundations, or associations supported by or seeking support from one or more businesses. Through its latest initiative, the President's Forum, Arts & Business is working with forward-looking businesses to develop a new model for creative partnerships between business and the arts. With the support of its patron, HRH The Prince of Wales, it is looking at stimulating ways for business, the arts, and society to interact.

Three Keys to Sponsorship Networking

For effective networking:

1. Join a local chapter of IFEA and/or ISES (use the contact information listed at the end of this section). Even if you cannot afford to attend a national convention of either of these two outstanding organizations, you can still network with local representatives. Most members of these organizations are quite willing to share—they want to talk to people who respect what they do.
2. Attend a convention or conference at the chapter level—this is an even better networking opportunity, as you can talk to event managers from many different organizations.
3. Attend a national convention of IFEA or ISES. Not only will you meet many more people, but you will be able to steal ideas from the best of the best. Europeans should contact CEREC, the European Committee for Business, Arts and Culture.

Remember, there is no use in reinventing the wheel!

Sponsorship Activities
1. Look at the following Web sites to find out more on how you can network:
www.ifea.com
www.ifeaeurope.com

www.sponsorship.com
www.ises.com
www.aandb.org.uk
www.aedme.org

2. List the reasons that it is important to network as an event manager.
3. Compare networking organizations (Figure 14-1) and determine which one is right for you.

Sponsorship Tool Kit

U.S. Organizations

International Festivals and Events Association (IFEA)
World Headquarters: 2601 Eastover Terrace, Boise, ID, 83706
Phone: 208-433-0950; Fax: 208-433-9812
www.ifea.com

International Special Events Society (ISES)
401 N. Michigan Avenue, Chicago, IL 60611
Phone: 800-688-4737; Fax: 312-673-6953
www.ises.com

International Events Group (IEG)
640 North LaSalle, Suite 600, Chicago, IL 60610-3777
Phone: 1-800-834-4850 or 312-944-1727; Fax: 312-944-1897
www.sponsorship.com

European Associations

IFEA Europe
c/o Netherlands Board of Tourism
Post Box 458
Leidschendam 2260 MG Netherlands
Phone: 31-70-3705296; Fax: 31-70-3201654
www.ifeaeurope.com

European Committee for Business, Arts and Culture (CEREC)
Francesca Minguella, Secretary General
c/o AEDME, C/Tuset, 8, 1° 2^a,
08006 Barcelona, Spain
Phone: 34 93 237.26.82; Fax: 34 93 237 22.84;
E-mail *contact@cerec.org;*
www.aedme.org

Arts & Business
Nutmeg House
60 Gainsford Street
Butlers Wharf
Londen SE1 2NY
Phone 020 7378 8143; Fax: 020 7407 7527
www.aandb.org.uk

ISES	IFEA	IEG
Annual Development Conference	Annual Convention	Annual Event Marketing Conference
Eventworld magazine	*Festivals* magazine	*IEG Sponsorship Report*
Local chapter networks	State/regional chapters	Sponsorship Seminar Series
CSEP Certification Program	CFE Certification Program	IEG Intelligence Reports
Regional education conferences	Affinity groups	Sponsordex
International Study of Event Management	Free member consulting	IEG Consulting
Periodicals, books, reports	Economic Impact Studies	Valuation Service
	Membership Directory	*Sponsorship Source Book*
	IFEA library	*Complete Guide to Sponsorship*
	Industry awards	
	Profits seminar	
	International seminars	

Figure 14-1
Three of the Best Organizations at Providing Information on
Sponsorship

CHAPTER 15

The Future of Global Event Sponsorship

What, sir, would you make a ship sail against the wind and currents by lighting a bonfire under her deck? I pray you excuse me. I have no time to listen to such nonsense.

NAPOLEON BONAPARTE, EMPEROR OF FRANCE (SPEAKING TO ROBERT FULTON)

IN THIS CHAPTER YOU WILL LEARN:

- How the Internet will influence events and their sponsors
- About the future growth of sponsorship
- The trends sponsorship is expected to follow in the future
- The effects of economic downturns on sponsorship

Napoleon Bonaporte's admonition to Robert Fulton is reflective of many events in the world and of resistance to change. But the future of events will be about change, as the following example relates.

David Jacobson, senior editor of the Exordium Group, wrote in the on-line newsletter, Exordium Group.Comment, that on July 17, 2001, Microsoft Network U.K. (MSN U.K.) and Elton John demonstrated the latest sponsorship trend and how the Internet will influence events and their sponsors in the future. He reported on how Microsoft sponsored Sir Elton's July 17 concert from the ancient Great Amphitheatre in Ephesus, Turkey, while the latter sponsored a cybercast of the concert on pay-per-view for broadband users only.

Through its sponsorship, MSN U.K. made maximum use of the Internet, helping to pave the way for event managers and sponsors.

"While the ability to pay to watch an Elton John gig online is hardly a fundamental human right, in a couple of years, watching live events on the Net will be as commonplace as watching them on TV," Jacobson quoted the *London Daily Mirror.*

The Elton John concert followed an earlier Microsoft Network sponsorship of a Janet Jackson concert, although the goals were different for that performance. The Jackson sponsorship included "trappings for tickets, ISP signups, chats and sweepstakes," wrote Jacobson.

Jacobson's story went on to report: "Elton John and Janet Jackson are coming at the same thing from different directions," said Niall MacAnna, special events producer for MSN in the United Kingdom. "In the United States, with Janet, it's about ticket giveaways and signups. With Elton, it's about the joys of the online experience."

Starting on July 2, 2001, fans were able to register at *MSN.co.uk/eltonjohn* to sign up for the event up to six hours before the virtual box office opened to the public. "Payment entitled users to see the full 90-minute concert live and to hear tracks from Elton's new album, 'Songs from the West Coast,' two months before its general release."

MSN limited Elton's cybercast to broadband users only, in hope of demonstrating the wonders of high-speed connections, and thus driving demand for such service and the special content it can deliver.

"We could get a flood of people at 28.8 or 56k, and that would rely on the excellence of their ISP," MacAnna said. "BT Openworld has been slow to provide fast services at home. We've aimed this at people at the office. That way we can provide quality and guarantee an experience. If it's open (to slower connections), you get a bottleneck and we can't control that."

MSN limited live streams to 130,000 for the live show. Archiving each show for seven days, MSN had a goal of delivering two million streams, MacAnna said.

"Regardless of how many streams MSN delivers, the wave of the future is starting to roll," Jacobson said.

Viewers paid £7 for a 100k connection or £10 for a 300k connection. "Pay-per-view services are the wave of the future as part of Microsoft's dot-net strategy," MacAnna said. "For these concerts, we're taking the next step first."

This sponsorship places little emphasis on sheer branding. "We'll never put the MSN butterfly behind the artist's head," MacAnna said. "It gets in the way, and when you're viewing, you're already using Windows Media. It's important not to stick a banner on an ancient column, and there has to be a certain amount of respect for the artist."

Instead, MSN will evaluate the sponsorship according to the revenue it generates from pay-per-view purchases and users' subsequent purchases of recordings and merchandise elsewhere on MSN Music. During the cybercast there was a link and a secondary banner promoting MSN Music.

"All banners . . . have a tracking device installed so we can see where people sign up and track where else they go on MSN Music," MacAnna said.

The Growth of Sponsorship

As we are now well into the Internet age, we can see that sponsorship marketing has come a long way in the last 20 years, and it promises to undergo even more changes in the next 20. Except for auto racing, tennis, and golf, there was little sponsorship in the special events field in 1980. For the most part, monies provided by the corporate sector were donations—very little, if anything, was expected in return.

According to the International Festivals and Events Association (IFEA), the first full-time sponsorship salesperson was not hired by a festival until 1984. Now most major festivals and other types of events have one or more sponsorship salespeople on staff.

When the Fiesta Bowl signed Sunkist as a title sponsor of the football game in 1985, NBC did not recognize the sponsor as such on the telecast, even though Sunkist was willing to purchase television advertising time. Networks were afraid that sponsorship dollars, especially those for larger events, were going to replace their own advertising revenue.

The next year NBC did recognize Sunkist (which purchased time on the telecast), and many other properties and networks followed suit. The television's networks also got into the sponsorship game. They now sell title and other sponsorships for many of the events they televise, along with sponsorship of replays, quarter scores, and many other segments of a telecast.

Currently, there is good news for people who sell sponsorship.

Sponsorship of events has grown 47 percent over a recent three-year period, according to the International Events Group (IEG) of Chicago, which publishes the *IEG Sponsorship Report* and tracks and analyzes sponsorship worldwide. The industry grew from $5.9 billion in 1997 to $8.7 billion in 2000.

Sports attracts the most sponsorship dollars (approximately $6.51 billion in 2001), but companies sponsor festivals and events more than any other type of event—47 percent of companies say they sponsor festivals, as compared with 25 percent that say they sponsor sports.

- There will be more sponsorship growth.
- Sponsorship of non-sports events will increase.
- Technology will provide for the largest trends.
- It will become increasingly important for sponsors to interface with consumers at events.
- There will be less commercialization, as sponsors will not want to offend consumers.
- Cause-related marketing will continue to grow.
- Ticket sales will continue to be tied to sponsorships.
- There will be fewer and larger sponsorships, as companies clamor for greater exclusivity.
- The list of different types of properties will continue to grow.
- Experiences, rather than impressions, will become even more important.
- Sponsors will continue to look for return on investment.
- Sponsorship will be used to target future customers.

Figure 15-1
Skinner's Predicted Trends for Sponsorship

We predict that there will be many major trends in sponsorship in the next ten years, including the 12 listed in Figure 15-1.

TREND NO. 1: MORE GROWTH IN SPONSORSHIP

Even with the slowing of the economy and the downturn of other sectors in the marketing industry, sponsorship fares better than traditional advertising. "Chiefly, when the economy cools, sponsorship has proven to be the most recession-proof communication," IEG wrote in its December 18, 2000, issue of The *IEG Sponsorship Report.*

This does not mean that event managers can sit back and relax during an economic downturn. It becomes even more imperative that they provide a tremendous amount of value (see Chapter 5) in sponsor packages. Sponsors will address the validity of every expense (whether marketing or otherwise) during downtimes, but sound event marketing decisions will survive. They will be anxious to keep sponsorship partnerships that lead to increased sales through business-to-business partnerships, exclusivity, activation, and good demographic fits.

After the events of September 11, 2001, several sponsors looked at their relationships with events, and those that addressed these needs and were proactive with their sponsors were the first to survive.

A Proactive Cherry Festival

Chuck O'Connor of the National Cherry Festival demonstrated a very effective way for event managers to deal with sponsors when a tragedy occurs, sending a communication, as shown in Figures 15-2A and 15-2B, to sponsors and other individuals immediately after the attacks.

Sponsorship Changing

Lesa Ukman says that her organization, IEG, did a survey of selected sponsors after the events of September 11. "Twenty-four percent of them said they were going to increase their sponsorship spending. Intuitively, companies have found that they have to go deeper beyond their pitches.

"Consumers are looking for substantive partnerships, and companies are looking beyond their products and services. They are using sponsorship to make their communities better. They are beginning

---

National Cherry Festival

To Sponsors:

I am writing to inform you of a Marketing and Sponsorship position paper we recently produced to respond to those wondering what the future holds for the sponsorship business in the wake of the horrific attacks of September 11.

The attached position statement will be posted on the National Cherry Festival Web site at www.cherryfestival.org and included in mailings and responses to businesses inquiring about our Corporate Sponsorship Program. I wanted to make sure that you, as a current Festival partner, were in the loop on this. I would welcome your comments and suggestions on this response, as well as any referrals to people you do business with whom you think may benefit from partnering with the National Cherry Festival as we plan our 2002 event scheduled for July 6 to 13.

On behalf of the Festival Board of Directors, our staff, and many volunteers, I want to thank you again for your investment. Partnership with you continues to ensure the overall quality of the Festival. We remain confident in our commitment to excellence and believe that these times will present many opportunities for our sponsor partners and us.

Sincerely,

Chuck

Source: Courtesy National Cherry Festival.

Figure 15-2a
Marketing and Sponsorship Letter

to give time off to employees who get involved in the community. They are looking at what their consumers are passionate about."

Global Growth
IEG predicted that U.S. sponsorship would grow 9.6 percent in 2001. Also according to IEG, global sponsorship would increase even more.

- European companies were predicted to boost spending 12 percent to $7.4 billion in 2001.

National Cherry Festival

Over the past few weeks, the National Cherry Festival's Executive Committee and staff have had an opportunity to absorb a number of conversations and reactions related to the economy and the future of corporate America on the heels of the tragic incidents of September 11. Many of our conclusions concur with business and marketing experts: If there ever was a time for companies to focus on the needs of their employees, customers, and communities, it is now. Lesa Ukman, president of IEG, the leading provider of independent sponsorship research, recently observed, "To stay relevant, marketers must find out what is important in their consumers' lives and whether their vision for their products and services is big enough to create profit for their shareholders while creating value for their communities."

Like you, we are all trying to get a grip on what the future will look like as it relates to our marketing and promotional strategies. We believe that forward-thinking companies will place heightened importance on building trust and loyalty with their employees and with consumers. We believe that companies will invest in experiential marketing—opportunities that connect businesses with their consumers and prospects—as a way to accomplish this, because they are the best option for businesses to earn consumer confidence and demonstrate their relevance to the lives of those consumers.

More than ever, key community special events like the National Cherry Festival, that reflect grassroots American values, will strike deep ties with their guests, your customers. For 75 years, families throughout the Midwest have come to the National Cherry Festival to participate and just plain enjoy themselves.

We are certain that the National Cherry Festival and its sponsorship program can truly answer the experiential marketing call. We can help companies show that they stand for the right things, while we create and maintain awareness for sponsors' brands and persuade consumers to prefer their products and services.

We are fortunate to have just gotten a green light from the U.S. Navy Blue Angels Flight Demonstration team for a patriotic return visit to the National Cherry Festival in 2002. We are also fortunate to have been invited to partner with Travel Michigan, an alliance that helped us build a more national presence last year, as that organization anticipates increased destination driving vacations next summer. All in all, we are positioned as a very desirable partner in an atmosphere conducive to success for sponsoring companies. I invite you to join us.

Source: Courtesy National Cherry Festival.

Figure 15-2b
Marketing and Sponsorship Position Statement (by Chuck O'Connor, CFE)

Despite being in a smaller community, the National Cherry Festival in Traverse City, Mich., is one of the country's best. Event managers were proactive with their sponsors following the events of Sept. 11. *Photo courtesy National Cherry Festival.*

- The Pacific Rim would see expenditures increase an additional 12 percent to $3.8 billion.
- South American countries would see the largest increase, jumping 17 percent to $2.1 billion.
- Including North America, worldwide spending would increase to $24.6 billion, a 12 percent increase.

TREND NO. 2: MORE NON-SPORTS SPONSORSHIP

Companies will continue to sponsor sports, but will increase their involvement in festivals, fairs, events, and causes.

Sponsors have done a good job in covering the sports market, but there is growth to be seen in the sponsorship of other events.

TREND NO. 3: TECHNOLOGY PRODUCING THE LARGEST CHANGES

As indicated earlier, the largest trend of all will be due to technology. We live in an era when there is far less verbal interaction between people. We e-mail everyone—even the person in the office next to us.

In this virtual world people are going to want to interact with other people more than ever, and there are very few places better to do that than at the ballpark, the local arts festival, a parade, or another such venue. Events—and therefore event sponsorship— are going to be more popular than ever.

We are also going to have to understand the changing habits of consumers. In the old economy, the merchandise producer was in charge, but as more and more people buy on-line, they take the lead and choose from many more products on the Internet.

Events will look for Internet sponsors, just as they seek radio, television, and print sponsors now. Use of the Internet, Web-site-sponsored promotions, and sponsorship-related content will grow more valuable.

TREND NO. 4: INCREASE IN FACE-TO-FACE MEETINGS

Events will receive more sponsorship dollars because:

- It will be increasingly important for sponsors to meet their customers face-to-face, and there is no better place to do that than at an event.
- Events will be ideal occasions for the sampling of new products.
- Events will also be conducive to experimental programs.
- Events will be cost-effective as compared with other forms of advertising.

TREND NO. 5: LESS COMMERCIALIZATION

At the conclusion of the 1984 Olympics, a spoof on sponsorship was produced for a broadcast convention.

The telecast began with the words: "American Express Presents the Bud Light Games of the 30th Olympiad, brought to you [presented in rapid succession] by AT&T, B&W, True Value Hardware, RCA, Black and Decker Tools, Sharp, 3M, Volvo, Seagram's, Magnavox, Avon, Nissan, Audi, Isuzu, Nuprin, and Gillette."

The spoof continued with an announcement for the GTE Sprint 4 x 100 men's relay race, which included teams such as "in Lane 3, the Italian team, presented by Pizza Hut . . . in Lane 5, the Goodyear U.S.A. team, presented by Chrysler and McDonald's . . . and in Lane 8, the Brazil Fruit of the Loom team."

The Radio Shack weather had winds of Northwest Airlines (NW) at 10 mph. It was a taxing and pressure-filled moment as runners got into position. "This moment is presented by H&R Block." And the starter's gun was presented by the National Rifle Association.

Although events generally have not produced anything close to the logo soup presented in the spoof, some (such as the 1996 Atlanta Olympic Games) have come under fire for overcommercialization, from consumers who say that they feel that they are being hit over the head by sponsor impressions.

Sponsors and events must pay careful attention to this area in the future, as both lose a lot in the wake of negative consumer reaction to too many sponsor banners.

TREND NO. 6: INCREDIBLE GROWTH IN CAUSE-RELATED SPONSORSHIP

It used to be that companies got involved in the community by making donations, and receiving very little recognition for them.

Sponsorship allows for companies to be involved in their communities *and to be recognized for their efforts,* and to create situations in which their employees feel good about where they are working. This is a trend that will continue to grow.

For example, Motorola in Phoenix has specific objectives when it sponsors events. The company wants opportunities that stress education, employee involvement, diversity, and environmental messages. In the Fiesta Bowl Parade, it sponsored a float for the Phoenix Union High School District, which is the most diverse school district in the state of Arizona.

For an environmental message, the company also stages the Motorola Cleanup of the parade route. In addition, they hold a day at the float pavilion, during which employees and their families receive a sneak preview of parade entries.

TREND NO. 7: TICKET SALES TIED TO SPONSORSHIPS

Ticket sales will increasingly be tied to sponsorships of large companies or retail-oriented firms. Events will encourage large companies to purchase tickets for employees and to provide giveaways, rather than just paying fees for signage and other benefits. This will allow an event to benefit from additional revenue from food and souvenir sales.

TREND NO. 8: FEWER AND LARGER SPONSORSHIPS

Sponsors will increasingly demand exclusivity. This will endanger an event's ability to attract associate sponsorships, as major sponsors will want to limit the number of companies getting visibility so that they can get more for themselves. However, events will be able to get larger fees from such sponsors.

"This will mean that a greater amount of our funding will come from a single source," says the Fiesta Bowl's Doug Blouin. "It's all about building a brand and identifying with something that is positive and very public."

A NOT-SO-SUCCESSFUL STORY

FEWER SPONSORS FOR ADELAIDE ARTS FESTIVAL?

The Adelaide Arts Festival, held each March in Australia, is known as one of the top ten arts festivals in the world.

The Festival has recognized, however, that it may have too many sponsors. A 1998 *Festival Booking Guide* shows the logos for one naming-right sponsor, four corporate sponsors, twenty official sponsors, five official suppliers, and two government agency sponsors.

With each additional sponsorship sold, the Festival has seen that its other sponsors have received less recognition. It has also realized that in such an environment, ambush marketing, be it deliberate or incidental, becomes a real concern, as many nonsponsors potentially reap the benefit of consumers' mistaken sponsorship associations.

TREND NO. 9: INCREASE IN THE TYPES OF PROPERTIES

In the past, you had to hold an event to sell sponsorship. But a growing number of unconventional properties have entered the arena: shopping malls, the film industry, trade shows, conventions, real estate developments, and others.

For the 2002 film *Spiderman,* at least four companies signed on a year early to be part of the film, amounting to about $40 million in additional paid media for the movie, writes Wayne Friedman in *Advertising Age.*

Shopping malls have seen a growth in sponsorship. Tony Wells, vice president of partnership marketing and sales for the Mills Corporation in Arlington, Virginia, says in *Shopping Centers Today,* "Customers can't buy 90 percent of the stuff they see in stadiums, while our customers are in a mind-set where they are ready to spend."

TREND NO. 10: SALES OF EXPERIENCES, RATHER THAN IMPRESSIONS

As mentioned earlier, it used to be sufficient to put sponsors' names on banners, brochures, and posters and in other traditional areas. Good event managers go beyond that by giving added value—creating positive experiences for the people they attract to events. These positive experiences will become increasingly important to sponsors in the future.

"In companies such as ours, sponsorship needs are varied, depending on timely promotions, new product introduction, and related target audiences," said Capital One's corporate meetings and event manager K Alferio. "Advertising reach and the potential stretch are key ingredients to any sponsorship strategy."

U. S. Bank also looks to build unique experiences through sponsorships. "We're in the third year of a deal with the hottest team in baseball," said the bank's Dennis Bash in July 2001. "We've created an affinity checking program around that sponsorship and have increased our sale of checking products tremendously, due to our ability to tie our brand with the Seattle Mariners."

The bank also looks for nontraditional hospitality opportunities, in which the only way people can have certain experiences is through their relationship with the bank.

"We did a batting practice event with the Triple A baseball team in Sacramento, the River Cats," said Bash. "We gave customers the opportunity to take batting practice, take infield/outfield, receive a special jersey, and have lunch at that ballpark. We never fail to get business when we do this type of event."

U.S. Bank also sponsors "Blues by the Bay" in Eureka, California. It invites musicians to come and join its customers at a lunch. "To blues fans, having the chance to talk with a name musician is just as important as a sports fan talking to a sports star, those experiences creating lasting memories for our customers," said Bash.

TREND NO. 11: SPONSOR'S CONTINUING SEARCH FOR RETURN ON INVESTMENT

Many sponsors used to be concerned only about community pride and involvement when they became associated with events.

"Events now have to understand that we are a business, responsible for profit and loss, and are interested in return on investment," said Dennis Boese, the Miller Brewing Company's corporate manager of fair and festival marketing.

"This is going to become even more important in the future. My scorecard has to list who we reached, the cost per attendee and impressions, and the numbers of cases sold. Event managers need to learn about our business."

TREND NO. 12: USE OF SPONSORSHIP TO TARGET FUTURE CUSTOMERS

Most of a company's marketing efforts are directed toward attracting customers today, and very little consideration is given to attracting future customers.

Lloyds, of the United Kingdom, gave a half million schoolchildren their first active involvement in the best of art, music, and drama through its sponsorship of TSB Artsbound.

Because of its sponsorship, Lloyds was able to support efforts that took youth to the National Gallery and other galleries, to the Royal National Theatre, and to other arts venues.

In addition to providing these opportunities, this sponsorship also allowed Lloyds to communicate its message to secondary school children when these potential customers were starting to think about where they might want to open an account.

Sponsors will desire a return on their investments more and more in the future: "Events now have to understand that we are a business, and responsible for profit and loss," says The Miller Brewing Company's Dennise Boese. *Photo courtesy of the Miller Brewing Company.*

These trends all point toward change in the world of sponsorship. Event managers must be visionary and not like Napoleon Bonaparte in the opening sentences of this chapter.

So, as you go out to sell sponsorship, be visionary. We wish you well in your future endeavors.

Three Keys to Successful Sponsorship Programs in the Future

For success in developing sponsorship programs in the future:

1. Pay attention to the trends of society; they will almost always affect the event world too. For example, when the environment became a hot issue in society, immediately several event recycling programs were created.
2. Non-sports and cause-related sponsorship will grow even more in the future, as sponsors become more sophisticated. If you are associated with one of these types of event, it is important to recognize this trend.
3. And even more, event managers are going to have to learn a sponsor's business and be extremely savvy in the marketing world.

Sponsorship Activities
1. Read *Megatrends 2000,* by John Naisbitt and Patricia Aburdene.
2. Read *The Popcorn Report,* by Faith Popcorn.
3. Read *Future Shock,* by Alvin Toffler.
4. List some of the things you have to consider in order to gauge the future of your event.

Sponsorship Tool Kit
Naisbitt, John, and Patricia Aburdene. (1990). *Megatrends 2000.* New York: Morrow.

Popcorn, Faith. (1991). *The Popcorn Report: Faith Popcorn on the Future of Your Company, Your World, Your Life.* New York: Doubleday.

Toffler, Alvin. (1970). *Future Shock.* New York: Random House.
Ukman, Lesa. (1999). *IEG's Complete Guide to Sponsorship.* Chicago: IEG.

Web Sites

www.exordiumgroup.com, The Exordium Group Inc., Cupertino, California, 408-973-0493.

APPENDIX 1

Resources—Sponsorship Books for Event Managers

Allen, Sylvia, and C. Scott Amann. (1987). *Drafting Contracts.* Charlottesville, VA : The Michie Company.

Allen, Sylvia, and C. Scott Amann. (1998). *How to Be Successful at Sponsorship Sales.* Holmdel, NJ.

Axtell, Roger E. (1994). *The Do's and Taboos of International Trade: A Small Business Primer.* New York: John Wiley & Sons, Inc.

Beckwith, Harry. (1997). *Selling the Invisible: A Field Guide to Modern Marketing.* New York: Warner Books.

Black, Henry Campbell. (2001). *Black's Law Dictionary.* St. Paul, MN: West Group.

Certo, Samuel C., Paul Peter, and Edward J. Ottensmeyer. (1995). *The Strategic Management Process.* Homewood, IL: Austen Press; Chicago: Irwin.

Davis, Keith. (1977). *Organizational Behavior: A Book of Readings.* New York: McGraw-Hill.

Feldman, Daniel C. (1983). *Managing Individual and Group Behavior in Organizations.* 3rd ed. New York: McGraw-Hill.

Finn, David, and Judith A. Jedlicka. (1998). *The Art of Leadership: Building Business-Arts Alliances.* New York: Abbeville Press.

Goldblatt, Dr. Joe. (2002). *Special Events: Twenty-First Century Global Event Management.* 3rd ed. New York: John Wiley & Sons, Inc.

Goldblatt, Dr. Joe, and Kathleen S. Nelson. (2001). *The International Dictionary of Event Management.* 2nd ed. New York: John Wiley & Sons, Inc.

Goldblatt, Dr. Joe, and Frank Supovitz. (1999). *Dollars and Events: How to Succeed in the Special Events Business.* New York: John Wiley & Sons, Inc.

Graham, Stedman, Dr. Joe Goldblatt, and Lisa Delpy, Ph.D. (1994). *The Ultimate Guide to Sport Event Management and Marketing.* Burr Ridge, IL: McGraw Hill.

Grey, Anne-Marie, and Kim Skildum-Reid. (1999). *The Sponsorship Seeker's Toolkit.* New York: McGraw-Hill.

Harris, Thomas. (1991). *The Marketer's Guide to Public Relations.* New York: John Wiley & Sons, Inc.

Hodgetts, Richard M. (1987). *Effective Supervision: A Practical Approach.* New York: McGraw-Hill.

Hopkins, Tom. (1982). *How to Master the Art of Selling.* Edited by Warren Jamison. New York: Warner Books.

Hopkins, Tom. (2001). *Selling with Dummies.* Indianapolis, IN: Hungry Minds, Inc., Warner Books.

Howell, John C. (1980). *The Complete Guide to Business Contracts.* Englewood Cliffs, NJ: Prentice-Hall.

Hoyle, Leonard H. (2002). *Event Marketing: How to Successful Promote Events, Festivals, Conventions and Expositions.* New York: John Wiley & Sons, Inc.

IFEA's Official Guide to Sponsorship. (1992). Boise, ID: International Festivals and Events Association.

Jauch, Lawrence R. (1988). *Business Policy and Strategic Management.* New York: McGraw-Hill.

Koontz, Harold, Cyril O'Donnell, and Heinz Weihrich. (1982). *Essentials of Management.* New York: McGraw-Hill.

Kotler, Philip. (2000). *Marketing Management: The Millenium Edition.* Upper Saddle River, NJ: Prentice-Hall.

Martin, Eric. (1997). *Festival and Event Legal Issues.* Boise, ID: International Festivals and Events Association.

Martorella, Rosanne. (1996). *Arts and Business: An International Perspective on Sponsorship.* Westport, CT: Prager Publishers.

McGonagle, John J. (1982). *Business Agreements.* Randor, PA: Chilton Book Company.

McIlroy, Andrew, and Sophie Ballastre. (1998). *The Business of Heritage.* Barcelona, Spain: CEREC (European Committee for Business, Arts and Culture).

Miller, Alex, and Gregory G. Dess. (1996). *Strategic Management.* New York: McGraw-Hill.

Naisbitt, John, and Patricia Aburdene. (1990). *Megatrends 2000.* New York: Morrow.

Neibert, Christopher, and Jack Withaim Jr. (1980). *How to Handle Your Own Contracts.* New York: Greenwich House.

Popcorn, Faith. (1991). *The Popcorn Report: Faith Popcorn on the Future of Your Company, Your World, Your Life.* New York: Doubleday.

Rapp, Stan, and Tom Collins. (1988). *Maxi Marketing.* New York: McGraw-Hill.

Rapp, Stan, and Tom Collins. (1992). *The Great Marketing Revolution.* New York: McGraw-Hill.

Rapp, Stan, and Tom Collins. (1994). *Beyond Maxi Marketing.* New York: McGraw-Hill.

Reed, Mary Hutchings. (2001). *IEG Legal Guide to Cause Marketing.* Chicago: IEG.

Salzman, Marian L. (1999). *Next: A Spectacular Vision of Trends for the Near Future.* Woodstock, NY: Overlook Press.

Schmader, Steven Wood, and Robert Jackson. (1997). *Special Events: Inside and Out.* Champaign, IL: Sagamore Publishing.

Schmitt, Bernd. (1999). *Experiential Marketing: How to Get Customers to Sense, Feel, Think, Act and Relate to Your Company and Brands.* New York: Free Press.

Schreiber, Alfred. (1994). *Lifestyle and Event Marketing.* New York: McGraw-Hill.

Sleight, Steve. (1989). *Sponsorship: What It Is and How to Use It.* New York: McGraw-Hill.

Toffler, Alvin. (1970). *Future Shock.* New York: Random House.

Tracy, Brian. (1995). *Advanced Selling Strategies: The Proven System of Sales Ideas, Methods, and Techniques used by Top Salespeople Everywhere.* New York: Simon & Schuster.

Ukman, Lesa. (2001). *IEG's Complete Guide to Sponsorship.* Chicago: IEG.

von Oech, Roger. (1990). *A Whack on the Side of the Head.* New York: Warner Books.

Periodicals for Event Managers

Advertising Age. Weekly; by Bill Publications, Chicago.

Amusements Business. Weekly; Box 24970, Nashville, TN 37202; 615-321-4250.

Association Management. Monthly; American Society of Association Executives, 1575 I Street NW, Washington, DC 20005; 202-626-2740.

Association Meetings. Bimonthly; Adams/Laux Publishing Company, 63 Great Road, Maynard, MA 01754; 508-897-5552.

Conference and Exhibitions International. Monthly; International Trade Publications Ltd., Queensway House, 2 Queensway, Redhill, Surrey RH1 1QS, England; (0737) 768611; International, 011 44 1737 768611.

Convene. Ten times a year; Professional Convention Management Association, 100 Vestavia Office Park, Suite 220, Birmingham, AL 35216-9970; 205-978-4911.

Conventions and Expositions. Bimonthly; Conventions and Expositions Section of the American Society of Association Executives, 1575 I Street NW, Washington, DC 20005; 202-626-2769.

Entertainment Marketing Letter. Twelve times a year; EPM Communications, Inc., 488 East 18th Street, Brooklyn, NY 11226-6702; 718-469-9330.

Event Solutions. Monthly; Virgo Publishing, Inc., Phoenix, AZ; 602-990-1101.

Events USA. Suite 301, 386 Park Avenue S, New York, NY 10016; 212-684-2222.

Event World. Bi-monthly; International Special Events Society, Indianapolis, IN.

Festival Management & Event Tourism. Quarterly; Cognizant Communication Corporation, 3 Hartsdale Road, Elmsford, NY 10523-3701.

ie: The Business of International Events. Quarterly; International Festivals and Events Association, Boise, ID; 208-433-0950.

IEG Sponsorship Report. Weekly; International Events Group (IEG), 640 North Lasalle, Suite 600, Chicago, IL 60610; 312-944-1727.

Public Relations Journal. 845 Third Avenue, New York, NY 10022.

Special Events Magazine. Monthly; Miramar Publishing Company, Malibu, CA 800-543-4116.

Trade Show and Exhibit Manager. Bimonthly; Goldstein and Associates, Inc., 1150 Yale Street, #12, Santa Monica, CA 90403; 310-828-1309.

APPENDIX 3

Organizations and Resources for Event Managers

American Marketing Association
311 S. Wacker Drive, Suite 5800
Chicago, IL 60606
800-262-1150
www.marketingpower.com
An association that supplies marketing professionals with the information, products, and services required to succeed in their jobs and careers.

American Society of Association Executives (ASAE)
1575 I Street NW
Washington, DC 2005-1168
202-626-ASAE
www.asaenet.org
A professional trade association whose members are executives in professional, trade, and civic associations, as well as those who provide services and products for this industry.

Association of Convention Marketing Executives
1819 Peachtree Street, NE, Suite 712
Atlanta, GA 30309
404-355-2400
www.acmenet.org
A professional trade association whose members are professional convention marketing executives.

The George Washington University Event Management Program
600 21st Street NW
Washington, DC 20052
202-994-1081
www.gwu.edu/emp
A university that offers event management certificate courses in cooperation with Johnson & Wales University.

International Association for Exposition Management
5001 LBJ Freeway, Suite 350
Dallas, TX 75244
214-458-8002
A professional trade association whose members manage trade and public expositions and provide services and products for this industry.

International Association of Amusement Parks and Attractions (IAAPA)
1448 Duke Street
Alexandria, VA 22314
703-836-4800
www.iaapa.org
A professional trade association whose members own, manage, market, and consult in the amusement park and attraction industry and provide services and products for this industry.

International Association of Assembly Managers
635 Fritz Drive
Coppell, TX 75019
972-255-8020
www.iaam.org
An association that comprises leaders who represent a diverse industry—entertainment, sports, conventions, trade, hospitality, and tourism.

International Association of Conference Centers
243 North Lindbergh Boulevard
St. Louis, MO 63141
314-993-8575
A professional trade association whose members own, operate, manage, market, consult, and supply goods and services for conference centers.

International Association of Conventions and Visitors Bureaus (IACVB)
2000 L Street NW, Suite 702
Washington, DC 20036-4990
202-296-7888
A professional trade association whose members manage and market

convention and visitors' bureaus for individual destinations and supply goods and services for these bureaus.

International Association of Fairs and Expositions (IAFE)
P.O. Box 985
Springfield, MO 65801
417-862-5771
www.iafenet.org
A professional trade association whose members organize and manage fairs and expositions.

Insurance Conference Planners Association
2810 Woodbine Drive
North Vancouver, BC V7R 2R9, Canada
604-988-2054
A professional association whose members are planners of conferences in the insurance industry.

International Council of Air Shows, Inc.
751 Miller Drive SE, Suite F-4
Leesburg, VA 20175
703-779-8510
www.airshows.org
Founded in 1968 as a trade and professional association by industry professionals to protect and promote their interests in the growing North American air show marketplace.

International Council of Shopping Centers (ICSC)
665 Fifth Avenue
New York, NY 10022
212-421-8181
A professional trade association whose members own, operate, manage, market, and supply goods and services for shopping centers.

International Events Group (IEG)
640 North LaSalle, Suite 600
Chicago, IL 60610-3777
Phone: 800-834-4850 or 312-944-1727; Fax: 312-944-1897
www.sponsorship.com
The leading company that tracks and analyzes sponsorship of sports, arts, music, causes, and events.

International Exhibitors Association (IEA)
5501 Backlick Road, Suite 105

Springfield, VA 22151
703-941-3725
A professional trade association whose members exhibit at international meetings.

International Federation of Festival Organizations
4230 Stansbury Avenue, No. 105
Sherman Oaks, CA 91423
818-789-7569
A professional trade association whose members organize festivals.

International Festivals and Events Association (IFEA)
World Headquarters: 2601 Eastover Terrace
Boise, ID 83706
Phone: 208-433-0950; Fax: 208-433-9812
www.ifea.com
The premier professional association for the special events industry, providing worldwide networking through education, training, publications, and trade shows for all types of event professionals.

International Institute for Event Leadership
55 Dorrance Street
Providence, RI 02903
401-861-0100
www.eventleader.org
An institute that offers education, research, and grants for event leaders

International Special Events Society (ISES)
401 N. Michigan Avenue
Chicago, IL 60611
Phone: 800-688-4737; Fax: 312-673-6953
www.ises.com
An umbrella organization representing all aspects of the events industry.

International Ticketing Association
250 West 57th Street, Suite 722
New York, NY 10107
212-581-0600
www.intix.org
An association that provides the definitive resource and forum for the international ticketing industry.

Johnson & Wales University
Alan Shawn Feinstein Graduate School

8 Abbott Park Place
Providence, RI 02903
401-598-4738
www.jwu.edu
A graduate school that offers an MBA in hospitality administration with a concentration in event leadership.

Meeting Professionals International (MPI)
1950 Stemmons Freeway, Suite 5018
Dallas, TX 75207-3109
214-712-7700
A professional trade association whose members include corporate, association, and other meeting planners, as well as those who provide goods and services for meeting planners.

Outdoor Amusement Business Association
1035 S. Semoran Boulevard, Suite 1045A
Winter Park, FL 32792
800-517-OABA
www.oaba.org
A membership organization providing services through proactive communication, education, and legislation promoting the continuation of the outdoor amusement industry.

Professional Convention Management Association (PCMA)
100 Vestavia Office Park, Suite 220
Birmingham, AL 35216
205-823-7262
A professional trade association whose members plan and manage meetings and supply goods and services for meeting planners.

Public Relations Society of America (PRSA)
33 Irvine Place
New York, NY 10003
212-995-2230
A professional trade association whose members are involved in public relations activities or supply goods and services for this profession.

Society of Corporate Meeting Professionals (SCMP)
1819 Peachtree Road, NE, Suite 620
Atlanta, GA 30309
404-355-9932
A professional trade association whose members are involved in corporate meeting planning and supply goods and services for this industry.

Stadium Managers Association
HHH Metrodome
900 S 50th Street
Minneapolis, MN 55415
612-335-3316
www.venue.org
A world council for venue management.

European Associations

European Committee for Business, Arts and Culture (CEREC)
Francesca Minguella, Secretary General
c/o AEDME, C/Tuset, 8, 1° 2ª,
08006 Barcelona, Spain
Phone: 34 93 237.26.82; Fax: 34 93 237 22.84;
E-mail contact@cerec.org;
www.aedme.org

IFEA Europe
c/o Netherlands Board of Tourism
Post Box 458
Leidschendam 2260 MG Netherlands
Phone: 31-70-3705296; Fax: 31-70-3201654
www.ifeaeurope.com

International Association of Professional Congress Organizers (IAPCO)
40 Rue Washington
B-1050 Brussels, Belgium
+32 26 40 7105
A professional trade association whose members are professional congress organizers.

International Congress and Convention Association
The International Meetings Association
Entrada 121
1096 EB Amsterdam, The Netherlands
+31 20 690 1171
A professional trade association whose members are travel agents, congress centers, professional congress organizers, and others involved in the organization and servicing of international meetings.

Directories for
Event Managers

Auditorium/Arena/Stadium Guide. Amusement Business/Single Copy Department, Box 24970, Nashville, TN 37202. A listing of venues for events.

Chase's Annual Events: Special Days, Weeks, and Months. Annually; Contemporary Books, Inc., 180 North Michigan Avenue, Chicago IL 60601. A listing of thousands of annual events.

IEG Directory of Sponsorship Marketing. International Events Group, 640 North Lasalle, Suite 600, Chicago, IL 60610; 312-944-1727. A listing of individuals and organizations involved in sponsorship marketing.

IEG Guide to Sponsorship Agencies. International Events Group, 640 North Lasalle, Suite 600, Chicago, IL 60610; 312-944-1727. A listing of sponsorship agencies.

IFEA's Festivals Membership Directory. Annually; International Festivals and Events Association, Boise, ID; 208-433-0950. A listing of IFEA's diverse membership of festival and event professionals and industry suppliers.

International Handbook. International Exhibitors Association, 5501 Backlick Road, Suite 105, Springfield, VA 22151; 703-941-3725. A listing of international exhibitors.

MPE Membership Directory. Annually; Meeting Professionals International. A listing of more than 10,000 individuals involved in meeting planning and related services.

Tradeshow and Convention Guide. Amusement Business/Single Copy Department, Box 24970, Nashville, TN 37202. A listing of venues and resources for events.

Who's Who in Association Management. ASAE Membership Directory. American Society of Association Executives, 1575 Eye Street NW, Washington, DC 20005; 202-731-8825. A listing of association executives (including meeting planners) and their suppliers.

Web Sites for Event Managers

Big Book
www.bigbook.com
Directory of addresses of any business in the United States, as well as maps and restaurant reviews.

Online Sports
www.onlinesports.com
The Online Sports Career Center is a resource of sports-related career opportunities and a resumé bank for potential employers within the many segments of the Sports and recreation industries.

Event Solutions
www.event-solutions.com
A Web site designed to solve your event problems and offer suggestions.

Exordium Group
www.exodiumgroup.com
Publishes on-line newsletter, Exordium Group.Comments.

ExpoGuide
www.expoguide.com
Listing of trade shows. Allows searches by alphabetical order, by date, and by location, and keyword searches. About 4800 shows.

APPENDIX 6

Video Resources for Sponsorship

Basic Road Map to Sponsor Success
Bruce L. Erley, APR, Creative Strategies Group
IFEA Video Library, Boise, ID
208-433-0950

Creating Sponsorship Materials and Making the Most of Them
Michael Marks, City of Santa Clarita, CA
IFEA Video Library, Boise, ID
208-433-0950

Beginning: The ABC's of Sponsorship
Ira Rosen, Entertainment on Location, Point Pleasant, N.J.
IFEA Video Library, Boise, ID
208-433-0950

APPENDIX 7

Sample Sponsorship Proposal

PORTLAND ROSE FESTIVAL
WATERFRONT VILLAGE
SPONSORSHIP PROPOSAL

Corporate Sponsor Main Stage

I. INTRODUCTION:

The Portland Rose Festival is one of the largest events in North America and Oregon's largest civic celebration, attracting two million people every year to its more than 80 events. Since the date of the first Festival in 1907, this gala event has grown into a 28-day extravaganza, including three colorful parades, a waterfront festival and exhibition area, a thrilling air show, a high-speed Indy car race, concerts, and sporting events.

II. DEMOGRAPHICS:

The Portland Rose Festival's 30-year-running, award-winning Waterfront Village has broad demographic appeal. With more than 500,000 guests, the event attracts families to its carnival activities, young families with toddlers to its Kids' Kingdom, young adults, singles, and couples to its music stages, office workers to noon-time food courts, etc. The event draws a diverse audience, with tented attractions such as the International Expo, featuring 70 cultural performers.

III. EVENT DESCRIPTION:

The Waterfront Village is Oregon's largest multiple-day event. Located along Tom McCall Waterfront Park in downtown Portland, it is attended by more than 500,000 guests over 10 days. Highlighted areas of the Waterfront Village include the Main Stage, Village Midway, Western Trail, and Kids' Kingdom.

The Main Stage is located just north of Salmon Street Springs Fountain at Waterfront Park. This stage is a highlight of the Waterfront Village and features great entertainment throughout the 10-day event, with premier local and regional performers. Each day, a top local radio station ties into the Main Stage to promote that day's entertainment lineup, with music tied to that station's format.

IV. **SPONSOR BENEFITS:**
(as calculated by independent valuation service)

Total Sponsor Benefits Value: $_____

- Title sponsorship for the **Main Stage** at the Waterfront Village. The Main Stage is the primary area for all staged entertainment at the Waterfront Village and is the main focal point for all activity in the adjacent food court area.
- **Sponsor** shall have use of the Rose Festival logo for its marketing and promotional use.
- The Rose Festival will provide **Sponsor** with a post-event media audit detailing all sponsorship-related benefits provided.
- **Sponsor** will have first right of refusal for renewing its sponsorship of the **Main Stage** for following years. Sponsorship must be renegotiated and the right of refusal exercised by September 30.

V. **WATERFRONT VILLAGE RECOGNITION:**
- RADIO:
The Main Stage will be promoted on Portland's top local radio stations. Each station will run $____–$1____ of 30 promotional spots promoting the Main Stage, which can include promotional activities (giveaways, contests, etc.). Promotional schedule runs mid-May–June 10.

Participating stations are:

KMHD	MIX 107
ROSIE 105	KUPL
KXL-AM	KISN
KGON	KXL
KUFO	KWJJ

Value (50% of media value): $_____

- PRINT

  The **Main Stage** will be featured in a 4C print campaign for the Waterfront Village in *The Oregonian,* with **Sponsor** receiving 20–30 words of copy, photo, and logo.

  Value (25% of media value): $_____

  WEB SITE

  The **Main Stage** will be featured on the Rose Festival's award-winning Web site, *www.rosefestival.org.* Last year the site drew 3.2 million hits and 175,000 unique site visits. Rose Festival will include promotional content, 4C logo, and link to Sponsor site.

  Value: $_____

- P.A. ANNOUNCEMENTS:
  - ✓ The Rose Festival will ensure frequent recognition of **Sponsor** during P.A. announcements made from the stage throughout each day's entertainment lineup.
  - ✓ The **Main Stage** will be included in the Rose Festival Hotline in *The Oregonian's* Inside Line. Inside Line will list the daily lineup of entertainment for the **Main Stage.**

  Value: $_____

- MARKETING AND PROMOTIONAL MATERIALS:

  The Rose Festival will recognize **Main Stage** sponsorship through name and/or logo inclusion in Rose Festival marketing and promotional materials. *Note:* Some materials may already be printed prior to sponsorship agreement.
  - ✓ 100,000 Rose Festival event brochures
  - ✓ 20,000 Rose Festival souvenir programs
  - ✓ 10,000 Waterfront Village pocket guides
  - ✓ 250 media guides distributed to all regional media. Several pages on the Waterfront Village will be included in the media guide.

  Value: $_____

- ON-SITE SIGNAGE:
  - ✓ Two (2) 7' × 19' **Sponsor** speaker scrims for the stage's speaker system.
  - ✓ Two (2) 5' × 5' **Sponsor** banners placed on the back wall of the stage, facing heavily trafficked Front Avenue (signage provided by Sponsor).

  Value: $_____

VII. **PROMOTIONAL OPPORTUNITIES:**
The Rose Festival encourages sponsor tie-in advertising and promotions. **Sponsor** and the Rose Festival will have a mutual agreement prior to any Rose Festival promotion.

VIII. **ROSE FESTIVAL HOSPITALITY:**
- Fifty (50) passes to the Waterfront Village Preview Night, featuring unlimited amusement rides.
- An invitation for two (2) to the Rose Festival Sponsor Recognition Reception the evening of the Fireworks Spectacular.

Value: $_____

IX. **SPONSOR INVESTMENT:**
The Portland Rose Festival Association is seeking a sponsor for the Waterfront Village's Main Stage, in exchange for the rights and benefits outlined herein, that will make the following commitment:

One-year commitment (2002): $_____
Two-year commitment (2002, 2003): $_____

We strongly encourage multiple-year commitments. Through independent research, it has been found that sponsorship value increases, and recognition grows, through consistent event property ownership.

Sample Letter of Agreement

Creative Strategies Group, Denver

February 20, 2002

Mr. Keith Villa
Coors Brewing Company
P.O. Box 4030/ NH 470
Golden, CO 80401

Dear Keith:

Thank you for your decision to return as an Official Sponsor of the 2003 Great American Beer Festival. We are delighted to have you back and are confident you will find this sponsorship to be among your most successful.

This letter will confirm the terms and conditions on which Coors Brewing Company (hereafter referred to as the "Sponsor") has agreed to sponsor the 2003 Great American Beer Festival (the "Festival") produced by Brewing Matters, a nonprofit organization.

1. The Organizers shall use their best efforts to conduct and promote the Festival to take place from *dates to be determined,* in Hall A of the Colorado Convention Center in Denver, Colorado.
2. **Sponsor Status.** The Organizers hereby grant Coors Brewing Company the right to be an Official Sponsor of the Festival. Sponsor shall have the right to use the name of the Festival and the use of its Trademark in advertising prior to, and through the end of, the

2003 calendar year in connection with this sponsorship. The name of the Festival is not to be used as an endorsement of any product or service. All such materials are subject to the Organizers' prior written approval, which shall not be unreasonably withheld.

3. **Naming Rights.** Sponsor shall receive proprietary naming and presentation rights for the Education Pavilion. Sponsor shall be recognized for its exclusive sponsorship of that program in all Festival collateral materials and advertising.

4. **Renewal.** The Sponsor shall be granted the first right of refusal for the Official Sponsorship of the 2003 Festival until December 31, 2002. If the Sponsor does not renew by that date, the category and the associated naming rights shall be considered open and available to others.

5. **Advertising and Promotion.** The Organizers shall provide the Sponsor with the following promotional rights:

   a. the right to four aisle or wall logo banners within the Exhibition Hall. Such banners to be provided by the Sponsor to the specifications of the Organizers as stipulated by municipal regulations;

   b. the right to have dominant logo recognition on Sponsor marquee banner inside Hall A of the Colorado Convention Center;

   c. the right to have name recognition on exterior Colorado Convention Center marquee banner;

   d. the right to have logo recognition in all print advertising *(Denver Rocky Mountain News)* placed by the Organizer in connection with the Show;

   e. the right to have rotating logo recognition and acknowledgment on Video Wall;

   f. the right to present a video presentation on Video Wall (maximum running time: 10 minutes);

   g. the right to have logo recognition on industry Sponsor marquee banner;

   h. the right to have Sponsor's Trademark appear in association with the Festival's logo in all collateral materials, including promotional posters, promotional kiosk cards, volunteer T-shirts, etc.;

   i. the right to have one full-page, four-color ad located on inside front cover of Official Festival Program;

   j. the right to be named as an Official Sponsor in all press releases issued by Organizers or at any press events;

   k. the right to have logo recognition on GABF's homepage on gabf.org, plus hot link to the Sponsor's Web site.
   Note: Sponsor responsible for all out-of-pocket expenses such as the cost of signage, promotional materials, mailing labels, etc.

6. **Hospitality Package.** Organizers will provide the Sponsor with the following package for hospitality purposes:
   a. 100 GABF Public Session tickets;
   b. 20 Invitations to Awards Ceremony;
   c. 10 Invitations to Judges Reception;
   d. 10 Tickets to Private Brewers' Gathering;
   e. Credentials for Coors Volunteers
7. **Sponsorship Fee.** In consideration of the full performance by Organizers of all of their obligations hereunder and all rights granted hereunder to Sponsor, Sponsor shall pay the Organizers a cash sponsorship fee of $22,000. A 50% deposit of $11,000 is to be returned with this agreement before February 1, 2003, with the remaining $11,000 to be paid on or before June 1, 2003.
8. Each party represents and warrants that it is free to enter into this Agreement without violating the rights of any person, that its trademarks do not infringe the trademarks or trade names of any person, and that it will comply with all laws and regulations pertinent to its business.
9. This Agreement does not constitute a partnership or joint venture or principal-agent relationship between the Organizers and the Sponsor. The Agreement may not be assigned by either party. It shall be governed by the laws of the State of Colorado. It is complete and represents the entire agreement between the parties.

If this accurately sets forth our Agreement, please sign both copies where indicated below and return one along with the deposit payable The Great American Beer Festival to Creative Strategies Group at 925 Main Street, Suite E, Broomfield, CO 80020.

Sincerely,

Wendy C. Burns
Sales Director, Creative Strategies Group
Sponsorship Agency for the Great American Beer Festival

Approved by:
By: _____
Nancy Johnson
Great American Beer Festival
736 Pearl Street
Boulder, CO 80302

Agreed and Accepted this _____ day of _____, 20____
By: _____
Title: _____
Coors Brewing Company

Sample Contract

PORTLAND ROSE FESTIVAL
&
XYZ, INC.

2003 SPONSORSHIP CONTRACT

This agreement is intended to serve as a contract between XYZ, Inc., P.O. Box 12345, Anycity, Anystate, 11111, and the Portland Rose Festival Association, 5603 SW Hood Ave., Portland, Oregon, 97201, to outline the terms and conditions of XYZ, INC.'S involvement in the 2003 Portland Rose Festival.

THIS SPONSORSHIP AGREEMENT COVERS THE FOLLOWING ROSE FESTIVAL EVENTS ON THE FOLLOWING DATES:

XYZ, INC. Opening Weekend featuring the Sponsor Fireworks Spectacular
- Thursday, May 29–Sunday, June 2 (fireworks Thursday and Friday nights only).

ABC, Inc. Grand Floral Parade Float and Kids Sweepstakes (Junior Judges Program)
- Saturday, June 7

I.   SPONSOR PAYMENT OBLIGATIONS:

IN CONSIDERATION OF SPONSORSHIP RIGHTS DESCRIBED IN THIS AGREEMENT, FOR SPONSORSHIP OF THE 2003 PORTLAND ROSE FESTIVAL, XYZ, INC. AGREES TO:

> **Pay total cash sponsorship fee of $_____ in the following payment schedule:**
> > **Total payment of $_____ due by May 15.**

II.   XYZ, INC. OPENING WEEKEND

XYZ, Inc. to provide the following items for this specific portion of the sponsorship:

1. Provide Portland Rose Festival Association an option of use of XYZ, Inc. refrigerated trucks for use at the Waterfront Village vendor commissary.
2. XYZ, Inc. agrees to host a "Welcome Tent" on Thursday, May 29 (Village opening night) at the Waterfront Village (location TBD). XYZ, Inc. agrees to provide a "presence" throughout the opening weekend by featuring autograph signings at various times and/or other welcoming activities.
3. XYZ, Inc. to the best of its ability will promote and advertise the Opening Weekend promotion and the Rose Festival through grocery bags, in-store signage, and promotions or through other store advertising.
4. PRFA must approve all uses of its logo by XYZ, Inc. Forward all uses to Sara Johnson, Sponsorship Manager, PRFA.
5. Participate in a promotion with Waterfront Village wherein any two proofs of purchase of XYZ, Inc. products may be redeemed for purchase of discounted tickets offering unlimited amusement rides at the Waterfront Village for Thursday, May 29 only (This promotion may be substituted by another Opening Weekend promotion when agreed upon by both parties).
6. XYZ, Inc. must provide six (6) 3′ × 8′ (approximate size) banners for the Opening Weekend activities (location TBD). XYZ, Inc. must provide its own corporate signage to the PRFA, Sara Johnson, by May 15.
7. XYZ, Inc. agrees to be a Rose Festival Court apparel donor, with the particular clothing items determined by an XYZ, Inc. apparel employee and the Court committee.

PRFA to provide the following items for this specific portion of the Sponsorship:

1. PRFA grants exclusive title sponsorship of the Opening Weekend promotion to XYZ, Inc. The Opening Weekend, after acceptance of this contract, will be referred to in all official PRFA publications and announcements as the "Rose Festival XYZ, Inc. Opening Weekend."
2. XYZ, Inc. will be included in all radio promotional announcements on Z100 and 1190 KEX supporting the Opening Weekend promotion, estimated at an approximate $_____ value.
3. PRFA will recognize XYZ, Inc. as the Title Sponsor of the promotion in all media releases to radio, television, and print associated with the Opening Weekend promotion. The XYZ, Inc. Opening Weekend will

be listed in Rose Festival highlight event schedules, including, but not limited to the following:

- Rose Festival Web site with link to XYZ, Inc. Web site.
- Calendar listing in 100,000 Spring Brochures, which are distributed regionally, nationally, and internationally in April.
- 20,000 Rose Festival Souvenir Programs.
- 10,000 Rose Festival consumer brochures.
- 5,000 Rose Festival membership brochures.
- 250 Media Guides, sent to local and regional news organizations in mid-May. The guides contain overviews of all events.

4. PRFA will include XYZ, Inc. as a Rose Festival major event in other Sponsor promotional opportunities and event listings for the nights that the XYZ, Inc. Opening Weekend promotion features fireworks (also dependent on other programming).

5. PRFA will provide prominent banner placement of six (6) 3' × 8' (approximate size) XYZ, Inc. banners at Waterfront Village during the Opening Weekend promotion (location TBD).

6. PRFA will provide a 10' × 20' booth for XYZ, Inc. during the Opening Weekend to use as a welcome area and/or promotions or on-site sampling. The exact location at the Waterfront Village and tent content to be mutually agreed upon by XYZ, Inc. and PRFA.

7. PRFA will work with XYZ, Inc. to develop in-store and media promotions to enhance involvement and value of participation and attempt to incorporate the distribution of the Rose Festival Souvenir Programs through XYZ, Inc. stores.

8. PRFA allows the use of its name and copyrighted logo on promotional materials produced by XYZ, Inc., with review rights reserved by PRFA.

III. XYZ, INC. KIDS SWEEPSTAKES AND ABC AIRLINES GRAND FLORAL PARADE FLOAT

XYZ, Inc. to provide the following items for this specific portion of the Sponsorship:

1. XYZ, Inc. is responsible for developing its float theme and coordinating any employee or volunteer support for completion of the float's flowering for the Parade.

2. Sponsor agrees to follow all parade rules governed by the Grand Floral Parade Steering Committee.

3. XYZ, Inc., to the best of its ability, will promote and advertise the Kids Sweepstakes Award contest.

4. XYZ, Inc. to provide clothing for Junior Judges.

5. XYZ, Inc. to provide one (1) 3' × 8' banner for placement at the Showcase of Floats. XYZ, Inc. to provide its own corporate signage to the

PRFA, Sara Johnson, by May 15.

6. XYZ, Inc. agrees to provide staffing for its Showcase of Floats booth. Hours for the event are Saturday, June 7, 2–9 P.M. and Sunday, June 9, 9 A.M.–5 P.M. Sponsor will be notified in writing if the hours are changed.

PRFA to provide the following items for this specific portion of the Sponsorship:

1. PRFA grants exclusive title sponsorship of the Kids Sweepstakes Award to XYZ, Inc. The Kids Sweepstakes Award, after acceptance of this contract, will be referred to in all official PRFA publications and announcements as the "XYZ, Inc. Kids Sweepstakes Award." The finalists selected as judges will officially be called "Junior Judges."

2. Coordinate and pay for the printing of entry forms and in-store information for the contest associated with the Kids Sweepstakes Award.

3. XYZ, Inc.'s float will be built to Sponsor's specifications by PRFA's official float builder, Float Builders, Inc. Through this contract, PRFA agrees to pay Float Builders, Inc. directly from the XYZ, Inc. sponsorship fee to cover all float building and operating costs. Sponsor has the option to work with Float Builders, Inc. to further float upgrades.

4. XYZ, Inc.'s float (a high-quality, flower-covered entry) will be eligible for all parade awards except the Kids Sweepstakes Award.

5. The parade entry fee and Showcase of Floats fee is included in this agreement for 2001.

6. Provide XYZ, Inc. with approximately one minute of in-focus coverage during the parade's seminational broadcast, which will be broadcast to 25 million TV households each year.

7. Include one (1) XYZ, Inc. logo in the banner used as a backdrop in the broadcast area.

8. PRFA agrees to display the XYZ, Inc. Float throughout the two-day Showcase of Floats.

9. Coverage of the XYZ, Inc. float and the XYZ, Inc. Kids Sweepstakes Award on the live broadcast by 1190 KEX.

10. PRFA to display one (1) 3′ × 8′ banner on the Showcase of Floats perimeter fencing. XYZ, Inc. to provide the one (1) 3′ × 8′ banner.

11. PRFA will provide a 10′ × 10′ booth at the Showcase of Floats area. PRFA will provide a covered area, one (1) table and two (2) chairs. XYZ, Inc. is responsible for staffing.

12. PRFA will provide the award banner to be marched in front of the winning Kids Sweepstakes Award float.

13. PRFA allows XYZ, Inc. to use its logo for marketing purposes, and to identify XYZ, Inc. as an "Official Rose Festival Sponsor." PRFA must

approve all uses of its logo by XYZ, Inc. PRFA requests that all uses be forwarded to Sara Johnson, PRFA Sponsorship Manager, at 555/555-5555 (fax) for approval.

14. PRFA agrees to recognize XYZ, Inc.'s Float and Kids Sweepstakes program by logo and/or name in the following publications:
   - Rose Festival Souvenir Programs
   - Showcase of Floats Programs and Maps
   - Grand Floral Parade page on the Rose Festival Web site

IV.   OTHER

A.   MEMBERSHIP AND ADDITIONAL HOSPITALITY BENEFITS

1. PRFA will recognize XYZ, Inc. as a prestigious *Queen's Rose* member of the Rose Festival and will extend to XYZ, Inc. the following benefits associated with that level.
2. An invitation for four (4) guests to the Rose Festival Sponsor Appreciation Evening.
3. Twenty-eight (28) Waterfront Village Midway Wristbands for Opening Night, Thursday, May 29.
4. Eight (8) passes to the special VIP Membership Airshow Chalet, which includes premier seating on Chalet row, VIP parking, a hosted luncheon, beverages, and Airshow programs.
5. Fourteen (14) passes to the Grand Floral Parade VIP Chalet, which includes catering and Souvenir Programs.
6. Ten (10) tickets for reserved Coliseum seating at the Grand Floral Parade.
7. Six (6) tickets to the Festival of Bands.
8. Ten (10) tickets to the Rose Society Rose Show.

B.   SOUVENIR PROGRAM AD

1. PRFA agrees to provide XYZ, Inc. with a full-page color ad in the Souvenir Program.
2. XYZ, Inc. agrees to provide the ad in the requested format and to pay all design costs associated with producing the final ad.

V.   TERMS AND CONDITIONS

1. Postponement or cancellation of the Rose Festival XYZ, Inc. Opening Weekend, Grand Floral Parade, or Showcase of Floats, for any reason beyond the control of PRFA shall not constitute a cause for refund on all or any portion of this sponsorship fee.
2. XYZ, Inc. has the right to upgrade the sponsorship at any time during the term of this contract as appropriate. The upgraded sponsorship fee would be negotiated separately, and a contractual amendment would be drafted to complete the contract.

3. PRFA shall secure and maintain throughout the term of this agreement all insurance for events of this stature and size, including but not limited to comprehensive general liability insuring itself and XYZ, Inc. against loss of liability out of or relating to any activities associated with any of the events outlined above.

4. PRFA agrees to defend, indemnify, and hold harmless SPONSOR, their affiliates, agents, employees, successors, and assigns from any and all liability, damages, claims, demands, actions, causes of action, attorney fees (including an appeal), cost and expenses of whatsoever nature arising directly or indirectly from or relating to any of the events described above.

5. This Agreement sets forth the entire agreement between the parties and takes the place of all prior verbal or written communication concerning the subjects of the Agreement. This Agreement may not be altered, modified, or changed in any way by either of the parties without the prior written consent of the other party.

6. Each of the parties hereto is an independent contractor. Neither party shall have the authority to act on behalf of the other or to incur obligation on behalf of the other.

7. If suit or action is instituted to enforce this Agreement or to determine any matter in controversy regarding this Agreement, the prevailing party shall be entitled to recover such sums as the court may judge reasonable attorney fees, including attorney fees on appeal and in collecting or enforcing any judgment order or decree.

8. Neither party shall without written authorization from the other party disclose to any third party the terms and conditions of this Agreement except as may be necessary to establish or assert rights hereunder or required by law; provided, however, either party may on a confidential basis disclose this Agreement to officials, officers, accountants, attorneys, or other individuals within each other's organizations with a "need to know."

9. By August 1, XYZ, Inc. and PRFA representatives will engage in a complete review of previous Rose Festival and discuss opportunities for improvements in all operational aspects including Sponsor recognition.

10. Renewal of this agreement for 2004 is subject to review and mutual acceptance in writing of these terms or revisions as negotiated by **August 1. Sponsor has first right of refusal on all events listed in this contract until August 1.**

AGREED TO BY:

_____   _____

Jane Director   Date
Senior VP/Director of Sales Promotion
XYZ, Inc.

_____   _____

Joe Smith   Date
Executive Director
Portland Rose Festival Association

Sample Benefit Report, Three Rivers Festival, Pittsburgh

SHOP 'n SAVE
SPONSOR BENEFITS REPORT

<u>TELEVISION</u>

PUBLICITY

- Inclusion within the "Ya Gotta Regatta" Preview Show airing on KDKA-TV2, Friday, July 27, 2002, at 7:30 P.M.
  - ➤ 1:21 Feature segment including an interview with SHOP 'n SAVE's Kathy Svilar.

Ad Value: $3,300.00
Publicity Value: $16,500.00

- SHOP 'n SAVE inclusion within the "Roar Before the Thunder" Preview Show airing on WCWB WB22 on Sunday, July 29, 2002, at 10:30 P.M.

Ad Value: $8,130.00
Publicity Value: $40,650.00

- SHOP 'n SAVE inclusion within thirty (30) of forty-six (46) Regatta News Broadcast Clips airing on KDKA-TV, WPGH-TV, WTAE-TV and WPXI-TV.

Ad Value: $154,620.00
Publicity Value: $773,100.00

- SHOP 'n SAVE opening and closing billboards in the WPGH FOX 53 live telecast of Regatta Thunder airing on Saturday, August 4, 2002, from 9:00 P.M.–11:00 P.M.

TOTAL AD VALUE: $166,050.00
TOTAL PUBLICITY VALUE: $830,250.00

COMMERCIALS

- 13 :30 Dedicated SHOP 'n SAVE Fixed News Commercials airing on KDKA-TV.

  Value: $10,930.00

- 12 :30 Dedicated SHOP 'n SAVE "Ya Gotta Regatta" Sweepstakes Fixed News Commercials airing on KDKA-TV.

  Value: $5,135.00

- 28 :30 Dedicated SHOP 'n SAVE Rotator Commercials airing on KDKA-TV.

  Value: $11,780.00

- 29 :30 Dedicated SHOP 'n SAVE "Ya Gotta Regatta" Sweepstakes Rotator Commercials airing on KDKA-TV.

  Value: $11,780.00

- 5 :30 Dedicated SHOP 'n SAVE Commercials airing on WPGH FOX53 during the live telecast of Regatta Thunder.

  Value: $2,850.00

- 22 :30 Dedicated SHOP 'n SAVE Commercials airing on WPGH FOX53.

  Value: $800.00

- 24 :30 Dedicated SHOP 'n SAVE "Ya Gotta Regatta" Sweepstakes Commercials airing on WPGH FOX53.

  Value: $2,475.00

- 16 :30 Dedicated SHOP 'n SAVE Commercials airing on WCWB WB22.

  Value: $1,060.00

- 23 :30 Dedicated SHOP 'n SAVE "Ya Gotta Regatta" Sweepstakes Commercials airing on WCWB WB22.

  Value: $290.00

- 25 :30 Dedicated "Ya Gotta Regatta" Sweepstakes Commercials airing on KDKA-TV.

  Value: $8,975.00

- 12 :60 Dedicated "Ya Gotta Regatta" Sweepstakes Commercials airing on KDKA-TV.

  Value: $5,550.00

- 12 :30 Dedicated "Ya Gotta Regatta" Sweepstakes Commercials airing on WPGH FOX53.

  Value: $1,565.00

- 10 :30 Dedicated "Ya Gotta Regatta" Sweepstakes Commercials airing on WCWB WB22.

  Value: $860.00

TOTAL COMMERCIALS: 231
12 :60
219 :30
TOTAL BONUS COMMERCIALS: 39
39 :30

TOTAL COMMERCIAL VALUE: $64,050.00

PROMOS

- 8 :60 SHOP 'n SAVE Logo-Tagged Sponsor Promos airing on KDKA-TV.

  Value: $6,300.00
- 16 :60 SHOP 'n SAVE Logo-Tagged Sponsor Promos airing on WPGH FOX53.

  Value: $9,990.00
- 15 :60 SHOP 'n SAVE Logo-Tagged Sponsor Promos airing on WCWB WB22.

  Value: $680.00
- 144 :30 SHOP 'n SAVE Logo-Tagged Sponsor Promos airing on KDKA-TV.

  Value: $61,855.00
- 36 :30 SHOP 'n SAVE Logo-Tagged Sponsor Promos airing on WPGH FOX53.

  Value: $1,750.00
- 48 :30 SHOP 'n SAVE Logo-Tagged Sponsor Promos airing on WCWB WB22.

  Value: $2,350.00
- 142 :15 SHOP 'n SAVE Logo-Tagged Sponsor Promos airing on KDKA-TV.

  Value: $52,320.00
- 51 :15 SHOP 'n SAVE Logo-Tagged Sponsor Promos airing on WPGH FOX53.

  Value: $3,350.75
- 34 :15 SHOP 'n SAVE Logo-Tagged Sponsor Promos airing on WCWB WB22.

  Value: $1,683.50
- 92 :10 SHOP 'n SAVE Logo-Tagged Thank-You Spots airing on WPGH FOX53.

  Value: $6,907.50
- 129 :10 SHOP 'n SAVE Logo-Tagged Thank-You Spots airing on WCWB WB22.

  Value: $4,765.00

TOTAL PROMOS: 715
39 :60
228 :30
227 :15
221 :10

TOTAL BONUS PROMOS: 315
14 :60
68 :30
12 :15
221 :10

TOTAL PROMO VALUE: $151,951.75

TOTAL TELEVISION VALUE: $1,046,251.70

<u>RADIO</u>
COMMERCIALS

- 100 :60 Dedicated SHOP 'n SAVE Commercials airing on 106 JAMZ WAMO.

  Value: $16,100.00

- 49 :60 Dedicated SHOP 'n SAVE Commercials airing on WISH 99.7 FM.

  Value: $4,460.00

- 50 :60 Dedicated SHOP 'n SAVE Commercials airing on 1320 WJAS.

  Value: $2,535.00

- 50 :60 Dedicated SHOP 'n SAVE Commercials airing on 1360 WPTT.

  Value: $1,750.00

- 100 :60 Dedicated SHOP 'n SAVE Commercials airing on WLTJ 92.9 Lite FM and Channel 97 WRRK.

  Value: $13,805.00

- 31 :30 Dedicated "Ya Gotta Regatta" Sweepstakes Commercials airing on 106 JAMZ WAMO.

  Value: $4,015.00

- 30 :30 Dedicated "Ya Gotta Regatta" Sweepstakes Commercials airing on 1320 WJAS.

  Value: $1,480.00

- 30 :30 Dedicated "Ya Gotta Regatta" Sweepstakes Commercials airing on 1360 WPTT.

  Value: $1,050.00

- 40 :30 Dedicated "Ya Gotta Regatta" Sweepstakes Commercials airing on WLTJ 92.9 Lite FM and Channel 97 WRRK.

  Value: $5,510.00

TOTAL COMMERCIALS: 480
349 :60
131 :30

TOTAL BONUS COMMERCIALS: 180
49 :60
131 :30

TOTAL COMMERCIAL VALUE: $50,705.00

PROMOS

- 100 :60 SHOP 'n SAVE Tagged Sponsor Promos airing on 106 JAMZ WAMO.
  Value: $14,695.00
- 110 :60 SHOP 'n SAVE Tagged Sponsor Promos airing on WISH 99.7 FM.
  Value: $10,490.00
- 101 :60 SHOP 'n SAVE Tagged Sponsor Promos airing on 1320 WJAS.
  Value: $5,075.00
- 113 :60 SHOP 'n SAVE Tagged Sponsor Promos airing on 1360 WPTT.
  Value: $3,850.00
- 99 :60 SHOP 'n SAVE Tagged Sponsor Promos airing on WLTJ 92.9 Lite FM and Channel 97 WRRK.
  Value: $12,865.00
- 170 :30 SHOP 'n SAVE Tagged Sponsor Promos airing on 106 JAMZ WAMO.
  Value: $22,975.00
- 165 :30 SHOP 'n SAVE Tagged Sponsor Promos airing on WISH 99.7 FM.
  Value: $13,980.00
- 143 :30 SHOP 'n SAVE Tagged Sponsor Promos airing on 1320 WJAS.
  Value: $6,880.00
- 170 :30 SHOP 'n SAVE Tagged Sponsor Promos airing on 1360 WPTT.
  Value: $5,950.00
- 339 :30 SHOP 'n SAVE Tagged Sponsor Promos airing on WLTJ 92.9 Lite FM and Channel 97 WRRK.
  Value: $47,830.00

TOTAL PROMOS: 1,510
523 :60
987 :30

TOTAL PROMO VALUE: $144,590.00

TOTAL RADIO VALUE: $195,295.00
PRINT RECAP

- 150,000 Regatta Schedule of Events Flyers distributed in sponsor locations, downtown areas, and Point State Park. SHOP 'n SAVE logo inclusion on the front cover and Title Sponsor listing.
  Value: $5,000.00

- SHOP 'n SAVE Inclusion within two (2) Regatta Bridge Party print advertisements in the *Pittsburgh Post-Gazette* printed on Sunday, July 29 and Wednesday, August 1, 2002.

  Value: $4,058.20

- Regatta Newspaper Supplement 431,172 distribution via *Pittsburgh Post-Gazette* (Sunday Edition).
  - ➤ SHOP 'n SAVE logo inclusion on the front cover.

    Value: $14,720.50
  - ➤ SHOP 'n SAVE Title Sponsor listing and logo inclusion.

    Value: $4,246.20
  - ➤ SHOP 'n SAVE location listing on the Site Map of Point State Park.

    Value: $14,720.50
  - ➤ SHOP 'n SAVE received four (4) full-page full-color advertisements.

    Value: $40,816.00
  - ➤ SHOP 'n SAVE inclusion within five (5) Regatta Sponsor one-half (1/2)-page black-and-white advertisements.

    Value: $12,950.00
  - ➤ SHOP 'n SAVE inclusion within three (3) Regatta Sponsor full-page black-and-white advertisements.

    Value: $15,306.00
  - ➤ SHOP 'n SAVE inclusion within two (2) Regatta Sponsor full-page full-color advertisements.

    Value: $20,408.00
  - ➤ One (1) full-page full-color "Ya Gotta Regatta" Sweepstakes advertisement.

    Value: $10,204.00
  - ➤ SHOP 'n SAVE Title Sponsor identity within eleven (11) editorials.
- SHOP 'n SAVE inclusion within eighty-one (81) Regatta print clips. (See Print Clip Report.)

  Editorial Value: $1,025,988.20
- Regatta Press Kit (1000 distributed) SHOP 'n SAVE feature release and inclusion within all other press releases.
- SHOP 'n SAVE Title Sponsor listing in the Regatta Anchor Awards Gala Program honoring Duquesne University President, Dr. John Murray, and Pittsburgh Steelers President, Mr. Dan Rooney.

TOTAL PRINT VALUE: $1,168,417.60

TENT/DISPLAY SPACE RECAP

- One (1) 40′ × 40′ high-quality modular display tent located in a high traffic area.

  Minimum Value: $17,000.00
- One (1) 48′ Kellogg's Semi and Kellogg's NASCAR race car displayed in the SHOP 'n SAVE tent in the Children's Village.

  Minimum Value: $16,000.00

TOTAL TENT/DISPLAY VALUE: $33,000.00

<u>SIGNAGE</u>

- One hundred (100) 4′ × 6′ City Street Pole Arm Banners with Event logo and Event Dates for a total of 600 feet of signage for a 7-week, 5-day period.

  Value: $1,925,000.00

- Twenty-five (25) City Billboard locations with Event Logo and Event Dates for a 4-week, 3-day period.

  Value: $281,250.00

- Ten (10) 3′ × 24′ Overhead Street Banners with Event logo and Event Dates for a total of 240 feet of signage for a 7-week period.

  Value: $175,000.00

- One (1) 40′ × 40′ North Shore Bridge Pillar Banner with Event logo and Event Dates for a 5-week period.

  Value: $70,000.00

- One (1) 8′ × 40′ SHOP 'n SAVE Children's Village Banner displayed in the entrance of the SHOP 'n SAVE tent.

  Value: $3,000.00

- One (1) 8′ × 40′ Portal Bridge Welcome Banner with Event Logo and Event Dates.

  Value: $3,000.00

- One hundred fifty (150) 3′ × 10′ SHOP 'n SAVE Banners displayed throughout Point State Park and the North Shore for a total of 1500 feet of signage.

  Value: $225,000.00

- SHOP 'n SAVE Banners displayed at the Regatta kickoff Press Conference and the Regatta Bridge Party on the Roberto Clemente Bridge.
- Seventeen (17) 2′ × 6′ SHOP 'n SAVE Pole Arm Banners displayed throughout Point State Park for a total of 102 feet of signage.

  Value: $25,500.00

TOTAL SIGNAGE VALUE: $2,707,750.00

<u>MISCELLANEOUS</u>

- 2,000,000 "Ya Gotta Regatta" Sweepstakes scratch cards distributed in 90 area SHOP 'n SAVE stores prior to the Regatta.

  Value: $200,000.00

- One (1) Tony the Tiger Hot Air Balloon entered in the Regatta Hot Air Balloon Rally.

  Value: $1,500.00

- Inclusion within Regatta interactive Web site.

  Value $2,500.00

- Eighty (80) V.I.P. Concert Series Seating wristbands for each of the four (4) Main Stage concerts for a total of three hundred twenty (320) wristbands.

  Value: $9,600.00

- Three (3) tables for ten at the Regatta Anchor Awards Gala held at the Westin William Penn Hotel.

  Value: $2,250.00

- Three hundred fifty (350) Hospitality Passes for the Regatta Thunder Fireworks Party held at the Carnegie Science Center.

  Value: $17,500.00

- Two hundred (200) hospitality passes for the IOGP Powerboat races aboard the Gateway Clipper Fleet's *Majestic*.

  Value: $10,000.00

TOTAL MISCELLANEOUS VALUE: $243,350.00

GRAND TOTAL VALUE: $5,394,064.30

Index